Sew Smart

with Wovens, Knits, and Ultrasuede® fabric

**by Judy Lawrence and
Clotilde**

**Professional
Methods
for the
Custom
Look**

**Fashion Art by Bernard Schorr
Diagrams by Judy Lawrence
Photography by Gene Larman**

HOW TO USE SEW SMART

As you read through this book you will see many words in italics. This indicates that these sewing terms, items, or techniques are explained further at some other place in the book. Refer to the index for the page numbers of these references.

Revised Edition Copyright 1982
by Judy Lawrence and Clotilde

Also known as *SEW SMART IN THE CLASSROOM*

First Printing	1977	Second Printing	1978
Third Printing	1979	Fourth Printing	1980
Fifth Printing	1981	Sixth Printing	1982
Seventh Printing	1983	Eighth Printing	1984
Ninth Printing	1990	Tenth Printing	1991

ISBN 0-8087-1261-6

Published by IBC Publishing Co.
1909 S.W. 1st Avenue, Ft. Lauderdale, FL 33315

Dear Reader,

SEW SMART has been written especially for you — to help you achieve the professional sewing results you have always wanted for knits and woven fabrics plus the information necessary to help you create beautiful Ultra Suede® fabric clothes. The techniques described in this book go beyond the ordinary sewing instructions and are written and illustrated in such a way that the beginner as well as the experienced seamstress can easily follow them. You will also find many useful sewing tips included in the text which will make your sewing experience easier and more enjoyable. A SEW SMART wardrobe with a custom look is now within your reach.

Happy sewing,

Judy and Clotilde

ABOUT THE AUTHORS

Judy began her sewing career as a young teenager and continued making her own and most of her family's clothes after she married and had children. She began her teaching career in the Los Angeles area in 1968 and wrote her first book SEWING KNITS after moving to Colorado in 1970. The second book SEWING KNITS MENSWEAR was published the next year, and both books have won wide acceptance as the text for knit classes in fabric stores and schools throughout the United States and Canada.

Judy worked as a consultant for a nationally known sewing machine company for two years. During that time she put together three knit courses including preparation of the teacher's manual, teaching aids, and training the firm's educational supervisors. The courses have been taught to thousands of students in the firm's sewing studios.

Well known as an author and lecturer, Judy has taught classes and conducted seminars all over the country. She met Clotilde at a workshop in the Los Angeles area in 1970, and their friendship and professional experiences developed into the co-authoring of this new book — SEW SMART.

Clotilde is a graduate of Miami University, Oxford, Ohio. After graduation, she worked for 20th Century Fox in the wardrobe department. She sewed commercially for boutique shops in Beverly Hills, learning many custom sewing techniques. Her curiosity about "how expensive designer clothes are sewn" was satisfied while making alterations on these garments. From this experience came many of the professional tips found in SEW SMART.

Clotilde taught adult sewing classes for an exclusive fabric store in Woodland Hills, California, for seven years — covering all facets of sewing, from basic sewing to tailoring to working with Ultra Suede® fabric. She conducted teacher seminars in the United States as well as England.

A love of antiques and sewing culminated in combining the two areas by collected antique sewing items. She has an extensive collection, some of which are shown in this book.

At the age of six. Clotilde picked up the needle and hasn't stopped sewing since. She makes all her own clothes and many garments for her husband and five children. Clotilde and her husband now live in Ft. Lauderdale, Florida. Since the publication of "SEW SMART", Clotilde has traveled the United States extensively giving seminars at Universities, fabric stores, and for Co-Operative Extension Agents. She and her husband manage a large notions mail-order company. When time allows, they indulge their fondness for racquetball.

TABLE OF CONTENTS

Sew Smart

An elegant French mother-of-pearl sewing case c. 1800. Needlecase, bodkin, thread winders, scissors, scent bottle and delicate thimble with the Palaise Royale insignia are set in a fitted walnut box lined with velvet.

WE'VE COME A LONG WAY

Yes, we've come a long way in the art of dressmaking. Our sewing sisters of long ago spent many days and even weeks of fine handwork creating their simple everyday wear or elegant evening fashions. We are fortunate that we can make a new outfit in a matter of hours, thanks to our modern sewing machine and the large variety of sewing tools that are available in every fabric store. While none of us would want to return to the good old days of dressmaking, we felt you would be interested in the story of the cloth and sewing tools we so casually take for granted. It is a fascinating as well as educational part of the history of mankind.

THE STORY OF CLOTH

From the earliest of days, the manufacture and sale of cloth has been of primary importance. The processes of producing it were closely guarded, and the sale of cloth was strictly regulated. Death by torture was the penalty for anyone revealing the secrets of silk making outside the borders of China. During the Middle Ages exile was the penalty for anyone caught smuggling wool out of England. It was a capital offense in England in the 1790's to export plans or parts of textile machines.

Sumptuary laws, or laws of dress, were enacted to keep the lower classes separate from royalty and the very rich. These laws prohibited the imitation of the styles of dress of the nobility. In ancient Rome, only free citizens were allowed to wear the long toga. Simple short tunics were worn by all non-citizens such as foreigners and slaves. The all-purple toga was permitted to be worn only by the emperor or by conquering generals. However, priests and magistrates could wear a purple border on their togas.

Plain togas were worn by the ordinary free citizen. If he wished to run for public office, he dusted his toga with chalk to show his intentions. The chalky white color was called "candida;" thus the office seeker became a "candidate."

During the Middle Ages in France, members of the nobility were allowed only four garments, while unmarried women were restricted to one gown! In 13th Century France laws governed the length of the hood adornments, the length of a train, and the cost of fabrics. In the 14th Century, long pointed toes were fashionable. A commoner was limited to a six inch toe, a gentleman could have a twelve inch toe, while a nobleman could have a twenty-four inch toe — these extended toes were held up by long chains attached to the waist.

Elizabeth I ruled that no one could wear a ruff wider than her own. No one with an income less than two hundred pounds a year could wear velvet or gold and silk embroidery — they could not be used on their horses either. Red garments were permitted to be worn only by the royal family; however, many commoners wore red flannel underwear in defiance of this edict. At one time in England, only members of the royal family were allowed to wear ermine. Sable was not permitted anyone below the rank of Earl; the middle classes had to be content with lamb or rabbit.

Naturally, the common people detested these laws. During the French Revolution, mobs attacked and demolished the Chantilly lace factory and even guillotined some of the lacemakers, all because the use of Chantilly lace was restricted to members of the French Court.

Laws also extended even to who was allowed to

1

make garments. Until Louis XIV gave seamstresses permission to make women's and childrens' wear, only tailors were permitted to make clothes.

The course of history has been intimately involved with the development of fabrics and fashion. For centuries, wool has been of major economic importance in England. To protect the woolen industry restrictions governed its use and sale. In 1326 Edward II ruled that commoners had to wear wool — only the nobility, clergy and those who paid forty pounds a year for rent were permitted to wear imported cloth. Even bastard sons of nobility had to wear only wool! In 1331 Edward III gave liberal franchises and protection to Flemish weavers to lure them to England, thus virtually destroying the Flemish wool industry. Elizabeth I ruled that every man, woman, and child over the age of six had to wear a woolen cap when out of doors on Sundays and holy days, or pay a fine.

In 1600, Elizabeth I had chartered the East India Company, and its ships were bringing back spices and calico from India in limited quantities. (The word "calico" is a derivitive of Calcutta, as the calicos initially came from that part of the world). The imported calicos were used as cheap clothing for servants and as bedlinens. In 1662 Catherine of Braganza of Portugal married Charles II of England, and the woolen industry met a formidable foe — calico. As part of Catherine's dowry, England was given free trading rights in Brazil and the Portugese East Indies; also, Tangiers and Bombay were ceded to England. With Catherine's marriage to Charles and, the increase in trade, calicos became very popular, making huge inroads into the English woolen market.

The Portugese particularly liked the painted calicos or chintz (chint is the Hindi word meaning spotted or varigated). A favorite pattern was the brightly colored "tree-of-life" design. Calicos became the rage in England, and by 1685 even the queen wore them. Calicos were hand dyed and painted by a very slow, tedious process until block printing came into use in the 18th Century. They were used everywhere, for gowns, petticoats, and bedclothes, including the draperies around the bed. Naturally the wool interests protested vehemently. Again, to protect the wool interest, in 1678 Parliament ruled that all corpses should be wrapped in a woolen shroud; this law remained in effect until 1814. In 1700 Parliament ruled that buttons and buttonholes had to be made of wool thread instead of silk.

A treaty with Portugal in 1703 tried to encourage wool trade by giving low duties on its imports. In exchange England received oranges and port. As a result, Englishmen who had been drinking claret turned to port.

Finally, in 1722 Parliament forbade the importation of Chinese silks and cottons from India — any use of calicos was strictly banned. These restrictions remained in effect for the next 52 years. Not even cotton printed in England could be worn or used in the home! The East India Company had to sell its chintz and calicos to the American colonies. In England, it became the fashion for ladies to do crewel embroidery on all sorts of garments using the popular "tree-of-life" pattern, thus simulating the forbidden calicos.

The width of English cottons was determined by the distance the shuttle could be thrown while weaving the cloth, approximately 36 inches. In 1733 John Kay invented the "fly shuttle" to compete with the three yard width of India cotton. On his loom, the shuttle was jerked by a thong attached to the weaver's wrist and the shuttle was thrown across the loom farther than a man could ordinarily throw the shuttle. Kay was hated and feared by the weavers who were afraid of losing their jobs. He fled to Paris where he died in poverty. It is now considered that his "fly shuttle" was the device that began the Industrial Revolution.

In 1771, Richard Arkwright made the first coordinated spinning mill which was driven by water power. English cotton could finally be spun fine and strong, enabling it to compete with Indian cottons. In 1790 the textile industry was begun in the American colonies by a run-away apprentice from the Arkwright spinning mill. He carried the plans for the water-powered spinning mill in his head to the new world. With Eli Whitney's invention of the cotton gin in 1793 an ample supply of raw material was available, and the American textile industry was off to a running start.

PINS AND NEEDLES

From the earliest of days, some form of pins and needles have been used. Until the 18th Century, they were so precious a possession that the loss of a needle was a disaster to an entire household. In Medieval days, some needles had a kink placed halfway between the point and eye, to prevent the needle from dropping out of the material and becoming lost. Pins and needles could be bought only at provincial fairs and markets or from traveling peddlers whose visits were infrequent. The fairs were attended by the wealthy and common people alike. Today we sometimes don't even bother to pick up a dropped pin or needle — let the vacuum cleaner do it!

The first pins may have been split from the spine of bird feathers, as the Latin root word pinna means feather. Certainly, spikes, thorns and fish bones were used as early pins. The Egyptians used small fish bones to secure the eyes of the dead. A type of lace called "bone lace" was so named as the pins used to make it were made of fish and chicken bone.

Pins were once made by filing fine wire to a point and twisting a finer wire around the opposite end to form the head. These heads often fell off and the rough ends would snag the material. A new type of pin was sought, and the French and Germans developed the art of wire-drawing, which was the basis of the modern pin. In 1797 pins with solid heads were being manufactured and came into general use.

Commemorative pin cushions, c. 1817. Made of cardboard, covered with printed silk, these were sold as souvenirs at the death of Charlotte (George III's granddaughter) in 1817. Around the pin cushion are mourning pins made from iron and coated with black enamel. The heads are bits of coiled wire.

In the 14th century pins were very expensive; they were considered appropriate gifts for a man to give to his sweetheart. "I'll give you a paper of pins, 'cause that's the way that love begins," is the first line of a folk song that was written around the fifteenth century. In France their sale was restricted by rules of the needlemakers' trade guilds. No pinmaker could have more than one shop for the sale of pins except on New Year's Eve and day, when all merchants were allowed to sell pins. It was the custom for a merchant to give a gift of pins or the money with which to buy them upon the completion of a sale: hence, the word "pin-money."

To protect the local industry, in 1483 Richard III prohibited the importation of pins, and Englishmen had to use the inferior iron wire pins that were made domestically. Henry VIII's wife, Catherine Howard, was allowed to introduce the fine brass pins that were then made in France. During Elizabeth's reign, a well-filled pin cushion was a necessity, as many garments were literally pinned together when worn.

In the Stone Age, sharp awls were used to puncture holes in skins, which were then "sewn" together with sinews. This "sewing" was used for many kinds of packages which had to be covered with an outer layer of cloth or skin for purposes of storage and transportation. When woven cloth was invented, a fine, thin needle with an eye could be used, and sinews were replaced by spun thread.

Supposedly the Chinese invented the steel needle to sew their fine silk fabrics. The steel needle was carried by traders to Damascus, which was a famous steel center. From there, the Moors brought needles to Spain. References in history call a steel needle a "Spanish Needle." Catherine of Aragon must have brought steel needles with her when she came to England to marry Henry VIII, as she was noted for her fine needlework.

A bodkin is a blunt edged long needle with a large eye. It was used for running drawstrings, ribbons and cords through casings in garments. In an age before elastics and zippers, bodkins were essential to men and women equally. Until the end of the

18th Century, the term bodkin and needle were interchangeable.

Delicately carved ivory bodkin case—5 inches long, c. 1800.

Needles and bodkins were kept in open-ended cases that were worn suspended by a cord hanging from the belt. As there was little personal privacy in the Middle Ages, men and women wore what small personal possessions they had suspended from their waists, such as pomanders, thimbles, pen-knives, keys, seals and scissors. Since the mistress of the chatelaine or castle wore these items, they became known as "chatelaines."

Needlemaking began in London in Queen Elizabeth's time. Needles were made in Threeneedle Street. This street was named for the coat-of-arms of the needlemakers guild, which consisted of three needles. The name today has been corrupted into Threadneedle Street. Due to economic restrictions, the needlemakers moved to the country and finally centered in Redditch, England, where there was the needed water power to run the stamping machines. Redditch is still a needle center of the world.

In Queen Anne's time, steel needles were in relatively good supply. At that time needles were kept in needlebooks with embroidered covers; however, the flannel leaves gathered moisture and the needles rusted. Tightly closed cylindrical needlecases were found to solve the problem of rust. These cases were made of many materials — wood, silver, ivory, mother-of-pearl and tortoise-shell; many were beautifully carved and inlaid.

18th century Dutch needlecase carved from a Coquilla nut.

Self-threading needles were available by the 19th century. They had a V-shaped notch at the blunt end to carry the thread. By now needles were plentiful and were sold in packets of special blue paper to prevent their rusting.

THIMBLES

In Central Europe in the Middle Ages, "thummels" or "thimels" were bell-shaped leather caps worn on the thumb — hence the word "thimble." Modern marine thummels are known today as "sailor's palms" and are necessary in sail-making.

Bronze thimbles have been found in Greek and Roman ruins, some of which have open tops, a style still used by modern tailors. These open-top thimbles leave the finger-tip free to pick up threads and pins — they are perfect for the seamstress with long fingernails.

Ordinary thimbles were made of brass or steel, while ornamental thimbles were made of silver and gold and often were capped with semi-precious stones; these were kept for fine needlework. Many thimbles were made of bone or ivory and delicate mother-of-pearl. China thimbles were popular in the mid-19th century, as their smoothness prevented snagging fine threads and fabrics.

In Siberia and Mongolia, brass thimbles were sewn on the borders of the garments as decorations. It was a common practice to give thimbles as betrothal or wedding gifts in small fitted cases in the shape of an egg or knife box. Many small thimbles have lasted through the ages; these were childrens' thimbles made in graduated sets. Children started sewing as early as four years of age!

Inlaid mother-of-pearl thimble case in shape of a Georgian knife box also contains packets of needles c. 1810.

SCISSORS

The origin of scissors as we know them today may have been with the 16th century Venetians. In Medieval days, scissors were kept in a sheath and hung from the waist. Folding scissors, invented during the Renaissance, were found in elaborate sewing cases or "etui" — a great word for crossword puzzle fans. In the mid-18th century, the Persians invented scissors in the form of a bird with the beaks serving as blades. The Dutch have laid claim to being the originators of the stork scissors.

Early steel scissors had ornamental handles which were made separately and soldered onto the shank.

They were very expensive. The common people had to use iron scissors. Scissors after the middle of the 19th century had the handles made in one piece. In the 18th century scissors were kept in metal sheaths to prevent their sharp points from tearing pockets and workbags and also to protect their delicate points.

Dutch scissors c. 1730. These have elaborate silver handles soldered onto steel blades.

MEASURING DEVICES

Measurements varied widely in early days. Ribbon tape measures winding into small cases, such as shells, were used early in the 17th century. Early ribbons were marked with embroidery or ink; stenciled or printed ribbons came into use at the beginning of the 19th century.

Georgian carved ivory tape measure c. 1810. The numbers are stenciled on a green silk ribbon.

5

Long before accurate yardsticks came into being, housewives had their own marked wooden measuring sticks. These were used to mark new ribbons for their needlework as well as to check that they received accurate measures from traveling peddlers from whom they bought ribbons and laces. From this usage we derive the meaning of the word "yardstick" to mean receiving a full measure of value.

Until the metric system was adopted in 1799, the whims of kings determined measurements. Henry I decreed that an English yard should be as long as his arm. A cloth-yard was equal to the length of a hunting arrow. Edward VI decreed that each yard of cloth should have 37 inches in it — an inch equaled the length of the first joint of the thumb. In some instances, an inch equaled three barleycorns laid end-to-end. How's that for accuracy?

Needlecases and other sewing tools such as tape measures, thimble cases and scissors were exquisitely made and were meant to be objects to be admired and treasured. In the 18th century needlework tools were called "toys," as they were sold in toy shops which were the equivalent of our modern gift shops. "Toy" referred to any small, expensive ornamental object. Ladies of that era had limited fields of interest open to them; of primary importance was their skill with a needle as well as skill at handwriting. Therefore, handwriting tools were frequently found mixed with the sewing tools. By the end of the Victorian age, ready-made clothes, mass production and the opportunity for higher education expanded women's interests so that sewing was not the center of a woman's life. Gone forever was the appeal of intricate, ornamental sewing tools; exquisite hand craftsmanship was a thing of the past.

SEWING CASES

In the 18th century sewing cases were called etui or "Lady's Companion," as they were compact traveling cases for ladies' sewing and household needs. These cases contained many items such as needlecase, thimble, stiletto, bodkin, tweezer, a memo pad (called an aide memoir), a small knife for cutting seams, pencil and other small personal items.

French silver gilt tools in a carved ivory case c. 1835.

A standing Georgian silver needlecase with thimble on top c. 1810, includes spindle for thread, powder shaker for keeping fingers dry. The needlecase is in the cylindrical stand. A seal is on the base of the stand.

BEFORE YOU SEW

As you approach each new sewing project, you should spend an adequate amount of time in the planning process, so that you choose a good, workable fabric-pattern combination. Some fabrics are not suitable for certain patterns; for example, a plaid fabric will not match along a raglan sleeve line, and a long A-line skirt would require almost twice the amount of yardage if a napped fabric is used. Not all fabrics can be used for all types of garments. A very ravelly fabric will not hold up in children's play wear or for sports clothes. Firmly woven fabrics are not suitable for draped or gathered styles.

Achieving the proper fabric-pattern combination becomes easier as you gain more experience. We want to hurry that process along by giving you some guidelines for choosing and cutting your fabric. Spend some time thinking about the finished garment before you make a purchase, and then spend more time thinking about the pattern layout, so that you use your fabric to its best advantage. One little slip-up during the layout and cutting process, on certain fabrics, can ruin the whole garment or send you back to the fabric store for more yardage.

Plan before you buy — plan before you cut. The time you spend at the beginning is well worth it, in order to create a garment of professional quality. Simple patterns and plain fabrics won't require much planning, but detailed patterns, using fabrics that must be matched, can take as much time for the planning process as for the whole sewing process.

FABRIC PROBLEMS

There are three basic types of fabrics used by home-sewers today: wovens, knits, and non-wovens, such as felt and the new synthetic suedes. Each type has many sub-types, which is what makes the world of fashion so interesting. Each type also has its own characteristics and problems. These should be understood so that you can handle each fabric the best way.

Woven Fabrics

Woven fabrics are made from many natural and synthetic fibers. They come in different weaves, weights, and combinations of yarns. Wovens have been the mainstay of the fashion scene for many, many years, and will always have a large part of the fabric market. A few of the problems found with woven fabrics are listed below.

* Woven fabrics tend to fray along cut edges, some fabrics more than others. Fraying edges require seam finishes of some kind.

* Some woven fabrics are "off-grain." This means that the lengthwise and crosswise threads are not at right angles. Off-grain fabrics will not hang properly, and cannot be matched at seamlines, if the pattern is woven in. Check for this problem on fabrics you plan to purchase, by folding the fabric crosswise, so that the selvages line up. Ideally, the crosswise thread and/or pattern should run along the length of the fold. A little variance is acceptable, but if the thread or pattern dips down more than ½" (13mm), save yourself some problems and don't buy the fabric.

GOOD

BAD

* Some off-grain wovens can be straightened by pulling on the bias and pressing. Permanent press fabrics are an exception, since they are heat or chemically set during the finishing process. However, the straightening process isn't always permanent, and after the garment is washed you are right back where you started.

* Permanent press fabrics have a firm finish that makes them difficult to ease or drape. Keep this in mind when choosing patterns that require these techniques. These fabrics also tend to be non-absorbing, which can make them feel warm.

* Woven fabrics don't have give, like knits, and so need more ease, making the garment appear somewhat larger. Knits are more suitable for active sports wear.

Knit Fabrics

Knits are the miracle fabric of our time, and we all love their easy care and the simplified sewing techniques. They are not without problems, though, and you should be aware of them so that you will have success with your sewing.

* The crosswise grain of most knit fabrics is not at right angles to the lengthwise rib (grain), because many of them are made on circular knitting machines, which produce a crosswise line that spirals up around the tube of fabric. It is impossible to straighten this crosswise line. Instructions will be given, later on, that will help you overcome this problem during the cutting process.

* Some printed, striped, and solid colored knits will be pressed during the finishing process in such a way that the crosswise grain is "off" more than it should be. Perhaps you have seen plaid or printed knits with the pattern dipping down as it approaches the center fold. There isn't any way you can use this fabric unless you buy extra, and throw away the crooked part, or you cut only non-visible, facing pieces from the crooked section. Unless you just have to have that fabric, you are better off leaving it in the store.

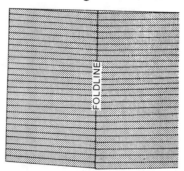

* Single knits tend to roll after they have been pre-shrunk. The rolling edges can be somewhat controlled by spraying with fabric finish or starch and then pressing.

* Most interlock knits will run like a nylon stocking in one direction. This tendency has nothing to do with the quality of the fabric. Find out the direction of the run by gently pulling across both cut edges of the fabric. Position the pattern pieces so that the runs go up the garment. This will prevent runs from forming at the neckline and shoulder seams. You can discourage runs at the bottom edges of hems and sleeves by straight stitching or zigzagging ¼" (6mm) from the edge of the fabric. Fortunately, manufacturers do check the direction of the run and print one-way prints in the correct direction.

* The lengthwise grain on a knit fabric is marked by the rib of knit loops that run the length of the fabric. The crosswise grain is more difficult to identify, but it is also marked by a line of knit loops that run across the fabric.

* Many knit fabrics have a permanent crease down the center. This must be avoided during pattern layout.

Non-woven Fabrics

Matted fabrics, such as felt and polyester fleece, non-woven vinyls, and the new non-woven, synthetic suedes such as Ultra Suede® fabric, are relatively new to the home-sewer. They are easy to work with because they do not fray, and one can take advantage of simple seam and construction techniques.

* Synthetic suedes have a nap, and require a nap layout so that you won't get different color shades on various parts of the garment.

Fabrics are usually folded and rolled so that the right side is to the inside. This is done to keep the fabric clean and also to avoid fading. However, not all fabrics are handled this way. If you are confused as to which is the right or wrong side, choose the side that appeals most to you. If anyone ever questions your choice, just tell them that's the way you like it! You can tell the right side of a knit fabric by gently stretching the crosswise edge. The fabric will roll to the right side.

Mark the wrong side of confusing fabrics with strips of transparent or drafting tape, or use tailor's chalk or a sliver of soap. This will help you put the garment together properly.

Carefully examine all fabrics for flaws before you have them cut from the bolt. As you well know, not all fabrics are perfect, and it is better to find the flaws at the store, rather than after you get home.

Check fabrics again, after they have been pre-shrunk. Sometimes the flaw is in the dye, and won't show up until it has been washed.

Don't hesitate about returning unsatisfactory fabric to the store, or refusing to buy inferior fabrics. Most fabric stores want to handle only quality goods, and appreciate your help in catching poor merchandise.

Pre-Shrinking Fabric

Most fabrics should be pre-shrunk before they are cut. This removes any fiber shrinkage, and allows the fabric to relax. After all, it has been stretched on a bolt for a fair amount of time, and needs to regain its natural size.

Pre-shrinking also removes any excess finishing materials in the fabric. Finishing chemicals can have a disagreeable odor, and they can also coat the machine needle, causing it to skip stitches.

Use the same method to pre-shrink the fabric that you will use to clean the finished garment. If you are going to machine wash and dry the finished garment, then pre-shrink the fabric using the same water temperature and dryer setting.

Cotton knits tend to shrink quite a bit, and more than once. We suggest that you pre-shrink them twice, using hot water and the highest setting on your dryer, even if you don't plan to do this afterward. This will guarantee maximum shrinkage before the yardage is cut.

Many other knits, including polyester double knits, will have a small amount of continued shrinkage if they are always dried in the dryer. You can prevent this problem by drip-drying the garments, or just partially drying them in the dryer.

Woolens, woven fabrics or knits should be pre-shrunk with steam, unless they are labeled "needle-ready." Send the yardage to a professional dry cleaner, or do it yourself by running the fabric through a coin-operated dry-cleaning machine.

Small amounts of wool can be conveniently pre-shrunk at home, in the dryer. Place the dry wool yardage in the dryer with some damp clothes. Run the dryer for about 10 minutes. The heat and moisture will remove the shrinkage. Lay the moist yardage on a flat surface to dry.

Other fabrics, that are going to be used for dry cleanable garments, don't usually have to be pre-shrunk. However, we suggest that you spread them out on a flat surface overnight to allow them to relax, before cutting.

If you find it necessary to press your fabric after it has been pre-shrunk, run the iron along the lengthwise grain rather than across the fabric. This will result in a smooth finish, and not stretch the fabric out of shape.

Measure your yardage before and after pre-shrinking. Make note of the amount of shrinkage, and keep this information handy when purchasing similar fabric.

PATTERN LAYOUT

Once you have selected your pattern and pre-shrunk the fabric, you are ready for one of the most important steps in the process of making a beautiful garment — "cutting out." No matter how expert your sewing techniques or how perfect your fit, you will have the "loving hands at home look" if your pattern layout and cutting procedure don't match your other skills. We're not just talking about cutting a straight line; there is more to it than that.

Take a look at designer clothes in an exclusive dress shop or nice department store. You will notice that grainlines are perfect, stripes and plaids match, and even the pockets on patterned or striped fabric are cut and sewn so that they match the garment perfectly. Patterned fabric will be cut so that the design will flatter the figure — no big roses on the bust or derriere. Great care is given to the cutting of small detail pieces, so that they add interest to the garment.

Since your paper pattern has been designed without any specific fabric in mind, the only help you receive in the layout process is an economical placement of pattern pieces, with grainlines in the proper position. Many times this is all you need, but some fabrics require careful positioning of the various pieces, so that you get a custom-look rather than a homemade look.

Some of the fabrics that require extra planning are: napped fabrics, plaids and stripes, diagonally printed or woven fabrics, and patterned fabrics that have a definite repeat or large motif.

There are some layout rules that pertain to all fabrics. Let's consider them first.

General Layout Guidelines

* Separate needed pattern pieces, and place the remaining ones back in the pattern envelope, so that they won't get mixed up.

* Trim away excess pattern tissue. However, it isn't necessary to cut-out the pattern pieces exactly.

* Press all the pattern pieces with a dry iron, to remove wrinkles. This makes cutting more accurate.

* Make any necessary alterations to the paper pattern before pinning it to the fabric.

* Extend the grainline on all pattern pieces, from the top to bottom edge. This makes it easier to place them on grain.

* Make a rough layout of all pattern pieces before you permanently pin them in place, or do any cutting. This will let you know if you are short of yardage, while there is still time to do something about it.

* The pattern grainline should run parallel to the fabric grainline. This is absolutely necessary for a properly hanging garment.

* The distance from the pattern grainline to the fabric fold or edge should be the same at the top and bottom of the pattern piece. Use a ruler or yardstick to help you measure exactly.

* Permanently pin the pattern pieces in place only after the grainlines are perfect and you are sure you have enough fabric.

* Pattern pieces can be placed right or wrong side up, if the fabric is folded double. If you are cutting one layer at a time, cut one piece with the pattern printing right side up, and the other piece with the pattern printing upside down. This makes sure you end up with a left and right garment piece.

* The selvage edge can be used only if it lies flat and does not pucker after pre-shrinking. It can be used on any straight-grain seam, such as the cen-

ter back seam of a skirt. This will give more stability to the seamline and reduce the sit-out problem in the seat area. Use the selvage edge along one side of waistbands. This reduces bulk, since you won't have to turn under a raw edge on the inside of the garment.

* Some fabrics will have a faded line along the fold, which is caused by gas fumes in the fabric store — not direct sunlight. Gas fumes are due to the formaldehyde used in the finishing process at the mill. These fumes will cause your eyes to smart if you ever happen to be in a fabric store just as they open up a new shipment of fabric. Check your fabric for a faded fold, and cut around it, or return the fabric to the store.

* Use a nap layout for napped fabrics, uneven plaids or stripes, and all knits. Place the pattern pieces on the fabric so that the tops all face the same direction.

Saving The Day
Sometimes the most careful planning will fail, and you will find yourself short of fabric. Check through the following list of suggestions to see if you can find the help that will save a trip to the fabric store.

* Cut facings and/or pockets, flaps, and cuffs from another fabric. Many times you see contrasting fabric used for collar, cuff and placket facings on ready-made shirts and jackets.

* Overlap the garment front and front-facing pattern pieces until the seamlines meet, and cut as one, for garments that have a straight front edge. This will give you two more seam widths of fabric, which is sometimes all you need.

* Change the grainlines of collars, yokes, pockets, flaps, and cuffs so they are cut on the bias. This will add interesting detail, as well as save fabric.

* Change the sleeve length to a shorter style.

* Face hems with another fabric, rather than making the usual turned-up hem.

Napped Fabrics
Napped fabrics have some sort of surface interest that influences the way light rays are reflected from the fabric. Even though a garment is made from one piece of napped fabric, it can look as though two different shades of fabric were used, if the pattern pieces are not placed on the fabric so that all the tops face in the same direction. You are probably most familiar with this problem on corduroys and velvet-like fabrics.

Knits and some woven fabrics have a nap-like effect because of the way they are constructed. Knits are made up of continuous rows of loops, with the tops facing in one direction. The closed ends of the loops reflect the light differently from the open ends. This makes for shading problems at seamlines, if all the pattern pieces are not cut using a nap layout. The same thing happens with textured wovens, if ridges or other surface interest are not symmetrical.

It is difficult to tell if some fabrics have a nap, and all too often you don't notice it until after the garment has been completed. Use this simple drape test if you aren't sure. Drape the uncut yardage from one shoulder to the other, letting as much hang down toward the floor, as possible. Stand in front of a full length mirror, in a well lighted room, or have a friend go out into the sunlight with you. If the fabric on one side of your figure looks slightly darker than the fabric on the other side, you have a napped fabric, and must use a nap layout when pinning the pattern to the fabric.

Most patterns will have a nap layout in the cutting guide, and it usually requires extra yardage. If your pattern doesn't tell you how much extra yardage is needed, you can find out by laying all the pattern pieces on a cutting board, keeping them within the same measurement as the fabric you will use. Many fabric stores will let you lay your pattern pieces out on the actual fabric you have chosen, so that you purchase just the right amount.

Check the direction of the nap by running your hand over the surface. Short pile fabrics, such as velvet and velveteen should be cut so that the pile runs up the garment. This will give a dark, rich color. Long pile fabrics should be cut so that the pile runs down the garment.

Most napped or nap-like fabrics can be cut double. However, you will find that fabrics with quite a bit of pile, such as velvet or fake furs, handle more easily when cut one layer at a time. Doing this will make each garment piece accurate in size and shape. Remember to cut one piece with the pattern printing right side up, and the other piece with the pattern printing upside down. This makes sure you end up with right and left garment pieces.

Care must be taken when cutting fabric pieces for collars and pocket flaps that turn down on the garment. These pieces should be cut so that the nap lies in the same direction as the fabric that they will lie against. You won't have to worry about the above problem if commercial pattern pieces are placed on the fabric so the printing all faces one direction.

Plaids

The correct use of plaids can make a stunning garment, but you must be aware of the careful planning required to match up everything. A little extra time spent in the layout process can eliminate most of the sewing problems. Keep the following points in mind when choosing your pattern and fabric.

Patterns of simple design, with a minimum of intricate detail, work best with plaids. Some patterns just aren't suitable, which will usually be stated somewhere on the pattern envelope. Avoid patterns with darts placed at angles, rather than on the horizontal or vertical line. Long curved darts, or seams that require some easing, such as princess lines, will also give matching problems.

Patterns cut from plaid fabrics will require more yardage than other fabrics. Yardage requirements will be given on the pattern envelope, or you will find the statement, "extra fabric needed for matching plaids." Small plaids will need approximately ½ yard (46cm) extra fabric, while large plaids will require more, sometimes up to 1½ yards (137cm). Plaids repeat at regular intervals, and it is this repeat factor that determines the extra yardage. Large distances between repeats will require more extra yardage than small distances between repeats.

There are basically two types of plaids: even and uneven. Even plaids have strong horizontal and vertical lines that repeat at regular intervals. The plaid is symmetrical in design. It looks the same from the top or the bottom, or from side to side.

Uneven plaids can be asymmetrical in either the horizontal, vertical, or both directions. The design will not appear the same if viewed from the top or bottom, or from one side or the other. Uneven plaids require more extra yardage than even plaids, and are somewhat more difficult to cut and match.

An easy way to tell if a plaid is even or uneven is to turn back a corner of the fabric, making sure that the selvage edge is parallel to a horizontal plaid line. Even plaids can be matched up along the diagonal fold, so that the design looks continuous. You will be unable to do this with an uneven plaid.

Careful thought should be given to the relationship of the plaid to the body. Avoid having a strong, dominant plaid line fall at the bust or hipline if you have a full figure.

12

Plan to have a dominant horizontal line of the plaid fall at the hemline. This will give balance to the finished garment.

Tall figures should have the dominant vertical lines centered on either side of the center front and center back lines. Short figures can wear the dominant vertical line on the center front and back to advantage.

Carefully position the pattern pieces for a front closing garment on the fabric so that the plaid matches when the garment is buttoned. This can be done by placing the center front lines on the same vertical stripe.

Match the plaids on the pattern pieces from the bottom up. The section of garment above the bust darts will not match, but the rest of the garment will.

Make all length adjustments on your paper pattern before pinning it to the fabric, so that you can tell exactly where hemlines will fall on the plaid.

Uneven plaids require a nap layout. Even plaids do not. If you are in doubt about your plaid, then cut using the nap layout, just to be safe.

You should match seamlines, not cutting lines, when you pin the pattern pieces to the fabric. Use notches and other construction marks as key points for matching.

Place the main front pattern piece on the fabric first, and then place the other pieces to match its placement.

Plaid fabric can be cut more accurately if it is cut one layer at a time. We're sure you know how difficult it is to fold a plaid fabric so that the plaid lines match up underneath each other. You will really save cutting time if you work with a single layer of fabric.

Position the main pattern piece as you want it on the fabric, and then lay the adjoining piece next to it so that the seamlines will match. Pin and cut. Flip these pieces over, so that the fabric rather than the pattern is up, and position them on the fabric so that the plaid lines up exactly. Pin and cut. You will

now have exactly matching right and left garment pieces.

Another method is to mark the plaid lines on the paper pattern, and then use these lines as a guide for cutting the matching piece.

Plaids should match across all vertical seamlines, including center front, sides and center back.

Set-in sleeves can only be matched at the front armhole. Use the sleeve dots and notches as guides remembering that you are matching seamlines rather than cutting lines. Raglan sleeves cannot be matched. Kimono sleeves will match only below the shoulder notch. Other things that should match are: the center back of the collar to the center back of the garment, if possible; pockets and flaps; and the joining line of two-piece outfits.

Design details, such as pockets, flaps, tabs, yokes, or stitched-on belts, can be cut to match the garment exactly, or cut on the bias for effect. If you want to match these details, it is suggested that they be cut after all the main pattern pieces have been cut, and construction marks transferred.

Place the small detail pattern piece on the garment piece in the proper position. Pin in place, and carefully trace the plaid lines onto the paper pattern. Pin this pattern to the fabric, matching up the plaid lines, and cut. You will get a perfect match every time.

Now that the cutting-out has been accurate and well thought out, the sewing should be a snap.

Checks

Follow the same basic rules for cutting plaids when working with checked fabrics. It is usually not nec-

essary to match up checks, ¼" (6mm) or smaller, unless it will be very obvious in the finished garment.

Consider cutting detail pattern pieces, such as collars, cuffs, and yokes, on the bias for an interesting effect. This also eliminates the need for matching.

Stripes

Stripes are fun to work with, and they can add lots of zip to your wardrobe. They present fewer cutting and sewing problems than plaids, and most of them can be solved by proper pattern selection and pattern layout. The following points should be kept in mind when cutting striped fabrics.

Did you know that corduroy and twill fabrics are considered to be striped fabrics, just the same as printed or woven stripes?

Not all patterns are suitable for striped fabrics; this information is usually given on the pattern envelope. The design lines of some patterns can conflict with the stripes and make a very unattractive combination. A rule to follow here is: the busier the fabric, the simpler the pattern.

There are two basic kinds of striped fabrics — balanced and unbalanced. Balanced stripes are like even plaids in that they are symmetrical and can be cut in either direction.

Unbalanced stripes are like uneven plaids and will require a nap layout and usually more yardage.

Examine your fabric before cutting to decide if there is a dominant stripe that should be placed in a particular position on the figure. Refer back to the plaid section for help with this problem.

Remember to match seamlines, not cutting lines, when placing the pattern pieces on the fabric. Use notches and constructions marks as guides for matching.

Balanced and unbalanced horizontal stripes should match at all side seams, and at the front of the armhole. Start matching from the bottom of the pattern piece, and remember that the stripes above the bust dart will not match.

A dominant stripe should fall at the hemline except when the pattern has a very curved hem, or if such placement will cause another dominant stripe to fall at the bust or hipline.

Plan the cutting of the vertical stripes so that the dominant stripe falls where you want it to on your figure. The stripes on flared skirts will form a chevron effect along the side seams. This effect is very striking when matched perfectly, so take care when laying these pattern pieces out on the fabric.

Diagonal stripes are not very common, but they do show up occasionally, and present a few problems of their own. Many patterns will state that they are not suitable for diagonal stripes or weaves, so watch out for this. Lapels on jackets will not balance when they are cut from a diagonally striped or woven fabric.

Chevron seams on flared skirts are impossible to achieve with some diagonals, and difficult with others. It is suggested that the fabric be cut so that the diagonal runs around the figure, with no attempt at chevroning.

Printed Fabrics

Printed fabrics are always very popular, and while many are just as easy to cut and sew as solid colored fabrics, some have to be matched, or cut with a nap layout, while others have large motifs that have to be carefully arranged on the garment.

Consider the different colors in your print. Which color do you want next to your face? Lay your pattern pieces on the fabric to achieve the desired effect.

How will the print best fit onto the finished garment? When cutting collars and cuffs, plan which bit of color or print will show on the finished side. A turtleneck pattern piece should be placed on the fabric so that the "show" section of the collar, features the print or color you want.

Carefully cut patch pockets so that they exactly match the fabric on which they are being placed.

This is a touch you will always see on expensive, designer clothes.

Border prints are fun to wear, and can be used for many exciting trims. They are unusually easy to match; just remember to start at the bottom. Use the border design to trim waistbands, cuffs, and necklines. This is one of Pucci's favorite looks.

Knits

We have all come to love the sewing and wearing ease of knits, yet they are not without their own set of layout problems. Some are caused by the way the fabric is constructed, while others are due to poor finishing procedures. You can't do much about the fabric construction, but you can, and should, refuse to buy poor quality fabric. No matter how good your sewing skills, you can't make a bad fabric look good.

Have you ever purchased striped T-shirt fabric, and then been unable to get the stripe at right angles to the lengthwise rib? No matter how hard you try to straighten the fabric, pin and push, you still can't do it. Well, don't get too upset, because you are trying to do the impossible.

T-shirt knits, as well as many other knit fabrics, are made on circular knitting machines, which make a tubular fabric. Some of the fabrics are left in the tube form, when they are sold in fabric stores, while others are split open along the joining line, and finished flat. By the way, the joining line looks like a big vertical flaw when the fabric is in the tube form.

Whatever the finished form, circular knits are all constructed so that the crosswise run of yarn spirals up the tube. When the tube is split open, the crosswise yarns or stripes will not be at right angles to the lengthwise rib.

Properly finished fabric will be "off" just a small amount. Poorly finished fabric can be really crooked. Carefully examine all knits to see how much "off grain" they are.

The amount of "off grain" can be determined by folding the fabric along the crosswise grain, until the selvage edges meet. Check the pattern or crosswise yarn along the fold. It should be as nearly parallel to the fold as possible. Anything up to ½" (13mm) is workable. Fabrics "off" much more than that are going to give you lots of problems.

OFF GRAIN

Because of this "off" grain problem, we suggest that you cut all knits that have to be matched in a single layer. This saves time in the long run and guarantees a perfect match along the seamlines.

Use an expanded, rather than a half pattern, when cutting pieces that have to be placed on a fold. Duplicate the pattern on a large piece of folded paper, and cut it out while the paper is still folded. This will give you an expanded pattern.

FOLDLINE
EXPANDED PATTERN

We have stressed how important it is to place pattern pieces on grain; now, we are going to tell you to ignore the grain, in favor of the print or stripe, when cutting knits. This is one place where the finished

look takes precedence over the grainline. Use the following guidelines to help you place your pattern pieces correctly.

* Place the pattern on horizontally striped fabrics so that the pattern grainline is at right angles to the stripe. Check this by folding down the pattern at the underarm points. The fold should be on or parallel to a stripe. Make sure you position the garment front, back and sleeves so the underarm points all lie on the same stripe.

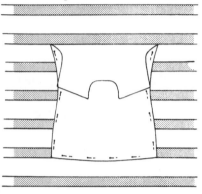

* Some printed fabrics can have the pattern printed crookedly on the fabric. Again, ignore the grainline, and position the pattern so that the print looks straight.

* Cut solid color knits with the lengthwise grain of the pattern on the lengthwise rib of the fabric.

* Many solid color velours have what we call an invisible horizontal stripe. This is probably caused by a variance in yarn color, and is really just a periodic, subtle change of color across the fabric. Treat this invisible stripe like a real one when you position the pattern on the fabric.

Other things to keep in mind when cutting knit fabrics are listed below:

* Cut the fabric so that the greatest stretch goes a-

round the body. This provides the most wearing comfort.

* Don't let the end of the fabric hang over the edge of the table when pinning the pattern in place and cutting the fabric. This will stretch the fabric and adversely affect the size of the cut pieces.

* Knits should be cut with a nap layout in order to prevent color changes at seamlines.

* Be aware of the permanent crease that runs the length of the fold on some knit fabrics. You will know it is permanent if it is still there after the fabric has been pre-shrunk. Avoid putting it down the front or back of a garment, unless you have some nice trim to cover it. The crease can be used down the center of sleeves.

CUTTING TIPS

Secure the pattern pieces to the fabric with enough pins to hold them in place, but not so many that the pattern begins to wrinkle. Many times *pattern weights* can be used in place of pins. They can save lots of time.

Always use a sharp pair of bent-handled shears, at least 8″ (20cm) to 10″ (25cm) long, when cutting fabric. Dull ones will chew up the fabric, and tire your hands. If you are left-handed, use a pair of left-handed shears.

Make long cuts, rather than short snips when cutting. This makes for more accurate cutting. Keep the shears constantly moving when cutting around curves.

Do not overcut. This means you should cut just around the pattern edges and not make cuts extending out into the fabric at each corner. You may need some of that extra fabric, so leave it intact.

Be aware of the width of the cutting line on your paper pattern. Some of them seem to be very wide, and, depending upon where you cut, they can affect the size of the garment. If you think you have a problem, measure the width of the seam allowance to see just where the cutting line should be.

Do not cut out fabric with pinking shears. This will make it very difficult to judge seam widths when sewing. Use your pinking shears after seams have been sewn.

If you ever have to enlarge a pattern piece, we suggest that you actually expand it with a piece of paper, rather than trying to rely on your memory when cutting.

MARKING FABRIC

Once the cutting job has been completed, your next step is to transfer the construction marks to the fabric. This can be done using various methods, and we always favor the easiest and most accurate.

Outside Construction Marks

Construction marks that fall along the outside edges of the pattern are easily marked with small clips into the seam allowance. An ⅛″ (3mm) clip is all that is necessary, and it doesn't weaken the seam allowance.

Use the clip method to mark the following construction marks:

Notches: Clip each notch, including all the points of multiple notches.

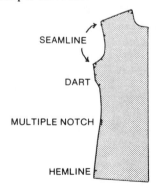

Hemlines: Mark the hem fold on each side of the pattern piece.

Seamlines: Mark if desired. This is not necessary if you have a *seam guide* on the throat plate of your sewing machine.

Dart Ends: Clip each end of the dart.

Zipper Openings: Clip the end of zipper openings.

Sleeves and Armscyes: Clip the dot at the top of the sleeves and the dots around the sleeve cap and armscye.

Other Details: Clip all other outside marks, such as pockets that go in a seam, special circles marking the end of stitching lines, center front and center back on garment and facing pieces, lapel notches, and also sections to be eased.

Inside Construction Marks

Inside details, such as pocket and flap locations, dart ends, pleats, and trim lines can be marked with a pencil, washable felt tip pen, or some sort of chalk. Fold fabric right sides together, this helps keep fabric clean and makes marking easier.

While the pattern is still pinned to the fabric, insert pins through all the inside construction marks, as shown. Always make sure the point the pin enters the fabric is the desired marking point or stitching line. It helps if you use a cutting board, so that the pins have something to hold them firmly in place.

Carefully turn fabric over. Place another pin or mark on the underside where the pins pierce through the fabric.

Garment pieces that are going to be interfaced, and have inside construction marks, should be marked after the interfacing has been fused or stitched in place.

Construction marks that have to be used on the right side should be marked as described above. Transfer them to the right side just before you have to use them.

Do this by running a short thread through the fabric, at the exact center of the mark. This method is more accurate than tailor's tacks.

GETTING IT ALL TOGETHER

The quality and variety of your sewing equipment greatly influence the look of your finished garment, and they can make the construction process simple or difficult. Having the right tools for each specific job is as important in the sewing room as any other place. A list of recommended sewing equipment is given below. Each item serves a definite purpose and makes sewing easier.

SEWING TOOLS

Of course, your sewing machine is the most important piece of sewing equipment you own. It really doesn't make too much difference what kind of machine you own, just as long as it is kept clean, well oiled, and in good repair.

Study your machine instruction book so you know how to use and care for your machine. It doesn't hurt to review it often just to remind you about certain points. One of the most important things contained in the instruction book is cleaning and oiling information. Perform these jobs frequently. We recommend a thorough cleaning and oiling of the bobbin area before each sewing session. Give your machine the proper care, and it will serve you long and well.

A secretary's chair is a good choice for the sewing room. It gives good back support, and can have the seat height adjusted. It is also handy because it rolls and turns.

Make sure your machine area is well lighted. A draftsman's lamp can be clamped onto the machine cabinet or sewing table; this is a must if you sew a lot at night.

Mount a small bulletin board over the sewing machine if you have a sewing room or fixed place for your sewing equipment. This is handy for pinning up pattern instruction sheets.

Machine Needles

Machine needles are almost as important as the sewing machine. Perfect stitching requires the proper size and type of needle, and a needle that isn't damaged or dull.

	Imported	Domestic
Needle sizes are marked by number. There is a different numbering system for domestic and imported needles. Compare the two systems at the right.	65	9
	70	10
	75	11
	80	12
	90	14
	100	16

Machine needles also have different point shapes. Each kind is used for a certain type of fabric.

Normal Sharp Point: This needle type pierces the fabric threads and is used for woven fabrics.

Light-ballpoint: The needle slides along the threads of the fabric until it finds a gap to get through, rather than piercing the fabric threads. It is used for knits which can run or develop holes if a sharp needle severs a thread.

Medium-ballpoint: This needle functions like the one above, but it is used for stitching elastic or elastic fabrics such as spandex. It is too blunt for other knits.

Wedge Point: Use a wedge point needle for leather or leather-like fabrics. It has small, sharp edges which cut through the leather.

Universal Needle: Many companies are now introducing a universal machine needle to the home sewing market. It comes in various sizes and has a modified ballpoint similar to the light-ballpoint described above. It is advertised as being suitable for both knits and wovens. Try it and see how you like it.

The needle chart below will help you choose the proper size and type of needle for your particular fabric.

Fabric Weight	FABRICS	Needle Size	Point Type
Sheer	Chiffon, Organza Lace, Voile, Crepe, Batiste	9-10	Sharp
	Sheer Tricot, Cire	9-10	Ballpoint
Medium Sheer	Wool Crepe, Jersey, Gingham, Challis, Coated nylon outerwear, Ultra Suede® fabric	11-12	Sharp
	Stretch lace, Power net, Swimsuit fabrics, Tricot, Lightweight Cotton and Polyester knits	11-12	Ballpoint
Medium	Seersucker, Flannel, Muslin, Gaberdine, Poplin, Broadcloth, Velveteen, Permanent press	14	Sharp
	Heavyweight knits, Sweater fabrics, Velour	14	Ballpoint
Medium Heavy	Denim, Quilted fabrics, Fake fur, Terry cloth, Heavy woolens	16	Sharp
Heavy	Upholstery fabric, Canvas, Duck, Sailcloth, Double-faced wool	16	Sharp
Leather	Kidskin, Patent, Synthetic suede, Cabretta, Calfskin, Upholstery vinyl	11 14-16	Wedge

Check your machine needles often for damaged points or dullness. A needle with a bent, dull, or rough point will have difficulty penetrating the fabric, and it can cause fabric damage, such as holes, snags, or pulled and broken threads.

Run your fingernail over the point of the needle to see if it is bent-over or rough. Check for dullness by looking directly down on the point. A dull needle will have a flat, shiny spot on the top.

It is possible to bend a needle out of the straight by hitting a pin or some part of the throat plate. **Do not** sew over pins; you are just asking for trouble. They can damage or break your needle. Pulling the fabric through the machine can cause the needle to hit the throat plate. Bent needles will cause skipped or uneven stitches; replace them.

Coated needles can interfere with perfect stitching. Chemicals used in the fabric finishing process can build up on the needle. Pre-shrink your fashion fabrics to remove excess finishing chemicals, and prevent the coating problem. Stitching through tape can also coat the needle. Change to a new needle if you have this problem.

Check and change your machine needles often. It is much cheaper to use a new needle than ruin a garment using a dull or damaged needle.

Thread

Choose the proper thread for your fashion fabric. The polyester and cotton-polyester threads that are now on the market can be used for nearly any fabric. They are available in a light-weight for sheer and lingerie fabrics, a medium-weight for most dress-making fabrics, and a heavy-weight for heavy-duty clothes and outer wear.

A heavy, polyester thread, designed for topstitching and buttonholes, is now available. It replaces silk buttonhole twist, and is much more practical because it is color fast and has a much larger color range.

Always use the same thread on the top and bobbin of the machine. Mis-matched thread (cotton on the top and polyester on the bobbin) is apt to cause stitching difficulties.

Match the thread size to the needle size. Thread that is too thick will break or fray.

Thread should be stored at a temperature of about 70° F (21° C) and a 65% humidity. Breakage can result with thread that is too moist or too dry. Thread also deteriorates with age. Don't expect thread that has been in your sewing room for four years to perform like fresh, new thread.

When selecting thread, choose a color one shade darker than your fashion fabric. Use a different color thread on the top and bobbin when stitching plaid or striped or printed fabrics. This makes the stitches less visible. Use a contrasting thread for machine or hand bastings.

Eliminate the problem of long tangled thread ends on stored spools by securing the ends to the spool with small pieces of transparent tape.

Thimble

A thimble is a must for hand sewing. Buy one that comfortably fits your finger, and learn to use it. It will feel awkward at first, but it prevents wear and tear on your fingertip.

Try a leather thimble if you don't like a conventional metal one. If you have gorgeous, long fingernails, use a thimble without a top. They are available at many notion counters.

CUTTING TOOLS

Many people feel that cutting-out is the hardest or least pleasant part of making a garment. It needn't be if you use the proper tools.

Cutting Board

A folding, cardboard cutting board is available at most fabric stores. It measures 40″ (100cm) by 60″ (150cm), and makes a nice surface for cutting. It can be placed on the floor or a table. We have even heard of people "cutting-out" on the bed.

The board is marked off in one inch squares, which are handy for all kinds of marking and measuring jobs. The thick cardboard also gives you a surface for anchoring pins when marking construction details and buttonholes.

Shears

Every seamstress should own a good, sharp pair of bent-handled shears. They should be 8″ (20cm) to 10″ (25cm) long. Buy left-handed shears if you are left-handed. Don't try to make do with right-handed shears.

Keep your shears sharp. Dull ones will chew up your fabric and give you very tired hands. Have them sharpened as necessary, and then hide them under your mattress so no one else can use them.

A small pair of shears about 6″ (15cm) long is handy to keep at the sewing machine for small clipping and trimming jobs. Hide these too. Kids think the small size was made just for them and their paper projects.

Invest in a good pair of pinking shears. These are available with either a zig-zag or scalloped edge. They are a good item to put on your Christmas or birthday "wish" list. Don't use your pinking shears for cutting-out.

Thread nippers are handy to keep at the machine for ripping seams, clipping into curves and cutting sewing thread when machine stitching. Contrary to what you might think, they work better if you don't put your thumb in the hole.   It's really for your third finger.

23

Pins, Pin Cushions and Pattern Weights

Long, thin large-head pins with glass or plastic heads are the most versatile in the sewing room. They are fine enough for your most delicate fabrics, and long enough to be used on thick or bulky fabrics. You can weave them into fabrics and they won't fall out. The large head makes them easy to find in your fabric (the heads don't bury down and get lost), and on the floor. Pins wear out, just like needles, so throw away all damaged, bent or dull pins.

A wrist pin-cushion is one of the most handy tools in the sewing room. Get used to wearing one, and you won't ever want to be without it when sewing.

Wrap a couple of layers of fabric around the head of the sewing machine. This makes a handy place to put pins that you remove from seams. Just make sure the fabric doesn't interfere with the threading or working of the machine.

Pattern-weights can be used in place of pins to hold the pattern to the fabric. They are available at most notions counters, or you can make your own from lead sinkers, or a collection of table knives and salt shakers.

MARKING AND DRAFTING TOOLS

A collection of various types of rulers and measuring devices makes pattern alteration and layout and garment construction easier.

Yardstick

Use a metal rather than a wooden yardstick. It is more accurate and doesn't develop rough edges that can snag fabrics.

See-Through Rulers

A see-through, plastic ruler is a great help for making pattern alterations. Use the kind made of thin, flexible plastic that has the surface completely marked off in red lines. It is more accurate and easier to use than the wide ruler with slots.

Curved Rulers

Curved rulers are available to help you alter curved pattern lines, such as armholes, hip and crotch curves. They are made of see-through plastic or metal.

Tape Measure

Buy a good plastic-coated, metal-tipped tape measure that is marked in inches on one side and millimeters on the other. Cheap, paper tape measures stretch or tear and are not always accurate. A 60″ (150cm) tape is the recommended size.

Tape measures are also available with a fiber board piece attached to one end. This is used to measure inseams; the fiber board piece is placed up against the crotch.

Short, 30″ (75cm), stick-on, tape measures are handy when stuck on the front edge of your sewing cabinet or sewing table. They can be purchased at most sewing counters. Don't stretch them as you press them in place, or they won't be accurate. Check the measurement with a yardstick for accuracy.

Hem Gauge

A hem gauge is a 6″ (25cm) long ruler with a sliding marker. It is used to accurately measure and mark hems.

Marking Devices

Pattern construction marks and seamlines can be marked with dustless chalk, tailor's chalk, a sliver of hand soap, or a pencil or felt-tip pen.

Always make a test mark on a scrap of your fashion fabric with a marking device to see if it is visible and can be easily removed without leaving any marks.

Dustless Chalk: Ordinary dustless, blackboard chalk can be sharpened in a pencil sharpener to a fine point. The chalk marks can be brushed off most fabrics. A metal chalk holder can be bought at most stationery stores. This will keep your fingers clean when using the chalk.

Tailor's Chalk: There are two kinds of tailor's chalk. One resembles ordinary chalk, except it won't mark unless it is moistened with the tongue or a small sponge. The soap type of tailor's chalk is easier to use and comes in a handy, flat square. It disappears when touched with a warm iron.

Sliver of Soap: Save those small pieces of hand soap. They can be used to mark fabrics. Their sharp edge helps you mark accurately. Soap marks can usually be removed with a warm iron.

Pencil and Felt Tip Pen: A pencil or washable, felt-tip pen can be used to mark darts and other small construction details. Just make sure the marks don't show through to the right side.

Pattern Paper

Pattern paper is available in a 45″ (113cm) width, marked off in one inch squares. It is useful for designing your own patterns and for pattern alterations.

A new product now on the market is a roll of 3″ (76mm) wide pattern paper that is marked off in half inch sections. It is handy for lengthening pattern pieces. Just tape or glue to the separated pattern pieces, using the marks to help you get things straight.

PRESSING TOOLS (see page 43)

MISCELLANEOUS SEWING EQUIPMENT

The following items are things we have found useful in our own sewing. You probably have some favorites that are not on this list, and you may find things listed that don't interest you. Use whatever ones work best for you.

Tape

A roll of Magic transparent tape and ½″ (13mm) wide drafting tape should be kept in the sewing room. Use the Magic rather than plain transparent tape because it can be written on, and won't leave a sticky residue on your fabric. Buy drafting tape rather than ordinary masking tape (even though they look alike) because it is less sticky. A word of caution: always remove tape from fabric as soon as possible. It is sometimes difficult to remove if left in place too long, and it can leave a mark.

Use the above tapes to mark wrong sides of fabric, to hold zippers in place for stitching, and to mark buttonhole locations, among other things.

Special sewing tapes are now on the market that can be used for basting and topstitching guides. Always follow the manufacturer's instructions when using these tapes.

Double Faced Tape: This tape is used to hold zippers in place before stitching, and for basting together leather and Ultra Suede® fabric seams.

Topstitching Tape: This tape is marked off and perforated in various seam widths. Use it for a topstitching guide.

Do not stitch through any of the above tape. They will coat your needle with a sticky substance and cause stitching problems.

Point Turner

Use this small plastic device to help turn neat points.

Beeswax

Run hand sewing threads through beeswax. This stiffens them and keeps them from tangling and knotting. Polyester thread builds up static electricity which causes thread to tangle and knot. Beeswax will help eliminate this problem.

Glue Stick

Use a glue stick for holding trims in place, and seams together before stitching. Buy one at a stationery store, or buy the one designed especially for sewing at your fabric store.

Fabric Glue

Liquid fabric glue is also available for the same above purpose. Be careful you don't get it on the right side of the fabric; it will leave a mark.

Scotch-gard® Spray

This spray can be used on finished garments to give them a water repellant finish. Follow the manufacturer's instructions.

Large Bobby Pin

Use a large bobby pin to help turn spaghetti straps. Directions for this procedure are given on page 265.

MACHINE STITCHING

Seams are basically used to hold your garment together. However, the sewing process requires more than just feeding the fabric through the sewing machine. The type of seam or seam finish used on a particular garment is determined by the fabric, the garment's use, and the pattern design. Professionally finished garments need perfect seams, and this section contains the information needed to help you make them.

THE BASIC SEAM

The basic seam is made by stitching two pieces of fabric together with a given seam width. Use the seam guide that is marked on the throat plate of your machine to help keep the seam width even. If your machine doesn't have a seam guide, purchase a seam guide attachment, or make your own with a wide strip of adhesive tape, following the instructions below.

Place the tape along side the presser foot, and mark a ¼″ (6mm) seam, measuring from the needle. Continue marking off ⅛″ (3mm) wide seams, up to 1″ (25mm).

Position the needle in the fabric ⅛″ (3mm) in from the cut edge, along the given seamline. Backstitch to the fabric edge, and then stitch forward to make the seam, backstitching at the end. Note: If the seam allowance is to be trimmed, do the backstitching at the point where the seamlines cross. This prevents the seam from pulling apart after the trimming.

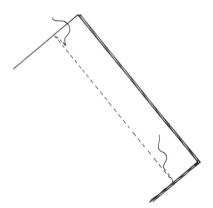

Hold the thread ends as you start stitching so they don't pull down into the needle hole. This is especially important if you are using the zigzag throat-plate when stitching on light-weight knits and woven fabrics.

Press the seam in the flat position to set the stitches, and then press the seam allowance open. Use a *seam roll* or paper strips to prevent a seam allowance impression on the right side.

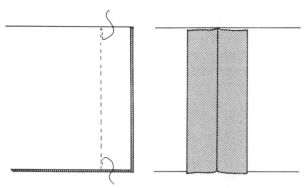

Seams can be *lockstitched* at the beginning and end instead of backstitched, if preferred. Do this by setting the stitch-length regulator at "0", then stitch up and down a couple of times in the same place. Remember to hold the thread ends at the beginning so they won't get jammed.

SEAM FINISHES

Many fabrics require seam finishes to keep the cut edges from fraying. The method you choose is determined by the fabric's characteristics.

Knit fabrics seldom need seam finishes since they don't fray. However, loosely knit fabrics look neater if the seam edges are overcast. A *Hong Kong* finish can be used on an unlined knit jacket for a neater inside appearance.

Pinked Seam Finish

Using sharp pinking shears, pink the seam edges after the seam has been pressed in the flat position, but before it is pressed open. This method can be used on most firmly woven fabrics.

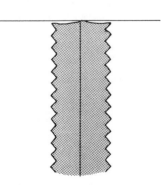

Overcast Seam Finish

Overcast the seam edges with a wide, machine zig-zag or by hand. Use this finish on loosely woven fabrics. Overcasting may leave an impression on the right side of some light weight wovens unless care is taken during the pressing process. Use a seam roll or paper strips to prevent seam impressions on the right side.

Turned and Stitched Seam Finish

Turn under a narrow hem, about ⅛" (3mm), on the seam edge and edgestitch. Use this method only on light-weight, firmly woven fabrics.

Bound Seam Finishes

Enclose the seam edge in a piece of bias fabric for a bound seam finish. Use either a purchased, double-fold bias tape, or cut your own bias strips from lining fabric and apply as for the *Hong Kong* finish. Use the bound seam finish for medium to heavy-weight fabrics.

Hong Kong Finish: Apply a ¾″ (19mm) wide strip of bias lining fabric to the right side of the seam allowance with a ⅛″ (3mm) seam.

Wrap the bias strip out over the seam edge to the wrong side. Baste in place and secure by *stitching-in-the-ditch*.

WELT SEAM

This seam is used on heavier fabrics for extra strength. It is also used as a decorative seam on many sports clothes. It consists of a basic seam that is then top stitched from the outside.

Make a basic seam, but trim one seam allowance to ¼″ (6mm) before pressing. Press the seam flat and then open. Now press both seam allowances to one side, covering the narrow seam allowance with the wide one. Turn the garment to the right side and topstitch, catching the wide seam allowance in place. Trim the wide seam allowance close to the stitching line if you are working with a white or pastel-colored fabric. This prevents a wide seam allowance from showing through to the right side. This is a good way to construct the side seams of any knit pants.

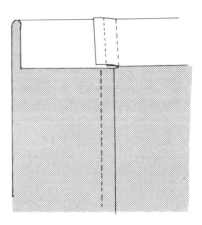

FLAT-FELLED SEAM

A flat-felled seam is a strong seam used for sports and children's clothes, especially those that have to be machine washed often. It can be sewn so that the overlapped portion appears on the outside or inside of the garment. Make your basic seam with the wrong sides together if you want the overlap to show on the right side of the garment; make the basic seam with right sides together if you want the overlap on the inside.

Trim one seam allowance to a scant ¼″ (3mm) and then press both to one side, as shown. Fold under the wide seam allowance, and position it so that it covers the narrow seam allowance. Edgestitch the fold of the wide seam allowance.

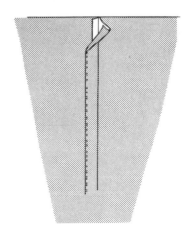

FRENCH SEAM

The french seam is used on sheer fabric to prevent raw seam edges from showing through to the right side. It can also be used for the side and underarm seams of blouses and shirts. This makes a strong seam because it is double-stitched, and it also serves as a seam finish.

Construct a basic seam, except position the fabric wrong sides together, and stitch just half the given seam width. Trim the seam to ⅛″ (3mm) and press the seam open and then to one side. Fold the fabric rights sides together, and stitch 3/16″ (4.5 mm) from the folded edge.

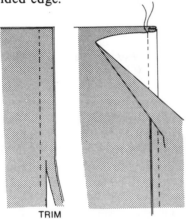

TRIM

LAP SEAM

The lap seam can be used on non-woven fabrics, such as felt, synthetic suedes, and real leathers. Firmly woven fabrics, such as blanket cloth and wool melton can also use a lap seam, in order to reduce bulk in the seam area.

Trim the seam allowance from one side of the garment, and lap this side over the other piece until the cut edge meets the seamline. Baste in place and topstitch with two rows of stitching ¼″ (6mm) apart. Trim the seam allowance on the underside close to the stitching line.

SEAM TECHNIQUES

Seams on various places of the garment require certain construction techniques. The following information will help you make those seams perfect.

Point and Curves

Shorten the stitch length as you stitch around all points and curves. This strengthens these seams so they don't fray away after they have been trimmed. It also gives you better control of your stitching because the machine is moving at a slower rate. Keep the machine moving at all times when stitching around curves. This guarantees a smooth stitching line.

Always take one or more diagonal stitches across corners and points to allow for turning room. This eliminates "rabbit ears" at the corners. Thick fabrics need more diagonal length than thin fabrics.

LIGHTWEIGHT FABRIC   MEDIUM WEIGHT FABRIC

HEAVY WEIGHT FABRIC

Enclosed Seams

Enclosed seams, such as the ones found on collars, cuffs, pocket flaps and facings, should be *graded*, trimmed and clipped as necessary to allow them to lie flat.

Grading: This is a technique used to reduce bulk when seam allowances are turned back on each other. The various layers of seam allowance are trimmed to different widths so they don't all end at one point. This is to prevent a distinct ridge from showing on the right side of the garment.

Trim the seam allowance to ¼″ (6mm) on average weight fabrics and ⅜″ (9mm) on heavyweight fabrics. Cut each layer a different width, leaving the seam allowance that is directly under the visible part of the garment the longest. This is usually the garment seam allowance, but it will be the facing seam allowance, in the lapel area only, on garments with a turnback lapel. Non-fusible interfacing should be trimmed close to the stitching line.

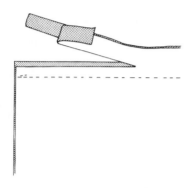

Bulky fabrics can have all the seam allowances graded in one cut if the shears are held at an acute angle to the fabric. This will result in a beveled edge, which is what grading is all about.

Trimming: Corners should be trimmed so they can be turned without unnecessary bulk.

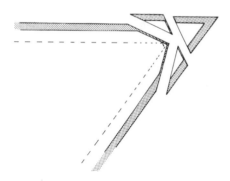

Clipping and Notching: Curve seams need to be clipped or notched in order to release the curve. Clip convex curves to the seamline at regular intervals. Notch concave curves in order to reduce bulk when the seam is turned and pressed. Pinking shears can be used for notching.

Pressing: Press open enclosed seams before turning the facing to the right side. Use a *point-presser* to help you press difficult to reach areas.

Seams can also be pressed open with the garment in the flat position. With the facing side up, press open the seam allowance with the tip of the iron.

Understitching: Facing seams are understitched to help keep them in place. Understitching also gives a firm edge on which to turn and press the facing. Understitch all facing seams except very short ones, as found on collar edges, or seams that might possibly show, such as the front facings of jackets or coats. The turned-back portion of the lapel can be understitched if you aren't topstitching the garment edges.

With the garment right side up, pull the facing out to the side and stitch along the facing edge, catching all the seam allowances.

Turn the facing to the finished position and press, rolling the seam to the facing side.

Staystitching

Curved and bias-cut edges should be staystitched to keep them from stretching out of shape. Stitch along the seamline for deeply curved edges, such as neckline and armhole curves, and stitch ⅛″ (3mm) from the seamline, within the seam allowance, for all other areas. Use a regular stitch length.

Easestitching

Easestitching is a technique used to ease a long piece of fabric to fit a shorter piece of fabric, with no visible gathers. It can be used around sleeve caps, backs of shoulders, elbows, flared hems, and the bust curve of princess line garments.

Easestitching is accomplished by holding your thumb, or the eraser end of a pencil, on the fabric behind the presser foot as you stitch with a regular stitch length. Let the fabric pile up for a bit, release, and then place your thumb or pencil back in position. You are hampering the normal feeding of the machine, and so the fabric tends to bunch up along the seam, but doesn't actually gather. Do the stitching just outside the seamline so that the ease stitching won't show on the finished garment.

Some fabrics ease in better then others, so it is a good idea to make a test run on a scrap of fabric before stitching on the garment. If it seems to be easing in too much, release the fabric periodically, and let some feed through un-hampered, or break the easestitching threads at intervals necessary to give the proper amount of ease. If it doesn't seem to be easing enough, take up some of the excess after the stitching has been completed by pulling up the bobbin thread at even intervals.

Stitching-in-the-Ditch

Stitching-in-the-ditch is sometimes referred to as stitching-in-the seam-well. It is a technique used to finish waistbands, secure facings, complete the backs of bound buttonholes, and hold edge finishes in place. Practice the technique on fabric scraps

until you get the feel of it. Some people find a zipper foot, rather than a regular foot, helps make the stitching easier. Try both to see which works best for you.

Stitch-in-the-ditch, or seam well on the right side of the garment. Shorten the stitch length so the machine runs slowly. This also helps the thread bury down in the fabric so the stitches won't show.

Eased Seams

Seams that require one layer to be eased to another should be stitched with the eased section on the bottom, and the smaller section on the top. The machine feed-dog tends to ease-in fabric, and this helps make the seam smooth.

Curved Seams

Curved seams, such as the ones found on princess line garments should be *staystitched* before they are sewn together.

Clip the convex seam almost to the stitching line to release the curve before you pin the two garment pieces together. *Easestitch* concave edges and then notch the seam allowance to allow it to lie flat when it is pressed open.

Corner Seams

Corner seams should be reinforced with *staystitching* before being sewn to the adjoining piece.

Stitch for about 1″ (25mm) on both sides of the corner, next to the seam allowance. Use a short stitch length, and pivot the fabric around the needle at the corner. Clip to the stitching line, and then pin the garment pieces together for the permanent stitching so you can see what you are doing.

Intersecting Seams

Press open and trim all seams before crossing them with another. This will reduce bulk in the seam area.

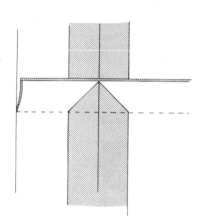

Special Fabrics

Special fabrics require slightly different seam techniques.

Knits: Make seams that can "give" with the fabric by using a stretch stitch, small zig-zag, or stretch the fabric slightly as you sew with a regular straight stitch. Synthetic threads are a good choice for knits because they are strong and have some built in "give". Press open knit seams if the fabric will hold a press. Fabrics that tend to roll should have the seam allowances trimmed to a scant ¼″ (6mm), and

edgestitched together, using one of the illustrated seams.

2 ROWS OF STRAIGHT STITCHING

STRAIGHT STITCH ZIGZAG COMBINATION

STRETCH OVERLOCK STITCH

Short Pile Fabrics: Corduroys, velvets, and velveteens sew more easily if you stitch in the direction of the nap. Many times hand-basting is required to keep the layers of fabric from shifting during the stitching process. Velvet must be hand-basted because it "creeps." Use a zipper foot or the narrow, straight stitch foot when stitching velvet. This helps reduce the creeping problem.

Long Pile Fabrics: Fake furs need a long stitch length, and they should also be stitched in the direction of the nap. The seam allowance can be pressed open and *catchstitched* in place, or trimmed to ¼″ (6mm) and edgestitched together.

Leather: Stitch leather with a special wedge-pointed needle. Do not use pins to hold seams together for stitching; use paper clips, double faced tape, or leather glue, since pins will leave permanent marks. However, pins can be used in the seam allowance. Use lap or welt seams on leather garments, or hold pressed-open seam allowances flat with leather glue or topstitching.

Bias-Cut Fabrics: When joining a bias-cut fabric to a straight-cut always stitch on the straight-cut fabric. This keeps the bias from stretching out of shape and gives a smooth seam.

Coated Fabrics: Use a medium size, ballpoint needle when stitching on coated fabrics such as cire. Use longer than regular stitch length, and hold the fabric taut in front and behind the needle. Stitch carefully so you don't have to unpick seams, since needle marks will remain. If your machine has difficulty feeding coated fabrics, sandwich the two layers of fabric between tissue paper. Tear away the paper after completing the seam. Another solution is to spray the presser foot area with ALL silicone lubricant to eliminate resistance. Wipe off the excess. DO NOT use WD-40 as it has an oil base.

Striped and Plaid Fabrics: Making perfectly matched seams on striped or plaid fabric is necessary for a custom finished garment. This can cause some problems, but the majority can be eliminated when cutting the fabric. Making sure the seamlines match when cutting-out the fabric is half the battle. Use one of the following matching methods when stitching the garment together.

#1 Pin the seams together at 1" (25mm) intervals, making sure the pin enters the top layer of fabric and leaves the bottom layer of fabric exactly on the edge of a stripe or plaid line. Leave the pins in the fabric until just before the needle comes to them. A slow running machine is a help here.

A new product called Disappearing Basting Tape holds fabric securely, sliminating any pinning or basting. It completely dissolves in the first washing.

#2 *Slipbaste* the seam before machine stitching. Working on the right side, turn under one seam allowance and overlap it to the seamline on the other section of the garment, matching up the plaid or stripe. Pin in place, and slipbaste to-

gether. Turn the garment to the wrong side and stitch the seam.

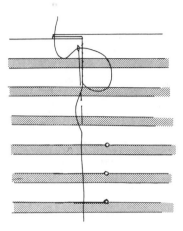

#3 The off-set technique works nicely on thick fabrics and knits. Make a test seam on fabric scraps to see how much you have to off-set the stripes to get them to match in the final seam. This works because the feed dog feeds the bottom layer of fabric through the machine faster than the upper layer.

With right sides together, position the fabric stripe of the top layer, behind the matching stripe of the lower layer. The amount of off-set is determined by the test scrap. Stitch a short section, checking to make sure the fabric is matching up. This technique may take a few tries to get used to, but it surely goes fast once you get everything working properly.

STITCHING DIRECTION

Unpicking Seams

Even the best seamstress has to unpick occasionally, and God loves a cheerful ripper! There are various ways of doing it. Try some of the following techniques and see if they don't make the process easier.

Stitches are sometimes difficult to see in dark fabrics. Run a piece of dustless chalk down the seamline; it will make the stitches stand out. The chalk can be brushed away after you are through.

Secure your garment under the presser foot of the machine when unpicking a long seam. This will hold the fabric securely so you can pull it taut, which makes the unpicking process easier.

Break a thread every four or five stitches, the length of the seam. Do this on the top rather than the bobbin thread side of the seam. Turn the garment over and you can easily pull the bobbin thread out.

BOBBIN THREAD

Bulky fabrics that tend to hide stitches should be carefully unpicked with thread nippers. Nippers are safer than a seam ripper. They are less apt to slip and cause fabric damage.

MACHINE BASTING

Use the longest stitch length on your machine when doing machine basting. Loosening the top thread tension will make the basting stitches easier to remove. Pull on the top thread at the end of the seamline and it will come right out of the seam. Just remember to readjust the tension before you start your regular stitching.

If you don't want to play with the tension, make basting removal easier by breaking a bobbin stitch

every couple of inches, then pull out the small sections of bobbin thread.

Use contrasting thread when machine basting so it will be easier to see.

TOPSTITCHING

Topstitching is used mainly for decoration, but it also serves to hold facings in place and seams flat. Topstitched seams will always stay neatly in place after repeated washings. This is great for knits and washable woven fabrics.

Always make sure the machine tension is balanced so you get a good stitch. It is a good idea to test stitch some scraps of your fabric to see how they will handle the thread and needle combination you have chosen for your topstitching. Stitch through 4 to 6 layers of fabric so you get a true picture of the topstitching results.

Topstitching can be done with regular or special polyester, topstitching thread. The special thread is heavier than regular thread and stands out nicely on the finished garment. If you don't have topstitching thread, you can achieve the same heavy look by threading two regular threads through the machine needle. Just make sure you use a large enough needle to handle the extra thread.

Try threading two threads on the bobbin also. When winding the bobbin, thread both threads through a large-eye needle to control them as they wind. Position the needle between the bobbin and winding guide. Using a double bobbin thread makes it unnecessary to break the thread at the roll line of a garment with a turn-back lapel.

Topstitching thread requires a size 14 or 16 needle. Experiment a bit to see which one works best for you. Some machines cannot handle topstitching thread on both the top and bobbin. Use regular thread on the bobbin if you have stitching troubles. Sometimes tightening the top tension will also help.

Topstitching should always be done with a long stitch length. You can get the look of a broken line of topstitching, seen so often on ready-to-wear, by using a darker color thread on the bobbin. Straight, even rows of stitching are necessary for a professional look. Use one of the following methods to help you achieve this.

#1. Use the seam guide on the throat plate of the machine as a guide for the edge of the fabric.

#2. Use the edge of the presser foot to help you measure equal distances between multiple rows of topstitching.

#3. Special topstitching tape is available that provides guide line of various widths. Follow the package instructions when using this tape.

#4. Use the right or left needle position to help measure topstitching widths. The right position gives a 1/8" (3mm) seam; the left needle position gives a 3/8" (9mm) seam.

#5. Topstitching lines that have to be done far in from the garment edge can be marked with chalk or a sliver of soap. Use a ruler to help you get the lines straight. Chalk marks brush off, and soap marks disappear when touched with a warm iron.

Always do the topstitching on the right side of the garment. A turn-back lapel should be topstitched on the garment side below the roll line, and on the facing side above the roll line. Change the stitching where the lapel breaks above the top button. Thread the ends through a hand needle and pull them through, between the garment and facing; tie in a knot or secure with a few invisible stitches.

The topstitching around the collar and lapel of coats and jackets should be done as shown at the right. Shorten the stitch length as you stitch in the

seam well; this keeps the gorge line nice and flat at the collar and lapel edge.

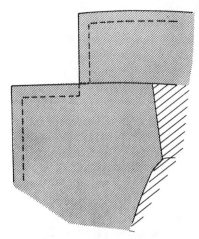

Buttons should not cover the topstitching line when a garment is buttoned. Add extra width to the center front of the pattern, or narrow the topstitching line if you anticipate a problem.

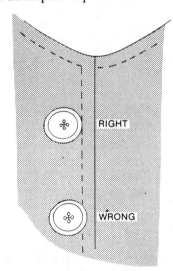

Garment edges and seams can be stitched with one or more rows of topstitching. Use matching, contrasting, or more than one color of thread. Some top-stitching patterns are given below.

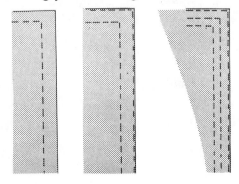

You will find that multiple rows of topstitching add body to the garment edge. Keep this in mind when considering hem finishes for sleeves, pants legs, and over-blouses.

An interesting look can be given to topstitched edges if a layer of polyester fleece is placed between the hem and garment fabric. This gives a padded look to the finished edge.

A padded look can be achieved along collar, cuff, and neckline edges if the seam allowance is trimmed just slightly short of the topstitching line. Trim the edges blunt rather than grading them. The seam allowance provides the padding for the garment edge.

Decorative stitches can be used for topstitching. Experiment with your machine to see what you can come up with. How about a straight-stitch, zigzag combination like the one shown.

STITCHING PROBLEMS

Occasionally you will run into stitching problems. These can be caused by a malfunctioning machine, a dirty, non-oiled machine, an incorrect thread and needle combination, or the gremlin under the table. A repair shop can fix your machine; you can clean and oil it, and also change the thread or needle size, but you can't do anything about the gremlin. If you try all the remedies listed below when you have stitching problems, and they still continue, blame it on the gremlin and put your sewing away until tomorrow.

Breaking Thread
Old, dried out thread will break more readily than new, fresh thread.

A machine needle with too small a hole will cause threads to break.

High needle temperature will also cause broken threads. Slow down the speed of your stitching. Synthetic fabrics generate more heat than natural fiber fabrics.

Threads made with short, rather than long fibers tend to "shave" at the needle, eventually causing breakage. Purchase long-fiber, polyester thread.

Rethread your machine. An improperly threaded machine will cause broken thread.

Thread catching in the notch on the spool edge will also cause breakage. Placing the spool on the machine with the thread notch on the bottom will help eliminate this problem.

Skipped Stitches
Using a ballpoint needle on a coarsely knitted or woven fabric will cause excessive deviation of the needle from the hook. The needle will slip along the fabric thread trying to find a gap to go through, which results in faulty loop formation. Change to a finer ballpoint or regular point needle.

Sometimes increasing the pressure of the presser foot will eliminate this problem. Adjust your machine accordingly. If it isn't possible to adjust the pressure on your machine, press your index finger against the toes of the pressure foot while you sew; this will give you the needed extra pressure. Just make sure your finger doesn't slip off and get caught by the needle!

Fabrics such as lingerie tricot and chiffon that tend to draw down into the needle hole can cause skipped stitches. Prevent this by using a throat plate with the small, round hole (straight-stitch throat plate). Holding the fabric taut while stitching also helps.

Bent needles, coated needles, or ones with damaged points can also cause skipped stitches. Change to a new needle.

Thread that is too thick or too thin for the needle size will interfere with the proper loop formation. Change to a different size needle.

Use a yellow-band needle, or drop your regular machine needle a small amount in the needle clamp to add extra length. This longer needle allows the top thread to get down to the bobbin hook better so it doesn't skip a stitch.

Uneven Stitching

Uneven stitching is caused by machine difficulties or by using the wrong size needle for the fabric. Thin, ballpoint needles used on coarse fabric will be pushed to the side, seeking a gap between the fabric threads. Use a heavier needle that can force its way better, or change to a sharp point needle.

Puckered Seams

Seams can pucker after washing if you use a thread that is made of a different fiber than the fashion fabric.

Thread tension that is too tight can also cause puckered seams. Synthetic thread should be sewn with a loose, but balanced tension because it has some built in "give".

Shifting fabric layers can also result in puckered seams. Pin or baste more securely.

Puckering can be reduced by holding the fabric taut while stitching. Hold the fabric in front of and behind the presser foot, but allow it to feed naturally —don't pull the fabric through. This stitching technique will solve 90% of your puckering problems.

STITCHING TIPS

Press open side seams only after the garment has been fitted. Sometimes creases are hard to remove if you have to let out a seam.

Add strength to corners of pockets and the ends of fly zippers with a bar tack. Use a narrow zigzag with a short stitch length. Test on a scrap or fabric until you get the desired look.

Mark seam widths with small clips in the fabric edge. This helps you start the seam at the correct width.

When topstitching, help your machine around corners and points by taking a stitch through the edge of the garment with a hand-needle and thread. Use the thread ends as a handle to help ease the fabric around the needle. Without this "helper," the presser foot has no traction and will stitch in place

or make shorter stitches, thereby ruining the look of the topstitching. To avoid a skipped stitch, make sure the needle is on the upstroke.

Always stop sewing with the "take-up" hook at the highest point. If you don't, you may unthread your needle when you start sewing again. Also, the bobbin has not completed its cycle and this may cause the thread to jam.

Use the edge of the wide, zigzag foot as a seam guide as much as possible. Many special, knit patterns call for a ¼″ (6mm) seam. This can be accomplished by running the edge of the presser foot along the edge of the fabric.

Use the right and left needle position to vary seam width, allowing you to keep the edge of the presser foot along the edge of the fabric as a guide. The needle in the right position will make a ⅛″ (3mm) seam and in the left position a ⅜″ (9mm) seam.

Note: On Viking machines, release the seam-former cam, and set the dials to "blue-blue-blue" for the right needle position. For the left needle position, engage the cam and set at the left-hand needle position.

Few machines have the stitch length regulator marked in stitches per inch. They are usually marked in numbers 1 to 4. This is the metric system of measurement and means the stitch length in millimeters. For example, a setting of 2 means a stitch length of 2 millimeters. Determine the number of stitches per inch by stitching on a scrap of paper, measuring off 1″ and then counting the stitches in that inch. Adjust your stitch length regulator until you get the desired stitch length.

Many times when topstitching, you will run into trouble when crossing bulky seams, such as ones found at necklines. The machine will begin to skip stitches, or they will become shorter because the presser foot doesn't function properly when it has to ride up over ridges of fabric. This problem can be solved by leveling the presser foot with a folded piece of fabric or piece of lightweight cardboard. Place this "helper" under one side or the back end of the presser foot to level the presser foot and help the fabric feed properly.

Learn to sew continuously. That is, sew all darts, facings, sleeve underarm seams, etc. in one continuous strip, connected by a few stitches. Sew as many seams as possible, then cut the pieces apart and have a pressing session. Remember though, you should never cross a seam that has not been pressed.

Use a "security blanket" when ending seams. This is a scrap of firm fabric that measures about 1″ (25 mm) by 3″ (75mm). Stitch across the blanket at the end of each seam. Snip the connecting stitches to release the garment. Cut the security blanket away from the next garment piece after you have started the new seam. The security blanket speeds your sewing along because: (1) you don't have to raise and lower the presser foot, (2) you don't have to hold the thread ends to keep the machine from jamming, (3) it eliminates cutting off long thread ends, making for neater sewing, (4) your needle will never come un-threaded, (5) you will save lots of thread. The security blanket also lets you check the stitch setting on your machine before you begin sewing. Someone may have worked with the machine since you last used it and changed the settings. If the needle point is damaged or dull, you will discover this on scrap fabric rather than your expensive fashion fabric. The security blanket also helps you get the seam started when you have to begin on the very edge.

Do not stitch over pins; pull them out of the seam-line just before you get to them. Hitting, or just ticking a pin, can damage the needle point, and then cause fabric damage. If you hit a pin when sewing at high speeds it is possible to break the needle and have a piece fly up in your face. DON'T SEW OVER PINS.

Vinyl fabrics can be difficult to stitch. Spray the machine bed with a silicon spray so that it becomes slick to the vinyl fabric. "Sandwich" the vinyl between layers of waxed paper if you don't have any silicone lubricant.

HAND STITCHING

Fine sewing still requires some hand stitching. You must know the basic hand stitches and this section will provide that information. First of all, let's discuss needles and thread.

HAND NEEDLES

Choose a needle that is compatible with your fabric and the job at hand. Use a long, thin needle when working on sheers, and a heavier needle for coarser fabrics. A short needle is good when doing small detail work such as hand-pricking a zipper. Long needles are handier for basting.

Needles come in various numbered sizes, from 1 to 24. The small number denotes a coarse needle while the large number denotes a fine needle. The most common sizes used for dressmaking are 6-10.

THREAD

Most hand sewing is done with the same thread you use on the machine. A single thread is generally used, but a double thread can be used when you need extra strength, such as for buttons or hand-sewn zipper.

Always thread your needle with the thread end that is cut from the spool to help prevent tangling. Cut the thread on a slant; this will make it easier to thread.

Thread sometimes gets tangled or knots up during hand sewing. Prevent this problem by cutting and threading the needle as directed above, running the thread through some beeswax, and using a relatively short thread length - 18″ (46cm) to 20″ (50cm).

Thread will sometimes build up a twist when doing certain hand stitches. Eliminate this problem by dropping the threaded needle occasionally and allow the thread to unwind before proceeding.

Use contrasting thread for basting so it will be easier to see and remove. Remove all basting done with regular thread before giving the garment the final press, otherwise it may leave a mark. Silk thread is a good choice for basting. You can press over this thread and not leave a mark.

HAND STITCHES

The following stitches are the ones you will use most frequently in your sewing.

Basting

Basting can be even, uneven or diagonal. Use even basting for holding seams together, uneven basting for marking the center front, holding up hems, and for holding the fashion fabric and underlining or interfacing fabrics together. Diagonal basting is used to hold interfacing to the garment before it is permanently stitched in place.

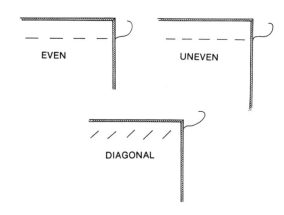

Slip Basting

Slip basting is used when matching plaid or striped fabric seams and for making fitting adjustments on the right side of the garment.

Turn under the seam allowance on one garment piece and lap it to the seamline of the other garment piece. Baste as shown, slipping the needle between the seam fold and bringing it out to catch a thread of the other layer of fabric.

Backstitch

The backstitch is the strongest hand stitch. It is used to repair broken seams in hard-to-reach areas and for attaching patch pockets from the wrong side.

Make the stitches 1/16″ (2.5mm) to 1/8″ (3mm) long. Always insert the needle in the end of the last stitch and bring it out of the fabric one stitch ahead.

Hand Prick Stitch

This stitch is used for hand finishing zippers. It is a variation of the backstitch.

The needle takes just a small bite into the fabric so that only a small stitch shows on the right side.

Whipstitch

The whipstitch is used to hold two finished edges together, such as on welt pockets and bound buttonholes.

Insert the needle in the fabric at a right angle to the edge so the stitches are slanted.

Fellstitch

This hand stitch is used to attach the raw edges of under collars to the garment and upper collar.

The stitches should be about 3/16″ (4.5mm) long, and 1/8″ (3mm) apart. They are at right angles to the fabric edge.

Slipstitch

This stitch can be used to hold hems and linings in place.

The needle runs along the fabric fold, and then comes out to catch just a thread of the other piece of fabric. Stitches should be ⅛″ (3mm) to ¼″ (6mm) apart.

Stabstitch

A stabstitch is used to hold shoulder pads to the armscye seam allowance. It is also used to secure the lower end of the zipper when applying an exposed zipper.

Insert the needle straight through the fabric from both directions so the thread is perpendicular to the fabric layers.

Blindstitch

This stitch is used for hems and holding facings in place. It should not be seen on either side of the garment. This is the type of hem that should be used on knits.

Catch just a thread or two of each fabric layer. Do not pull the threads tight, otherwise the hem will show on the right side.

Catchstitch

The catchstitch is used over raw edges to hold the interfacing in place, or for woven fabric hems.

Stitch from left to right for a right-handed person, and from right to left for a left-handed person. In either case, the needle is always inserted in the fabric opposite to the stitching direction, as shown.

French Tack

French tacks are used to attach two layers of fabric that require some space between them. Linings are attached to coat hems with French tacks, and tie belts can also be held in place with a French tack.

Using a double thread, work a few stitches back and forth between the fabric layers, as shown. The length of the stitch determines the length of the tack. Blanketstitch over the strands of thread.

Arrowheads

Arrowheads are used to accent the ends of pockets, buttonholes, and at the top of slits of pleats in shirts. They add a professional finishing touch.

Use a single thread of buttonhole twist or top-stitching thread. Mark the outline of the arrowhead with fine stitches or chalk. Make a few small stitches in the corner of the arrowhead to secure the thread end and construct the arrowhead following the illustration below.

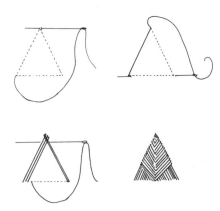

An arrowhead shape can be cut out of Ultra Suede® fabric or real leather and top stitched in place for a different look.

Chain Stitch Carriers

Chain stitch carriers are used to hold belts in position, or they can be used to hold two layers of fabric together that require a long linking thread or for a thread eye to accommodate a metal hook.

Thread the needle with a double thread, knot it and run it through *beeswax*. Secure the thread to the wrong side of the garment with several small backstitches. Insert the needle in the fabric and pull it through to the right side.

Make a small stitch on the right side and bring up a large loop of thread.

Hold the loop open with the thumb and forefinger of the right hand. Hold the thread end taut with the fingers of the other hand.

Form another loop with the second finger of the right hand, as shown.

Release the first loop, allowing it to close down on the double thread. Open up the new loop with the thumb and forefinger and repeat the process until the chain is the desired length.

Finish the chain by inserting the needle through the last loop and pulling it tight. Stitch through to the wrong side of the fabric at the desired spot, and secure the chain on the wrong side with a few small back stitches.

A PRESSING PROBLEM

Pressing as you sew is one of the most important concepts of the sewing process. All seams must be pressed, either open or to one side, before they are crossed with another seam. Careful pressing of all garment edges before they are turned to the right side is absolutely necessary for a perfect edge. We can't stress proper pressing techniques enough. They are very important to a professionally finished garment.

Having the proper pressing tools is half the battle. Knowing when and how to use them is the other half. Check through the list of recommended tools to see what your sewing room needs. Each one serves a definite purpose, and speeds garment construction along to a perfect finish.

PRESSING TOOLS

As you will see, there are many pressing tools available today. Buying them all at once would take a fair investment. However, if you purchase them over a period of time, or put them on your wish list for birthdays and Christmas, you will soon have what you need, without a big dent in the budget. It is possible to substitute home-made tools for some of the ready-made ones. This saves money, and some of the home-made tools work better than the purchased ones.

Iron
The iron is obviously the most important pressing tool. We recommend the kind that has the surge of steam feature, as well as the regular steam or dry option. Get one with a large water capacity, and follow the manufacturer's instructions about the proper water, and recommended method of cleaning

the iron. Treat your iron kindly, and it will give you years of good service.

Ironing Board
An adjustable ironing board is a great help in the sewing area. Lower it to table height, and place it right next to the sewing machine, so you don't have to get up everytime you need to use the iron. You will be surprised at how much time this saves, and what a convenience!

Use the type of ironing board cover you prefer. Just make sure it is kept clean. Change or launder it as necessary.

Make your ironing board neater by using spring clamps to hold the cover taut. These are available at most hardware stores and are well worth the few dollars they cost. They can be re-used whenever you change covers.

Iron All®
An Iron All is an attachment that fits over the sole plate of the iron. It is made of a thin, strong, space-age material that is framed in metal. The surface is perforated so that the steam can get through.

It functions like a pressing cloth, and helps control the heat of the iron, so that you'll never have to worry about scorching a fabric, or leaving a shiny, iron mark. It is one of the best of the new sewing aids, and we strongly recommend that you get one at your fabric store. We leave ours on our iron all the time.

Iron Safe

This is a new product similar to the Iron All® except that it has a Teflon® coating on the pressing surface. Fusible interfacings or web will not stick to it, and it glides over fabrics more readily.

Pressing Cloths

There are a variety of pressing cloths available at most notion counters. Some are made of see-through fabric, while others are made of more heavy material.

You can either buy one or use some square of fabric you have around the house. Many people like old sheeting or muslin. Use whatever works best for you; just remember to launder your pressing cloths often.

We like to use Handy Wipes® for pressing cloths. They are a good size, and hold moisture well. It is easy to keep a package with your sewing supplies.

Paper Strips

Another useful pressing aid is paper strips. Heavy brown paper can be purchased in pad form, but this is quite expensive when you consider how much it costs to cut up brown kraft paper or a brown paper bag. Small and large envelopes can also serve the same purpose, which is to prevent seam impressions from showing through to the right side of the garment. They are easier to handle than paper strips.

Hem Guide

Metal hem guides can be used to help you press-up even hems. They have various hem widths marked on them. A heavy piece of poster board can be used for the same purpose. Measure and mark your own hem widths.

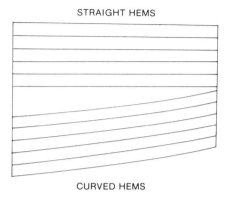

Point Presser

A point presser is a wooden tool that is used to help press open seam allowances, especially in hard-to-reach areas, such as collars and lapel points.

A pencil, rolled in several layers of fabric, or a wooden cooking spoon, can serve as a substitute point presser for hard to reach areas.

Tailor's Board

This device is an all-purpose pressing board that combines the point and flat surface of the *point presser* with various curves and extensions for hard-to-reach places. It can be purchased with or without a collection of padded covers.

Sleeve Board

A sleeve board is used for pressing open sleeve seams. There are various styles available. A stationary, one sided, sleeve board works well, but the folding kind that has two different sized pressing surfaces is very handy.

A seam roll can be used in place of a sleeve board, if necessary. See the information immediately below.

Seam Roll

Ready-made seam rolls are about 13″ long. They are useful for pressing open short seams because the rolled surface prevents the seam allowance from making an impression on the right side. A longer seam roll is more efficient for pressing long seams.

Make your own long seam roll by getting a heavy, cardboard tube from a fabric store. This is the kind of tube used for rolls of corduroy or suede cloth. Cut the tube to a handy length or leave it long to press pant leg seams all at once. The best thing about this seam roll is that it's free.

Tailor's Ham

A tailor's ham is used for pressing curved seams, darts, and curved areas of the garment. Pressing over a rounded surface helps build in garment shape.

Tailor's hams are covered with two fabrics. One side is covered with wool and the other side is covered with cotton. Use the wool side up when you are working with wools or softly napped fabrics and the cotton side when working with most other fabrics.

Tailor's Mitt

This pressing aid is used for hard-to-get areas that need steam shaping. The mitt is covered with two different fabrics, just like the ham. It also has a pocket on one side so that it can be slipped over the sleeve board. It is used this way when you have to steam sleeve-caps.

Clapper or Pounding-Block

A clapper or pounding-block is the same thing. They just are called by different names. This tool is used to help flatten seam and garment edges.

Many times an iron will leave a pressing mark where a combination of steam and the clapper will not. It is usually the best way to flatten out seam areas of bulky or resilient fabrics.

Steam the area to be pressed, and then quickly strike the area with the clapper, holding it in place for a short time until the heat and moisture have dissipated.

An ordinary child's wooden block can be used in place of a clapper. Use an unpainted one that fits your hand easily.

Needle-Board

A needle-board is used for pressing velvet or velvet-like fabrics. It prevents the pile from being crushed by the iron.

A substitute needle-board can be made from a folded bath towel, covered with a layer of velvet. This works well, and probably is more practical than buying a needle-board, unless you sew lots of pile fabrics.

Brush and Tape

A good clothes brush is nice to have for the final touch-up. It is also handy for keeping your fabric lint-free during the construction process.

Three inch wide masking tape is also useful for removing lint from fabric. In fact it is a good thing to have in your suitcase when you travel. It keeps you lint-free the easy way.

PRESSING TECHNIQUES

Using the proper pressing technique is just as important as using the proper pressing tool. It is possible to over-press as well as under-press. Use the guidelines below to help you get that smooth look.

Co-ordinate the iron temperature setting with the fiber content of the fabric. An iron that is too cool won't do the job, and an iron that is too hot can scorch or melt your fabric. If you are in doubt about the proper iron setting, test the heat on a scrap of fabric before you press the garment.

Always use an up and down motion, rather than a back and forth motion when pressing. PRESS, DON'T IRON. This keeps the fabric from stretching and reduces the possibility of making new wrinkles.

Steam-press seams in the closed position before you do anything else to them. This sets the stitches and makes for a smooth seamline. Handle darts this way, too.

Always press each seam before it is crossed by another seam. It is impossible to have a well pressed garment if you leave everything to the end.

Finger-press seams just ahead of the steam iron, to help them open all the way. Be careful not to get the iron so close to your fingers that they burn.

Press open seams along all facing edges before you turn the facing to the right side. This can be done with the help of a *point presser*, or you can use the technique shown below.

With the facing side up, open up the seam allowance with the tip of the iron, and press. Work all around the facing.

Fold both seam allowances over to the facing side, as shown, and press again. This makes the turning and finishing process much easier.

Roll seams to the underside when pressing all faced edges. A garment with a turn-back lapel should have the seam rolled to the facing side, below the roll line, and rolled to the garment side above the roll line. This keeps the facings from showing on any visible part of the garment.

Press curved seams over a curved form, such as a tailor's ham, in order to preserve their shape.

Use a moist pressing cloth when you need more moisture than your steam iron can produce.

Prevent seam, hem or dart impressions from showing on the right side by placing an envelope or strip of heavy paper between the two layers of fabric, when pressing. Use the same technique whenever you press pleats, so that the underside of the pleat isn't impressed on the right side. The envelope-paper technique is also good when pressing the mitered corner of sleeve and back vents.

Use a clapper or pounding block to set creases. This technique works particularly well on polyester knits or other resilient fabrics. Place a towel-covered wooden block or cutting board under the section to be pounded, so that you have a firm surface to work on.

Most pressing is done from the wrong side. This prevents press marks and keeps hem, dart, and seam allowances from showing through. If you do need to press on the right side, let the steam do the work for you. Hold the iron above the fabric, rather than actually touching the fabric. This is usually all you need; however, if you feel more pressing is required, protect the right side of the fabric with a press cloth, before touching it with an iron.

THE INSIDE STORY

Interfacing fabric is an important part of most garment construction. It provides the support and firmness so necessary in well-made clothes. Some of the areas usually interfaced are collars, cuffs, button and buttonhole areas, facings, pockets and flaps, waistbands, sleeves and hem edges, and belts and straps.

There are many different interfacings available in fabric stores today. You need some knowledge of each in order to choose the one most suitable to the garment you are making. Make a habit of reading hang-tags, bolt-ends and other consumer information provided by the interfacing companies. This will give you the necessary information for making the right choice.

FUSIBLE INTERFACINGS

Fusible interfacings are a fairly recent development for the home-sewer. Ready-to-wear has utilized fusible interfacings for years, but it has been just recently that a fusing agent was made that would make a permanent bond when applied with an ordinary steam iron. Fusible interfacings have been eagerly adopted by the home-sewer because they are quick and easy to use. Some of their advantages are listed below.

* Fusible interfacings are fused to the fashion fabric so that the two layers can be handled as one.

* Seam allowances can be removed from the interfacing before fusing in order to reduce thickness and bulk in the finished seam.

* Small detail pieces, such as pocket flaps or welts,

are easier to work with if the interfacing can be fused in position.

Fusible interfacings are available in woven or non-woven fabrics, with or without stretch, and in light, medium and heavyweights. Keep these characteristics in mind when selecting an interfacing to go with your fashion fabric.

NON-FUSIBLE INTERFACINGS

There are many non-fusible interfacings available to the home-sewer that can be used for fabric of light to heavyweight. These can be used for most interfacing applications. However, they won't give as flat a finish at seamlines and garment edges as fusible interfacings since they are usually included in the seam.

CHOOSING THE RIGHT INTERFACING

Keep your fashion fabric in mind when choosing an interfacing. Your choice should be governed by the desired finished look. The old rule of a lightweight interfacing for a lightweight fabric and a heavyweight interfacing for a heavy fabric just doesn't work. Details on garments made from lightweight fabrics sometimes need the firmness and support of a medium or heavyweight interfacing. Many heavy-weight fabrics need just a lightweight interfacing; a heavy interfacing might create too much stiffness and/or bulk.

A good procedure to use when selecting an interfacing is to drape the fashion fabric over various interfacings to see which combination is going to give the desired hand or appearance. Sometimes you will find it necessary to use two different interfacings fabrics on one garment in order to get the right look in different areas. For example, you might need a firm, medium-weight interfacing for cuffs and pocket details, but a more supple, lightweight interfacing for the roll collar.

Interfacings with an all-bias or crosswise stretch are ideal for knit garments. They add the needed support but still retain the "give" of the knit. Be sure to cut the interfacing pieces so that the stretch goes around the body. This will provide the most wearing comfort.

Non-stretch woven interfacings can also be used for knits. However, it is suggested that they be cut on the bias when covering large areas of the garment so that the interfacing "gives" with the knit.

Fusible interfacings can be used for nearly all interfacing requirements. Non-fusibles can be used anywhere too, but they sometimes require some hand work. They are not quite as easy to handle as a fusible interfacing that is bonded to the fashion fabric.

Some delicate, lightweight, snythetic fabrics cannot stand the heat needed to apply a fusible interfacing. A non-fusible one should be used in this situation.

Tailored garments can be made with either a fusible or non-fusible hair canvas. The fusible hair canvas works best with synthetic fabrics. It is quick to use and eliminates the need for hand padding stitches. Non-fusible hair canvas is a better choice for natural fiber fabrics because they mold and shape nicely and can really take advantage of hand padding.

Interfacings are made in various colors. The most common is white, but you will see some cream, grey and black interfacings. Use the darker colors only on dark or heavy fabrics where the color will not show through.

Machine buttonhole areas should always be supported by some type of interfacing. If you use lining or under-lining fabric that is color-matched to the fashion fabric, you will avoid a line of white showing along the edge of the buttonhole. If you have to use white interfacing, camouflage the white line with a matching colored pencil or pen.

APPLYING THE INTERFACING

Read the manufacturer's instructions for the recommended application methods for your chosen interfacing. Proper application is the key to a nice looking garment. The following points apply to both fusible and non-fusible interfacings. Special helps for fusible and non-fusible interfacings will be given afterward.

* Some interfacings tend to shrink, wovens more than non-wovens. Unless the hang-tag or bolt-end states differently, it is advisable to pre-shrink all interfacing fabrics. Non-fusibles can usually be pre-shrunk in the washing machine and dried in the dryer. A rule to follow is to use the same method to pre-shrink the interfacing that you will use to clean the finished garment. Fusible interfacings should be placed in a sink of warm water and then allowed to drip-dry. DO NOT pre-shrink these fabrics in the washer; that will cause the fusing material to come off.

* Cut all interfacing pieces accurately. Cut on the same grain line as the garment piece when using a woven interfacing. Exceptions are bias cuts for knit garments and collars. Stretch interfacings should be cut with the stretch going around the body.

* Apply the interfacing to the wrong side of the garment piece that will be visible on the finished garment. For example: interface the upper pieces of collars, cuffs and pocket flaps; apply interfacing to the visible side of waistbands, front bands and plackets; apply the interfacing to the wrong side of the facing when the garment has a turn-back lapel. Doing this will prevent "shadowing through" of the seam allowances. This is especially important on light-weight or sheer fabrics.

* Trim away the interfacing at corners and points, as illustrated, before applying to the fashion fabric. This will eliminate bulk in these areas and allow them to turn smoothly.

Fusible Interfacings

Fusible interfacings have application requirements other than those listed above because of their special finish. Since the interfacing is held to the garment by a bonding process, it is possible to remove seam allowances from all interfacing pieces before they are fused to the fashion fabric. This reduces thickness at seams and garment edges. Corners and points of the interfacing should also be trimmed as shown above, for the same reason.

Fusibles are easy to work with if you just keep in mind the following points.

* Follow the manufacturer's instructions exactly when bonding the interfacing to the fashion fabric. If an imperfect bond is made, the interfacing will blister and pull away from the fabric in the first washing or cleaning. It is very difficult, if not impossible, to re-bond the interfacing after this happens.

* Make sure you get the proper bonding instructions when you purchase the interfacing. Each interfacing seems to require a slightly different technique, and what works with one doesn't necessarily work with another.

* The factors necessary to a successful bond are: proper iron temperature, steam, if needed, and adequate pressing time. An iron that is not heated to the proper temperature will not completely melt the fusing material, and you will end up with an imperfect bond. Too hot an iron will scorch your fabric. Some fusibles call for a dry iron, while others need steam. If you suspect that your steam iron isn't putting out enough moisture, place a damp press-cloth underneath the iron during the fusing process. A certain number of seconds of heat, steam and pressure is necessary for a perfect bond. Follow the recommended pressing time to the second. Remember, it must be done right the first time, so be patient and count the seconds on a clock.

* Fuse-baste large pieces of interfacing to the garment before starting the fusing process. This is done by positioning the interfacing over the garment piece and then touching the tip of the iron to the interfacing at various key points to hold the interfacing in place. This prevents the interfacing from slipping while fusing smaller sections.

* Occasionally small pieces of fusing material will stick to the ironing-board cover. This can be prevented by covering the ironing board with a piece of sheeting or an old pillow case. Keep this handy so that you can use it whenever you fuse interfacing.

* Fusible interfacing should completely cover the garment piece to which it is being applied. Failure to do this will leave a visible line on the right side of the garment, where the interfacing ends.

WRONG   RIGHT

Interface all garment pieces when making a blazer from cotton velveteen. This supports the fabric, giving the garment an elegant look. Non-interfaced velveteen blazers can look like old dish cloths after a few wearings. The interfacing also prevents seam allowances from "shadowing through" to the right side.

Non-Fusible Interfacings

Non-fusible interfacings are held in the proper position by including the interfacing in the seamline or by trimming away the entire seam allowance and catching the interfacing to the fashion fabric by hand. The first method is used for more interfacing applications while the second method is used on a tailored garment.

Trim non-fusible interfacing seam allowances so that just 1/8″ (3mm) is left. Pin the interfacing to the fashion fabric and catch the interfacing in the seam.

Trim non-fusible interfacing as close to the seamline as possible when *grading* and turning an enclosed seam. This reduces bulk in the seam area.

FUSIBLE WEB

Another product that is related to fusible inter-facing is fusible web. This consists of a thin web of fusing material. It is available as narrow, pre-pack-aged strips or in wider widths by the yard. It is used to bond two layers of fabric together, and it can be used to put up hems (a quick way to do that) and hold appliques or patches in place while stitching. It is also a handy item for many craft projects. Because the fused web adds some firmness to fab-rics, it can also be used across the top of pockets and at hem and sleeve edges to add a bit of crisp-ness. Remember to carefully follow the fusing in-structions that come with each brand of web so that you get a perfect bond.

NOTES

DARTING AROUND

One of the secrets of a nice fitting garment is perfect darts. Since they build the garment's shape, they should be of the proper size, accurately positioned, and stitched so that they can function as designed. Darts that are too long or too short, too high or too low, can ruin the look and fit of an otherwise perfect garment.

A perfect dart will have the following characteristics:

* It will be directed toward the fullest part of the figure.

* It will end ½" (13mm) to 1" (25mm) short of the fullest part of the figure.

* It will be the correct width.

* It will have a smooth point that doesn't bubble or pucker.

You have probably seen darts that don't display the above characteristics. The most common fault seems to be darts that are not positioned properly. However, before we start solving problems, let's review the various types of darts found on patterns.

TYPES OF DARTS

Different types of darts are used in pattern design. Some are just functional, while others add design interest, as well as shape. Plain, functional darts should be as inconspicuous as possible. Darts that combine design and shape should be accentuated, by stitching or fabric treatment, so they add interest to the finished garment.

Straight Darts

The horizontal bust dart and vertical waistline darts are good examples of straight darts. They are generally just functional darts, giving shape to the garment. However, they can have one of three different shapes, as illustrated below.

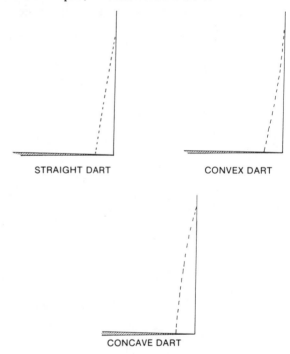

STRAIGHT DART   CONVEX DART

CONCAVE DART

Straight darts are used mostly at the bustline, elbow, below the waist, at the neck or shoulder, and above the waist on the back of the garment.

Concave darts are usually used above the waist in the midriff area. They can have a small or large outward curve. The more curve, the closer the fit.

Convex darts are perhaps the least used shape. They are found wherever the body curves outward, such as over a round tummy. They can also be used at the bust, if the figure is extremely full. Convex darts are used at the hip when a dart replaces the side seam.

Note: Have you ever wondered how to tell the difference between convex and concave? An easy way is to relate the word "concave" to the word "cave." Caves go in, so concave curves also go in. Look at the illustration above, to see what we mean.

The dart shape marked on your pattern can be changed if you want a different type of fit. Body-hugging clothes will use more curved than straight darts. Just match the dart curve to the body curve, and stitch away.

Curved Darts

The curved darts that we refer to in this section are different from straight darts with curved stitching lines. A curved dart is actually drawn along a curved line, and it is used as a style line in women's fashions.

Curved darts should be carefully marked, matched and pinned before they are stitched so that the dart doesn't ripple.

Double-Pointed Darts

Some darts have points at each end. They are used in the waist area of one-piece dresses, and coats and jackets. They usually have curved sides, which can be curved more for a closer fit.

Open Darts

Most darts have a fold down the middle. Some will be open, or part of a seam.

Extra wide darts, especially curved darts, usually have an open middle. Sewing these darts is like sewing two seams together. The open middle reduces the bulk in the dart area and makes a smooth curve.

Darts can also become part of an intricate design, which requires a seam rather than a fold.

French Darts

The French dart is not really a dart type; rather, it is the way the dart is positioned. It angles from somewhere on the side seam up to the bust.

The French dart can start at the hip or closer to the waist. It can be either straight or curved.

One thing should be kept in mind when working with long French darts. They are not suitable for fabrics that have to be matched. The fabric pattern will be "off" the length of the dart.

DART PLACEMENT

The proper placement of darts is the key factor in their fit. When taking bust measurements, always wear the same foundation garment as you will when wearing the completed garment. Make sure the shoulder straps are properly adjusted. A high bustline is more youthful than a low bustline.

The first and most important rule to remember is that darts should always point toward the fullest part of the figure. This means the high point of the bust, tummy, derierre, shoulder area, or elbow.

The second rule is this: darts should end ½" (13mm) to 1" (25mm) short of the fullest part of the figure. Darts that are sewn too close to the full point will "peak," and darts sewn beyond the full point will be very unattractive.

The third rule is that the dart width must accommodate the fullness of the figure. Obviously, an A-cup bust will need less dart width than a D-cup bust.

The Proper Position

As stated above, darts should be directed toward the fullest part of the figure. Let's use the bust dart as an example.

Too High: This dart is directed above the high point of the bust, so it releases the fabric fullness above the bust. This will cause wrinkles above the bust, and perhaps tightness below. This is a very common fitting fault.

Too Low: This dart is directed below the high point

of the bust, which releases the fullness below the place it is needed.

Just Right: This dart is directed toward the high point of the bust, releasing the fabric fullness where it should be. Garments should be fitted this way.

Since patterns are not custom designed, it is up to you to check the dart placement on each pattern before you cut your fabric. Dart position is not always the same on every pattern, so you cannot make a general rule about how much you have to raise or lower the dart. Check each pattern!

Locate your high point by measuring down from the middle of the shoulder seam, to the high point of the bust. Mark that measurement on the pattern.

Measure the distance between the high points of the bust with a tape measure. Divide by two, and measure in that amount from the pattern center front, at the level of the previous mark. Place a dot to mark the high point location.

Check to see if the dart is properly positioned by placing a ruler along the dart center line, as shown. The edge of the ruler should go right through the high point mark. Raise or lower the dart if it is not correctly positioned.

How To Alter

There are two ways of changing the bust dart location. One works best if very little change is required. The other method should be used if a major change is required.

Re-drawing Method: Use this method when you are moving the dart just a small amount, ½″ (13mm) or less. A *see-through plastic ruler* is a great help here.

Position the ruler parallel to the dart foldline, so that the edge intersects the high point mark. Draw a new foldline. Measure the distance between the old and new foldline.

Redraw the other dart lines by positioning the ruler parallel to the lines, keeping the distance between the old and new lines the same as measured above.

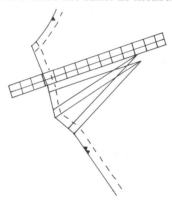

Cut and Fold Method: Use this method when you have to make a large change. This method will retain the proper shape at the end of the dart, so that you have a smooth side line after the dart has been stitched.

To raise the dart, cut the pattern below the dart and up around the point, making sure the vertical cut is parallel to the center front. Use a ruler to mark the cutting lines so they are straight.

Fold the pattern until the dart is directed toward the high point mark. The fold should be at right angles to the center front, and the vertical cut edges should meet evenly. Tape the fold in place; and fill in the gap below with an extra piece of paper, and redraw the side of the pattern.

Lengthen the dart by extending the dart center line, and locating the new length on it. Redraw each side.

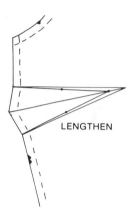

Lower the dart by going through the same process, except make the first cut above the dart.

Change the position of vertical darts by redrawing each side parallel to the original. Use the cut and fold method for curved darts.

The Proper Length

Darts should not be sewn all the way to the fullest part of the figure. The fabric should be released slightly short of the fullest part so that the dart doesn't "peak." Underarm darts should end 1" (25mm) short of the high point, while waistline darts should end ½" (12mm) to 1" (25mm) short of the high point, whichever gives the best appearance for a particular figure and fabric combination.

Short darts should be lengthened, and long darts shortened, so that the fabric fullness is released where it does the most good.

How To Alter

Adjust the length of the dart only after it has been properly positioned.

Shorten the dart by marking the right length on the dart center line, and redrawing each side, as shown.

The Proper Width

The dart width should properly relate to the cup size of the bust, or the fullness of other parts of the figure. Figures with full curves need wider darts than figures with straighter curves. Patterns are designed for a standard body shape, and you will have to alter dart widths if you deviate from this standard.

Darts that are too wide will cause wrinkles in the bodice, and the garment will look too big, even though it fits elsewhere.

Darts that are too narrow will cause the garment to bind over the bust, making you think you might need a larger size, even though you know it will be too big elsewhere.

How To Alter

Dart width alterations are best done in muslin. Once you see just how wide your bust dart should be, you can easily compare it to darts on all patterns, and make the necessary alteration.

Small Bust: Construct and try on the muslin. Pin tucks across the chest, and down over the bustline, as shown, until you get the proper fit.

Transfer the alteration to the pattern by slashing and overlapping. Reduce the width of the dart the same amount as the width of the horizontal fold.

Large Bust: Construct and try on the muslin. Slash the pattern, as shown, and fill in the gaps with strips of muslin. Adjust the gaps until you get a comfortable fit.

Transfer the alteration to the pattern, increasing the dart width by the width of the horizontal slash.

DART CONSTRUCTION

Bulging, puckered, or pointed darts are very unattractive. Stitching perfect darts is simple if you understand what is going on.

Marking

First of all, the dart must be accurately marked, using the pattern as a guide. It is best to mark the dart right after the garment piece is cut, before it has been allowed to shift. Misplacement can happen quite easily if the pattern piece is picked up and moved.

Mark the ends of the dart with small clips. Mark the point of the dart by inserting a pin through both layers of fabric at the dart point. Lightly mark the fabric with pencil or chalk, where the pin goes through.

Insert pins along the sides of double pointed darts, and mark as above.

Stitching

Pin the dart, right sides together, sticking pins through each construction mark. Check to make sure the pins are accurately placed on each side of the dart. Pin from the wide to the pointed end of the dart.

Always start stitching at the widest point of the dart. Backstitch at the beginning of the stitching, and gradually taper to a point at the end of the dart. The last three or four stitches should be exactly on the fold. Continue stitching a few stitches off the edge of the fabric.

Note: Darts that are stitched with an abrupt point will "peak" when worn.

Raise the presser foot and needle, and pull the fabric toward you about ¾" (19mm). Lower the presser foot and needle and take a few stitches in the fold of the dart, with the stitch length regulator set at 0. This secures the thread ends, and you can clip them close without having to worry about their coming loose. This process beats tying knots in the end of all your darts.

Continuous-thread Dart

Darts in sheer fabrics should be made with a continuous thread so the knot and thread ends can be eliminated at the point of the dart. Darts stitched on the right side of the garment for decorative effect should also be stitched with a continuous thread. Follow the instructions below for the continuous thread dart.

Unthread the machine needle. Pull a long thread out of the bobbin and insert it through the eye of the machine needle, opposite the direction in which it is usually done. Tie the bobbin thread to the spool thread, and pull the bobbin thread up through the thread guides. Wind enough bobbin thread on the spool to stitch the dart.

Start the dart stitching at the pointed end. This is the one time you should start stitching at the end. Make sure the needle goes into the fabric exactly on the fold. Stitch the dart to the wide end, backstitch and cut the threads. Rethread the machine for each dart.

Pressing

Horizontal darts are pressed downward, and vertical darts are pressed toward the center of the body. Open darts are pressed open. Work from the wrong side and use a good steam iron. Place an envelope between the dart and fabric so an impression won't show through on the right side.

Darts in bulky fabrics should be slashed open, trimmed if necessary, and pressed open. Handle wide darts the same way, slashing to within ½" (13mm) of the point. Squash the point flat, and press.

Darts in sheer fabrics look best if they are stitched twice and trimmed to ¼" (6mm). Press the dart in the proper direction, and then overcast the raw edges by hand.

SEWING TIPS

Clip double pointed darts, as shown, so the curve is released, and they lie flat.

Double pointed darts can be topstitched for a different look. This is a good technique for bulky or resilient fabrics.

Trim away fusible interfacing, within dart lines, before fusing it to the fashion fabric. Use the cut edges of the interfacing for a stitching guide. This process reduces bulk in the dart area.

Bust darts can be removed from a pattern by making a fold across the pattern that is the width of the dart. You might want to do this when using a stretchy knit with a darted pattern.

FOLDLINE

Back shoulder darts can be eased in, rather than stitched in, when using knit fabrics. This reduces bulk at the shoulder seam.

The shape at the open end of a dart has a direct relationship to the length and width of the dart. If you make any length or width adjustments, you must also change the end shape.

Draw in the new dart lines, and tape an extra piece of paper to the pattern at the dart end.

If you are underlining a garment with darts, stitch down the center of the dart through both the fashion fabric and underlining. This holds the fabric layers together along the fold, resulting in an accurately stitched dart.

Fold the dart along the new stitching lines, and press the fold down or toward the center of the body, just as it would be done in the finished garment. Trim along the edge of the pattern while the dart is still folded. This gives you the proper end shape.

FACING FACTS

Facings are an important part of the sewing process. You should know how to handle them properly so that all your faced edges are smooth and flat, without any of the facing "peeking" to the right side. Many ideas for professional touches are given in this section, as well as basic construction information.

FACING ADAPTATIONS

A simple facing is a piece of fabric cut in the same shape as the garment piece to which it is being sewn. Sometimes the facing is the same width as the garment piece, as in cuff or pocket flap facings; sometimes it is just a narrow strip, as in neckline or armhole facings. Let's see just how you should go about making your own facing.

Lay a piece of pattern or tissue paper over the garment edge to be faced. Trace around the edges and then draw in a lower facing line, so that the facing is about 3″ wide. Use this traced-off pattern to cut the facing.

Some faced edges will include one or more darts; i.e. the back of the neck, or the waistline of a skirt or pants. The dart should not be included in the facing, in order to reduce bulk.

Fold out the dart and trace along the garment edges. Draw a lower facing line making the facing approximately 3″ (76mm) wide.

FOLDED DART

Sometimes it is advantageous to combine two facing pieces into one. This can save fabric, reduce bulk in the seam area, and simplify the construction process. Some facings that can be cut all-in-one are the back and front armhole facings, the back and front neckline facings, armhole and neckline facings, and the garment front and front facing.

Armhole Facings

Eliminating the seam at the shoulder of the armhole facing reduces bulk in that area. Construction time is speeded up because you are working with one rather than two pieces of fabric.

Combine the two facing patterns by overlapping the shoulder seams until the seamlines meet; tape or pin them in place. Use the grainline on the front facing piece when cutting the fashion fabric. Mark the shoulder seam with a small clip.

Thickness can be reduced in the underarm area by off-setting the underarm seam of the facing. This is a good technique to use for bulky fabrics. Make this alteration before you eliminate the shoulder seam.

Overlap the facing pattern until the underarm seams meet, and tape in place.

Measure 1¼″ (32mm) toward the back, and draw a line parallel to the underarm seamline. Cut the facing apart along this line.

CUT

1¼″ (32mm)

Add a ⅝″ (16mm) seam allowance to each cut edge. Don't rely on your memory for this addition.

ADD
SEAM
ALLOWANCES

Now you can eliminate the shoulder seam, as described above, and make a very neatly faced armhole.

If you ever decide to change a set-in sleeve armhole to a sleeveless armhole, you will have to make your own facing. Use the following directions.

First of all, raise the underarm point by taping on an extra piece of paper to the front and back pattern pieces and drawing a new underarm line ½″ (13mm) above the given line.

Take the underarm in ½″ (13mm) also; this prevents "gaposis." Always try on the garment before finishing the armhole to see if you need to make further adjustments.

Overlap the front and back pattern pieces until the shoulder seams meet. Pin in place. Lay a large piece of pattern or tissue paper over the armhole area and trace the outside edges. Draw another line making the facing 3″ (76mm) wide. Make the facing grainline parallel to the grainline on the front pattern piece.

Neckline Facings

The back and front neckline facings can be combined so that the shoulder seam is eliminated. Just overlap the two pattern pieces until the seamlines meet, and pin in place. Cut the fashion fabric using this combined pattern, remembering to mark the shoulder seam with a small clip.

Neckline-Armhole Facings

Sleeveless, scoop-necked garments usually require a facing at both edges. Since separate facings tend to leave ridges that show through to the right side, combine the neckline and armhole facings for a smoother finish.

Lay a large piece of pattern or tissue paper over the front pattern piece. Trace around the edges as shown, marking the center front as a fold. Draw in a lower facing line that curves up over the bust. This curve is necessary to allow the facing to lie smooth-

ly over the bust area. Cut out the new facing pattern.

Go through the same procedure for the back facing, curving it in the shoulder blade area, and marking the grainline the same as the pattern back. Cut out the back facing pattern.

Use these two new patterns to cut the fashion fabric. Application methods for this type of facing are given at the end of this section.

Garment Front and Front Facings

The garment front and front facing can be cut all-in-one when the front edge is a straight line. This gives one less seam, and it is a good way to reduce thickness at the garment front edge when working with a bulky fabric.

Overlap the front and front facing pattern pieces until the front seamlines meet. Tape or pin in place. Use this modified front pattern to cut the fashion fabric. The front edge will now be a fold rather than a seamed edge.

stitched technique works well with most light-weight woven fabrics. It is too bulky for knits.

Method #2: Stitch ⅜" (9mm) from the facing edge and trim the edge with pinking shears, or overcast the raw edge with a zig-zag stitch. Use this method for knits or woven fabrics that don't fray easily.

FACING APPLICATION

We suggest that interfacing be applied to the wrong side of the garment rather than to the facing to prevent seam allowances from "shadowing through" to the right side. However, if you are using a fusible interfacing at a neckline or armhole edge, apply the interfacing to the facing piece. Fusible interfacing usually leaves a line where it ends, and you don't want that to show on the right side of your finished garment.

Unstructured garments that have turn-back lapels should also have the interfacing applied to the facing rather than the garment piece. This gives a firm look to the visible part of the lapel and prevents the seam allowance from "shadowing through."

Edge Finishes

The free edge of the facing should be finished in some manner. You should use the method that gives the flattest finish for your particular fashion fabric so that facing ridges won't show through to the right side. The finished edge of a facing is called a clean-finish.

Method #1: Press over a ¼" (6mm) seam allowance and edgestitch. If you have difficulty turning this narrow seam allowance, stitch ¼" (6mm) from the facing edge. Then turn the seam allowance back along this stitching line and edgestitch. Use whatever method works best for you. This turned and

Method #3: Face the facing with a lightweight fabric. Instructions for this technique are found on page 75. This gives a beautiful inside finish, and is a good way to handle fabrics that fray.

Method #4: Use the Hong Kong Finish for heavy fabrics. See page 27 for instructions.

Stitching

Facings should always be slightly smaller than the comparable garment piece so that the facing rolls to the underside and doesn't show around the finished edge. This can be achieved by laboriously trimming ⅛" (3mm) away from all facing edges before you stitch them to the garment. However, since you must trim the garment seam allowances after stitching, why do it twice? Make the facing smaller by the way you pin it to the garment. Just follow the instructions below.

Position the facing against the garment piece, right sides together, so that the facing extends beyond the garment edges 1/8" (3mm). Pin in place and stitch with the given seam allowance, measuring in from the garment rather than the facing edge. This off-set will make the finished facing slightly smaller than the garment. Caution: Do not make facings smaller on silk blouse-weight fabrics. The facing is made smaller to compensate for the thickness of the fabric which is not necessary on thin fabrics.

Stitch all facings carefully so they have a smooth finish. Shorten the stitch length around all corners and sharp curves, remembering to take a diagonal stitch across the corners to provide turning room. Keep the machine constantly moving while stitching curves. This makes for a smooth line. Make sure all seam widths are exact. Use a seam guide or mark the seam widths with a small clip at the beginning and end.

Finishing

The secret to a smooth facing line is in the trimming and turning procedure. First of all, trim the interfacing close to the stitching line if you have used a non-fusible type.

Press all seams in the flat position to set the stitches.

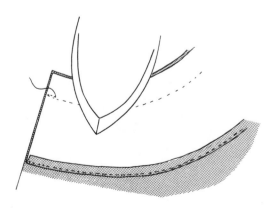

Grade the seam allowances. Average weight fabrics should be trimmed to about ¼" (6mm). Trim closer for thin fabrics and slightly wider for heavy fabrics. Seam allowances that lie just under the visible part of the garment should be left the longest. The seam can be graded in one quick operation by holding the scissors at an acute angle and cutting both seam allowances at once. This will make a beveled seam edge.

Clip the curved areas using just the tips of your shears. Clip just to the staystitching or stitching line, making sure you don't cut any threads. The clips should be perpendicular to the seamline and evenly spaced. Deeply curved sections will require closely spaced clips, while more shallow curves need fewer clips. (A good rule of thumb is that the clipped curve can be held open in a straight line.)

Occasionally turn the facing to the finished position, while clipping curved areas, to see if you are making enough clips. An uneven edge indicates the need for more closely spaced clips.

CLIP MORE CLOSELY

Pinking shears can be used to trim curved seam allowances, if desired. They trim and clip in one operation.

Press open the seam allowances to facilitate the turning process. A *point presser* will help you get in those hard-to-reach areas, or you can use the technique described below.

With the facing up, use the tip of the iron to press open the seam allowances.

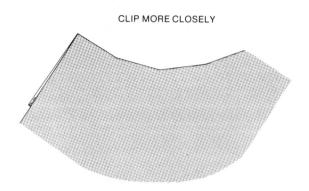

After they are all pressed open, press both seam allowances over to the facing side. This gives a firm turning edge.

Understitch the facing edge. This keeps the facing in place and also gives a firm turning edge. Turn the facing to the finished position and press, rolling the seam to the underside. Make sure all corners are sharp and curves are smooth.

Some facings need to be tacked in place so they won't flip out to the right side. This applies mostly to armhole, neckline, and waistline facings. Never completely stitch down the entire outer edge of a facing unless the garment has been lined or underlined; otherwise it will show on the right side giving that "loving hands at home" look. There are three methods you can use. Choose the one that works best for your particular garment.

Method #1: Pin the facing in position and *stitch-in-the-ditch* on the right side of the garment. Shorten your stitch length so the stitches will bury in the seamline. This technique can be used with most wovens and knits.

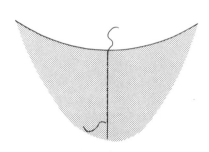

Method #2: Hold the facing in place with a small piece of fusible web placed between the garment seam allowance and the facing. Never fuse the whole facing to the garment. This will usually show on the right side.

Method #3: With the facing and garment seams aligned, catch the facing edge to the garment seam allowance only, as shown.

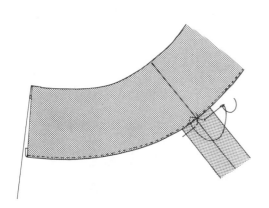

edge of the facing at the top of the armhole, and from the edge of the garment around the lower part.

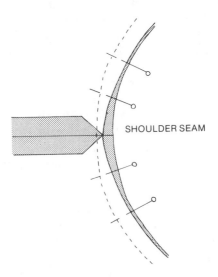

Press, *grade,* and clip the seam allowance. Press open the seam allowance at the top of the armscye, and *understitch* the facing seam. Turn the facing to the finished position, rolling the seam ⅜" (9mm) to the underside at the top of the armscye, and just slightly to the underside around the rest of the armscye. Tack the facing into position, using the method most suited to your fabric and garment.

FACING TECHNIQUES

The following facing techniques can be used on many garments. They give a smooth, professional finish to the faced edge.

Off-Set Sleeveless Armhole Facing

The off-set sleeveless armhole facing is a good technique for thick fabrics. It moves the facing edge ⅜" (9mm) back from the garment edge, at the top of the armscye, so there is less bulk at the finished edge.

Prepare the garment and facing by stitching the shoulder and underarm seams, pressing them open, and then *clean-finishing* the facing edge.

Pin the facing to the armscye so that the facing extends ⅜" beyond the garment edge at the top of the armhole, and ⅛" (3mm) around the rest of the armscye. Stitch the facing in place taking the given seam allowance. Measure the seam width from the

Bias Finished Sleeveless Armhole

Many ready-to-wear garments will use a folded bias strip, rather than a shaped facing, for sleeveless armhole finishes. You will see this technique used on many designer clothes. It is easy to do and can be used for both knits and wovens.

71

Knit fabrics can use a strip cut across the stretch of the fabric rather than a bias cut. You can use a self-fabric strip if the knit is not too bulky. Thick knits should have the armhole strip cut from a lighter-weight knit that is color matched to the garment fabric.

Stitch and press open the shoulder and underarm seam of the garment. Trim the armscye seam allowance to ¼″ (6mm). Measure the circumference of the armscye. Cut the trim strip 1½″ (38mm) wide and ½″ (13mm) longer than the armscye measurement. This allows for ¼″ (6mm) seam allowances.

Join the strip ends into a circle with a ¼″ (6mm) seam, right sides together. Press the seam open. Fold the strip in half, lengthwise, with the wrong sides together. Press the fold.

Pin the cut edges of the strip to the right side of the prepared armhole, placing the strip seam at the underarm seam. Stitch together with a ¼″ (6mm) seam.

Clip the seam allowance and turn the facing strip to the inside. Press the edge, rolling the seam to the underside, and hold in place by edgestitching around the armhole. This stitching will hold the facing strip in position.

Combined Neckline-Armhole Facings

There are various methods of applying the combined neckline-armhole facing. Not all the methods given in pattern instructions give the professional finish you want. The three methods found below will solve that problem. Each one is suitable for a different situation, so make sure you read the instructions before you start to work.

Pull-Through Method: This facing technique is used for garments that have a center back or center front opening and a finished shoulder width of at least 4″ (10cm). This width is necessary to allow you to pull the back section of the garment through the shoulder area without making the garment look like it has been through the wringer. This technique can also be used for fully lined vests. Handle the lining pieces as though they were the facing. Do not use this method for full length dresses or jumpers. Pulling that much fabric through the shoulder can damage the finished look of the fabric. Prepare the garment by stitching and pressing open the shoulder seams. Stitch and press open the facing shoulder seams and *clean-finish* the lower edges.

Position the facing against the garment, right sides together, pulling the facing ⅛″ (3mm) out beyond the garment edge at the neck and armscye. Pin in place and stitch with the given seam width. Press, *grade* and clip the seams.

Turn the facing to the finished position by pulling the back garment sections through the shoulder. Press the garment edges, rolling the seam to the underside.

PULL THROUGH

Finish the underarm seam by stitching the garment and facing in one operation. Make sure the underarm seams exactly match, and the seam allowances are pressed up into the facing when stitching.

MATCH
SLEEVE SEAMS

This technique can also be used for a garment with a collar. Pin and stitch the collar to the garment neckline before the facing is pinned in place. Continue as directed above.

Sleeveless Scoop-necked Facings: Sleeveless, scoop-necked garments that pull over the head require a different facing technique. Prepare the garment and facing by stitching and pressing open the underarm seams. *Clean-finish* the facing edges.

Pin the facing to the garment, right sides together, extending the facing ⅛″ (3mm) beyond the garment edge. Stitch the neck and armscye edges with the given seam width. Be exact, so that both shoulders are the same width. Backstitch at each shoulder seam. It is important that the backstitching be done at the shoulder <u>seamline</u> rather than the shoulder edge because the shoulder seam allowance will be trimmed. Press, *grade,* and clip the seam allowances, and turn the facings to the finished position.

Working on the inside, press the neck and armscye edges, rolling the seam to the facing side. *Understitch* these edges as far as you can go. Trim ⅜″ (9mm) from each shoulder seam.

TRIM

Pin the front and back shoulder, right sides together, leaving the facings free. Reach in from the back (between the facing and garment back) and pull the shoulder seams out between the back and back facing. The front shoulder unit is now "sandwiched" between the back shoulder and back facing.

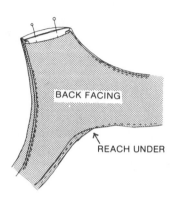

Finger-press the seams and pin them so they match exactly. Stitch the shoulder seams around in a circle, taking a ¼″ (6mm) seam.

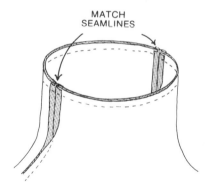

Pull the garment to the right side and press the shoulder area from the wrong side. You now have a nice, smooth finish with no lumpy shoulder seams that have been whipped together.

Shoulders narrower than 1½″ (38mm) need a slightly different technique since they are very difficult to stitch in the circle.

Position the shoulders and prepare for stitching as described above, but stitch flat across all four layers of fabric.

Make sure the shoulders are exactly the same width; otherwise you will have a "jog" at the seam when finished. Turn the garment to the finished position and press the shoulder area from the wrong side.

Sleeveless Garment With Collar: This is an excellent finish when a full or drop-lining is used in a garment with a collar. If a lining is not wanted, use the combined neckline-armhole facing, as described on page 67.

Prepare the garment and lining (facing) by stitching and pressing open the shoulder seams. IMPORTANT—backstitch where the seams cross, rather than at the edge of the fabric. Prepare and attach the collar and zipper according to the pattern instructions. Stitch and press the underarm

74

seam of both the garment and lining (facing). The garment is now finished except for the armscye.

Trim the garment armscye ⅜″ (9mm). Trim the lining (facing) armscye ½″ (13mm).

Arrange the garment and facing in the finished position, wrong sides together. Turn under a ¼″ (6mm) seam allowance at the top of the shoulder and pin in place.

¼″ (6mm) SEAM
TURN UNDER

Reach in from the back between the garment and lining (facing), grab the pinned seam allowance at the shoulder, and pull to the wrong side. Don't let the pin fall out while doing this, or you may twist the pieces incorrectly.

REACH IN

Begin stitching at the shoulder, taking a ¼″ (6mm) seam, making sure the cut edges of the garment and lining (facing) are kept even. Continue stitching around the armscye, lining up the underarm seams. This looks like a mess while you are doing it, but take heart—it will all turn out in the end.

Clip the curved areas, *understitch* if desired, and press the armscye edges for a neat finish.

FACING TIPS

Faced Facings

The technique of facing the facing gives a custom inside finish to your garments. It is a good way to handle fabrics that fray easily.

Cut the facing pieces from the fashion fabric, and then cut another set of facing pieces from a color-matched, lightweight fabric such as batiste or organza.

For an armhole facing, join both the fashion fabric and facing fabric into a circle. Trim and press open the seams. Pin the two facings right sides together, and stitch the outer edge with a ¼″ (6mm) seam. Press, *grade,* and clip the seam allowance.

Turn the facing right side out. Press again, and edge stitch.

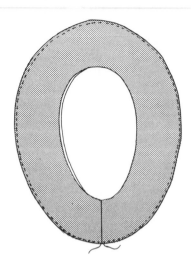

Now apply this faced facing to the garment edge in the normal manner. Other facings, such as neckline and sleeve facings can be handled in this manner.

Facing Sheers

Garments made of sheer fabrics present some problems when it comes to facings. They always show, which isn't very attractive. You can handle this problem in several ways.

Underline the garment so that the facings won't show, or use a drop-lining to eliminate the facings entirely. These methods aren't practical if you want to retain the sheer look.

The neckline and armhole edges that require facings can be finished with matching or contrasting bias binding.

If you have to use a facing, use the faced facing technique. This will look the nicest. If your sheer fabric is printed, use a solid color fabric to face the facing so the print doesn't show through to the right side.

Waistline Facings

Waistline facings can be used on skirts and pants instead of a waistband finish. If one always wears overblouses, or has a short waist, the faced waistline is usually more comfortable to wear, and it also eliminates the problem of rolling waistbands.

Cut the waistline facing pieces as described in the first part of this section.

A full lining (drop-lining) can also take the place of waistline facings for a skirt. Apply the lining as for the facing, hand stitching around the zipper opening. *Understitch* or topstitch the waist edge to hold the lining in place.

Facing Thick Fabrics

A lightweight fabric should be used for facings when your fashion fabric is thick. This will reduce bulk in the seam areas and along the facing edges. Color match the facing fabric to the fashion fabric.

Back Facings On Ready-To-Wear

Many ready-to-wear garments will have extra wide back facings. This is done to give the garment "hanger appeal", but wide facings are a bother when the garment is worn. They always seem to flip to the outside.

Solve this problem by trimming the facing to 2½" (64mm) and using one of the *clean-finish* methods to finish the cut edge.

Short of Fabric?

Facings can be cut on the cross-grain rather than the length-wise grain if it will save fabric needed for something else.

COLLAR CAPERS

Professional quality garment construction always shows up in the finished collar. Perfect collars don't just happen. They are the result of careful work at each stage of construction and a complete understanding of how collars work.

A well made collar will have the following characteristics: each side of the collar is identical in size and shape; the collar fits smoothly around the back of the neck, hiding the neckline seam; the collar points lie flat against the garment; the undercollar doesn't show; and the collar either hugs the neck or stands away, as designed. If your finished collars don't always fit this description, then you can benefit from the techniques given in this section.

ANATOMY OF A COLLAR

Before we go much further, it might be a good idea if we clarify the various collar terms that will be used.

Stand: The section of collar that stands up around the neck. Not all collars have a stand and not all stands are of the same width. Some are cut as part of the collar and some are cut separately.

Fall: The collar section that folds over the stand. It must be wider than the stand in order to cover the neckline seam.

Roll-line: The line on which the fall rolls over the stand.

Outside edge: The finished edge of the collar.

Neck edge: The edge of the collar that is sewn to the garment neck edge.

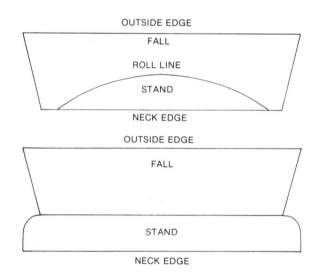

BASIC COLLAR STYLES

Even though you see many different collars on garments and patterns, there are just three basic collar styles. The various looks are achieved by size and shape changes and small details. If you learn how to properly construct the three basic styles, you can give any collar a custom fit and finish.

The three basic collar styles are: the flat collar, the partial-roll, and the full-roll collar. Each one is used for a specific fashion look, and fits the body differently.

The Flat Collar

The flat collar has a very deep curve at the neck edge. In fact, it will almost match the neckline curve of the garment. It lies flat against the body with just a slight roll up the neck. It can be cut to many shapes and sizes.

Since the flat collar has no stand, it is always applied with a full neck facing so that the neckline seam allowance can be pressed down into the garment. If the collar and neckline seam allowances are allowed to go up inside the collar, (the techniques of finishing without a facing,) the seam allowances will interfere with the smooth roll at the neck edge.

The facing can be either a full fitted facing or a strip of bias-cut fabric. Since the full width of a flat collar lies against the garment, you can secure the lower edge of a bias-cut facing by machine and not have to worry about the stitches showing.

The Partial-Roll Collar

The partial-roll collar has a slight curve to the neck edge. It rolls higher up the neck than a flat collar, but the stand is always shorter than the fall. The size of the collar and shape of the outside edge can be varied to give different looks.

A partial-roll collar can be applied with or without a facing. The facing is used when the stand is not high enough to allow for turned up neckline seam allowances.

The Full-Roll Collar

The full-roll collar comes in two styles: the straight, full-roll collar, which can have the stand cut as one with the collar or as a separate piece, and the convertible, full-roll collar, which will fit more snugly around the neck than the straight collar.

The neck edge of the full-roll collar is either straight or convex. Straight, full-roll collars are the kind used on shirts and blouses. The convertible, full-roll collar has a convex neck edge, and is the style used on tailored suits and jackets with turn-back lapels.

NECK EDGE

NECK EDGE

Note: Because of the shape, it is easy to mistake the neck edge for the outer edge on a convertible, full-roll collar. Keep this in mind as you apply the collar to the garment.

Full-roll collars, either straight or convertible, can be applied without facings because the stand is high enough to allow the neckline seam allowances to be turned up into the collar.

The stand-up or mandarin collar and the turtleneck collar are modifications of a full-roll collar; the fall has been completely removed and only the stand remains. Shawl collars can be made from either a full or partial-roll collar.

UPPER AND UNDER COLLARS

Each collar consists of an upper and under collar. The upper collar is the piece that shows on the finished garment. The under collar acts as a facing to the upper collar.

The under collar should always be smaller than the upper collar for two reasons. First, it helps the collar roll smoothly and stay in its proper position; second, it prevents the under collar from showing around the edges of the finished collar.

Patterns featuring some type of flat or partial-roll collar usually give just one pattern piece that is used for both the upper and under collar. The under collar is made slightly smaller during the stitching process (see below).

Patterns featuring a full-roll collar usually have separate pattern pieces for the upper and under collar. If you compare the two pieces you will see that the under collar is indeed smaller. This size difference provides the nice roll that is so important to this collar style.

The amount of size difference between the upper and under collar is governed by the thickness of the garment fabric. Thick fabrics require a greater difference than thin fabrics. Patterns are designed with average fabrics in mind, so you may have to increase the width of the upper collar by ¼" (6mm) to ⅜" (9mm), depending on the fabric thickness. Make this change at the outer edge of the upper collar. Do not trim the outer edge of the under collar; this will affect the stand-fall relationship and can result in the neckline seam showing around the back of the neck.

The under collar pattern for a convertible, full-roll collar is cut on the bias, unless a double knit fabric is used. Under collars cut from double knit fabric should be cut across the stretch; the center back seam can be eliminated. Bias-cut under collars are seamed at the center back so that the grain runs the same way on each end of the collar. This makes sure the ends of the collar are identical in shape after they have been stitched.

COLLAR CONSTRUCTION

As stated above, proper construction techniques are the keys to perfect collars. Each step should be carefully done, following the instructions given below.

Interfacing

Interfacing adds the shape and body so necessary to a perfect collar. Choose the style and weight of interfacing that complements your fashion fabric. Fusible interfacings are a good choice for collars because they allow you to trim away the seam allowances, thus reducing bulk. Non-woven interfacings can also be used, if desired.

Collar interfacing should be applied to the wrong side of the upper collar, except for collars on tailored coats and jackets. This is contrary to many interfacing instructions, but it makes for a nicer collar finish because the interfacing will prevent the seam allowances from "shadowing through" on the right side of the finished collar. This is especially important on lightweight fabrics.

The convertible, full-roll collar, used on tailored jackets and coats, should have the interfacing applied to the under collar in order to give more support to the stand. Sometimes an extra piece of interfacing is applied to the stand area only, for greater firmness. If the under collar is going to be applied by hand, and a fusible interfacing is being used, trim away the seam allowance plus an extra ⅛" (3mm) before fusing the interfacing in place. This ensures that the interfacing will not be visible around the edge of the collar after it has been stitched in place.

The grainline or direction of stretch on the collar interfacing will affect the way the collar rolls. Woven interfacings should be cut with the collar on the lengthwise grain for a sharp crease along the roll line, and on the bias for a softer roll. Non-woven interfacings should be cut with the stretch running the length of the collar for a soft roll line, and on the lengthwise grain for a sharper crease. Collar interfacing for knit fabrics should be cut across the stretch or on the bias, in order to preserve the stretch of the fabric and give a soft roll.

Collars that have separate stands should have the outside stand piece interfaced. If you want even more support, interface both the inside and outside stand piece.

Fusible Interfacing Application: Cut the interfacing using the collar pattern. Trim away all seam allowances and the corners, as illustrated. Fuse in place, carefully following the instructions for your particular brand of interfacing.

Fuse an extra patch of interfacing to the collar points. This helps keep them neat and flat.

Non-Fusible Interfacing Application: Cut the interfacing using the collar pattern. Trim only the corners, and machine-stitch the interfacing to the collar seam allowance. Stitch just ⅛″ (3mm) outside the given seamline. Trim the interfacing close to the machine-stitching.

Stitching

Pin the upper and under collar pieces together, right side to right side.

Collars that have the upper and under collar pieces cut from the same pattern should be pinned with the under collar extending out beyond the upper collar by about ⅛″ (3mm). This makes the under collar smaller after the stitching has been completed.

Collars that have separate pieces for the upper and under collar should be pinned so that the edges are even. You will have to ease the upper collar to fit, since it was cut slightly larger.

Stitch on the upper collar side, and hold the collar pieces taut while stitching so that the upper collar doesn't pucker.

Shorten the stitch length and take one or two diagonal stitches across the collar points. This diagonal stitching provides turning room and helps make fine collar points. The length of the diagonal is governed by the fabric thickness. Thick fabrics need more turning room than thin fabrics. The short stitch length at the points strengthens that area and allows you to trim the seam closely without having it fray away when you turn the points. Use a short stitch length on collar curves and any other detailed shapes.

Trimming

Trim the collar seam allowance to approximately ¼″ (6mm). *Grade* the seam allowances so that the upper collar seam allowance is longest. This can be easily accomplished by holding the scissors at an acute angle so that a beveled cut is made.

Trim the points, as shown, so that they mitre neatly when turned. Do not trim loosely woven fabrics too close to the stitching, or the seam allowance will fray away before you get the point turned.

Trim curves with pinking shears. This eliminates the need for notching and clipping.

Pressing

Steam press the collar flat after you trim the seams but before you turn it to the right side. This sets the stitching and gives it a more professional look when finished. Now, press the collar seams open, using either a *point-presser* or the method described below.

With the under collar up, press open the seam allowances, as shown.

Now press both seam allowances over to the under-collar side. This helps set the edge.

Understitch the long collar edge if you are not going to topstitch the finished collar. This gives a hard edge to turn on.

Finishing

Turn the collar to the right side; finger-press the edges, rolling the seam to the under collar side. Use a *point-turner* or threaded needle to coax the points out fully. Do not use scissors; the points can very easily make a hole in the fabric.

Steam-press the collar edges, rolling the seam to the under collar side. This makes sure the under collar doesn't peek through to the right side. Bulky or resilient fabrics, such as polyesters, will get a flatter edge if a *clapper* is used.

When working with a partial-roll or one-piece full-roll collars, it is suggested that you roll them over your hand into their finished position and then place some pins along the roll line. The under collar will extend a little below the neck edge of the upper collar. Trim the under collar until it is even with the upper collar. This shortens the under collar so it will stay properly positioned. It also helps to build in the collar roll.

Collar With Separate Stand

The upper part of this type of collar is constructed according to the above instructions. Apply the separate stand as directed below.

Sandwich the upper collar portion between the two stand pieces; the interfaced, outside stand piece should be against the under collar. Match up construction marks, making sure equal amounts of stand extend beyond both sides of the collar. Stitch as indicated, remembering to shorten the stitch length as you go around the stand curve.

Trim the seam allowances, pinking the curves; turn to the right side and press. The seam on each end of the stand should not be rolled to the underside; keep it on the edge.

TOPSTITCHING

Topstitching is an attractive detail used on many collars. It can be done with a matching or contrasting color, using either regular or buttonhole thread.

Various looks can be given to a collar just by using different topstitching patterns. See the Top Stitching section on page 35.

Collars are topstitched at two points of garment construction. This depends on the type of collar.

* Flat and partial-roll collars that have full or front facings are topstitched before they are applied to the garment neck edge.

* Partial-roll and full-roll collars without front facings, using either the wrap or double-stitched method of application, are topstitched after the collar has been applied.

* The convertible, full-roll collar, even though it has a front facing, is also topstitched after the collar has been applied.

APPLICATION TECHNIQUES

There are quite a few methods of applying a collar to the garment neck edge. The method you use is determined by the type of collar and whether a front facing is given.

Prepare the garment for the collar by stitching and pressing the shoulder seams. *Staystitch* the garment neck edge and clip to the stitching at regular intervals so that the neckline can straighten out to match the collar neck edge.

Collar With A Facing

Collars with neckline facings are attached to the garment using the "sandwich" method; the collar is sandwiched between the garment and facing. This technique can be used for both of the collar styles shown below.

Flat collars can use a full, fitted neckline facing, while partial and full-roll collars should have just the front faced. Directions are given for both finishes.

Fully Faced Collars: Stitch and press the facing shoulder seam, and *clean-finish* the free edge of the facing. A bias strip, instead of a full, fitted facing, is sometimes used around necklines that have center-back zippers. The construction technique is the same as for the full facing.

Pin the collar to the neck edge, making sure the distance between the collar edge and the front edge of the garment is the same on both sides. Position the facing over the collar so all the neckline edges are even. The collar will be sandwiched in between the garment and facing. Check again to make sure the collar edges are of equal distance from the front edge of the garment.

Stitch the collar to the garment, starting at each front edge, joining the stitching at the center back. Collars should always be stitched in this manner so that drag doesn't accumulate around the neckline and distort the way the collar lies in the seam.

Front Faced Collars: Garments with a partial-roll or full-roll collar will sometimes have just the front of the neckline faced. The seam allowances at the back of the neck are turned up into the collar and the open seam at the back of the neck is closed by hand. *Clean-finish* the free edge of the facing before applying the collar.

Pin and stitch the under collar only to the neck edge, starting and ending about 1″ (25mm) in front of each shoulder seam.

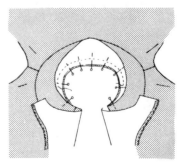

Fold the facing back over the collar so that it is sandwiched in between the garment and the facing. Pin in place. Check to make sure the same amount of fabric extends beyond the collar edge on each side of the collar. Adjust the facing folds if necessary. Stitch each side of the collar from front to back.

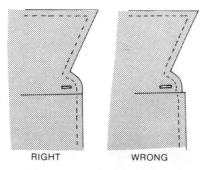

Collars with separate or cut-on stands should be positioned so that their edges are right on the front edge of the garment. The facing should fold back snugly over the collar edges.

Make sure the facing is pulled snugly around the collar edges when stitching, otherwise you will get a "stair-step" finish.

RIGHT   WRONG

Trim the neckline seam allowances, turn the facing to the inside and press the seam allowances up into the collar, around the back of the neck.

Clip the upper collar to the seamline, at the shoulder seams. Turn under the seam allowance and close the remaining open seam by hand or machine.

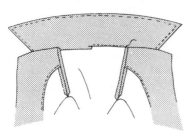

A man's knit shirt will use a slightly different finishing technique. Press both collar and back neckline seam allowance down into the garment, and hold in place with a line of topstitching ⅛" (3mm) from the neckline seam. Trim away excess seam allowance.

Collars Without Facings

Many shirts and casual jackets have stitched-on front bands and no neckline facings. The accompanying collar style always has a stand, either cut-on or separate. There are two techniques that can be used to apply these types of collars.

The "wrap" method works best for collars with cut-on stands. The "double-stitched" method is more suitable for collars with separate stands.

Either of these collar methods makes a finish that allows the wrong side of the fabric to show when the shirt or jacket is unbuttoned at the neckline. Fabrics with very obvious wrong sides will not be as attractive as fabrics with more similar right and wrong sides. Keep this in mind when selecting your fabric and pattern.

Prepare the garment by stitching and pressing the shoulder seams. Apply the front band and finish the other side of the garment front as directed in the pattern.

Wrap Method: Pin and stitch the under collar only to the neck edge, right sides together. The seam at the front edge of the collar should be right at the garment front edge and the seam allowance should be pressed open. Stitch from the front to back on both sides of the collar.

Mark the location of the shoulder seams on the neck edge of the upper collar with small clips.

Now wrap the upper collar snugly around the front edge of the garment so that the right side of the upper collar is against the wrong side of the shirt. Pin in place as far as the shoulder seam, if possible, matching the clips with the seam. Check inside to make sure nothing is folded over or caught where it shouldn't be.

Stitch each side of the collar as far as you can go, making sure you keep the front edge wrapped snugly and the collar seam pressed open in order to avoid a "stair-step" finish. Stitch both sides from front to back, sewing just below the first stitching line so that it will be covered when the collar is finished. Trim the seam allowance.

Clip the upper collar to the seamline at the point where the stitching ends. Turn under the remainder of the seam allowance and close the seam by hand.

Double Stitched Method: This application method can be used with any partial-roll or full-roll collar. However, it is almost a must for collars with separate stands or the popular, stand-up type of shirt band. You need a certain amount of maneuvering room to use the wrap method, and many stands and shirt bands are not wide enough to provide it.

The collar is constructed according to previous instructions with the following exception.

Press under and trim the neck edge seam allowance of the outside stand or under collar before you stitch the two layers of stand or collar together.

Pin the inside stand piece or the upper collar to the wrong side of the neck edge. Position the collar so that it is a scant 1/16" (1.5mm) from the front edges. Start stitching on each side of the collar 1/8" (3mm) less wide than the given seam width. Trim the seam allowance and press it up into the collar stand.

Fold the collar over and pin in the finished position around the neck, making sure the stitching line is covered on the right side. At each front edge, push the seam allowance up into the collar 1/8" (3mm). Make sure the edge of the garment fills the collar all the way out to the edge. Pin in place. Topstitch the lower edge of the collar, stitching from front to back on each side.

Note: If you don't want topstitching around the collar, you can apply it in reverse and do the second stitching procedure by hand on the inside neck edge. Just pin and stitch the outer band or under collar to the right side of the neck edge to begin with.

COLLAR TIPS

Occasionally you will find a nice ready-made garment that has the problem of "under collar peek-a-boo." This happens quite often on shawl-collared coats. Eliminate the problem by taking the needed size tuck along the fold of the under collar and catching it in place by hand. This is much simpler than re-making the entire collar.

Collar and lapel points, on garments with turned-back lapels, are cut larger than the matching collar or garment piece. This helps these points lie flat against the body after they have been stitched and turned. A good way to control this extra size is to fold the point along the diagonal, right sides together; weave a needle along the fold, as shown. This

pin takes up and controls the ease while you stitch the collar point to its facing.

Collars with a separate stand can be changed to a collar with a cut-on stand by overlapping the collar and stand pattern piece until the seamlines match. Tape or pin in place and use this modified pattern to cut the collar.

UP YOUR SLEEVE

Different sleeve styles make up a large part of the fashion picture. The variety of sleeve shapes is large, and the various details that can be used to change the basic look seem endless. Sleeves are an important part of any garment, and your construction techniques should be flawless so that the custom look you want is reflected in the sleeves.

A perfectly made sleeve is a credit to your sewing ability, whether you use a simple short sleeve or a tailored sleeve, complete with placket, cuff and button. Once you have mastered the basic sleeve techniques, you can then improvise and add designer sleeve details to your wardrobe of custom clothes.

The information contained in this section is to help you sew the sleeve into the garment correctly. Construction details for traditional sleeve vent and cuff styles are also given. This information will help you make perfectly finished sleeves on every garment.

BASIC SLEEVE STYLES

There are three basic sleeve styles in the fashion world: the set-in sleeve, the raglan sleeve, and the kimono sleeve. Each basic style has variations which can change the look quite a bit. Set-in sleeves can have fullness added to the sleeve cap for a puffed finish. The raglan sleeve can be made from one piece of fabric, with or without a shoulder dart, or from two pieces of fabric with a seam down the middle of the sleeve. A gusset can be added to a kimono sleeve, or the width at the underarm can be extended to make a dolman sleeve. There are some other variations of these sleeves, but the basics remain the same.

Raglan and kimono style sleeves are quite easy to construct. Most sewing problems appear with the set-in sleeve. Before we start solving construction problems, let's look at some set-in sleeve patterns, and compare their shapes and functions.

Set-in Sleeves

There are two basic sleeve-cap shapes for a set-in sleeve. Each one was designed for a specific purpose, and these should be understood so that you can use each shape where it functions best.

We will refer to the first shape as the tailored, set-in sleeve. It has enough height in the sleeve-cap so that it fits in the armscye without any wrinkles. The shape below the sleeve-cap will vary with the sleeve style.

The second set-in sleeve shape can be called the shirt sleeve. It has a very shallow cap that allows for much freedom of movement. The sleeve is usually cut wider than the tailored set-in sleeve. Vertical folds will appear on this sleeve when it is worn.

The shirt sleeve should be used only for men's and boys' dress and sports shirts and on casual knit T-shirts. While it gives plenty of room for body movement, it doesn't provide the slim, tailored fit that is desirable in most other garments. The tailored set-in sleeve gives a more fitted look, though it loses some of the wearing ease in the process.

All this is academic if you use and follow only printed patterns, since they will have the sleeve shape needed for that particular style. However, if you begin to do some style changes or designing on your own, you should know just how the two set-in sleeves will affect the look and feel of the finished garment.

SLEEVE PROBLEMS

As stated above, the most common sleeve construction problems exist with set-in sleeves. Most of these problems occur in the sleeve-cap. Either too much ease is allowed, or you have difficulty handling the ease and sewing the sleeve into the armscye. Other problems result from sleeves that are too narrow for the arm, incorrect armscye size, and sleeves that don't hang properly. Solutions to all these problems are given below.

Sleeve-Cap Ease

Sleeve-cap problems result when the pattern allows too much ease or the chosen fashion fabric is not supple enough to handle the allowed ease. Examples of these fabrics are: real and fake leathers, hard finished, firmly woven fabrics such as denim or permanent-press fabrics, and most knits.

Real and fake leathers, such as synthetic suedes and vinyls, need very little sleeve-cap ease because of their non-supple nature.

Firmly woven or stable fabrics will not ease-in as much or as easily as softer, more supple fabrics. Too much ease in the sleeve-cap will produce puckers or even unsightly tucks or gathers. This is an eye-catching advertisement for "home-sewn."

Knits have ease problems for two reasons. First, they are usually made of synthetic fibers which are not as supple as natural fibers; second, they have quite a dense construction, which makes them difficult to compress or ease-in. Knits also need less

cap ease because the fabric itself has built in ease. The amount of ease given in most patterns, unless they are designed for knits only, is usually too much.

The recommended amount of sleeve-cap ease for various fabrics is: 1½″ (38mm) ease for supple fabrics and 1″ (25mm) ease for knits, firmly wovens, permanent press, and real or fake leathers.

It is suggested that you check the sleeve-cap ease on your paper pattern before you cut the fashion fabric. If you make a habit of this, you will soon develop a feel for the amount of ease each type of fabric can handle, and you won't run into problems when you set the sleeve into the armscye. Making ease alterations on the paper pattern is much easier and more accurate than trying to make them on an already cut-out sleeve.

Determine the pattern ease allowance by overlapping the front and back pattern pieces until the shoulder seams line up; pin in place. Walk a tape measure around the armscye seamline, from the underarm seam to underarm seam. This is easy to do if you place the tape measure on edge. Make a note of this measurement.

Now measure around the sleeve seamline from underarm seam to underarm seam, with the tape measure on edge. The difference between the two measurements is the allowed sleeve-cap ease.

90

Cut the sleeve apart where the armscye and underarm seam meet. Make two to four slashes in the sleeve cap as shown. Make a slash for each ¼" (6mm) of ease you need to remove.

Overlap each slash up to ¼" (6mm) and pin. Recheck the sleeve measurement and adjust the slash overlaps until you have the right amount of ease. Tape the slashes in place; tape the sleeve back together and use this altered pattern to cut the fashion fabric.

Note: Sleeve lining pattern pieces should be altered the same as the garment sleeve pattern.

The usual solution for the above problem is to cut down the top of the sleeve cap. If too much is removed at the cap, the height of the cap is changed so much that you will end up with a shirt sleeve rather than a tailored sleeve.

Setting-In Sleeves

Sometimes sleeve-cap problems aren't really the result of too much ease; they are caused by the inability to handle the ease correctly. If the ease isn't evenly distributed around the cap, then puckers or tucks will result, and the sleeve will not hang correctly.

The easiest method to use for setting the sleeve into the armscye is to *easestitch* around the sleeve cap between the notches. Stitch just outside the given seamline. This stitching usually eases up the sleeve cap just the right amount. However, some fabric will ease more than others. If you find the sleeve-cap has become too small, break a few threads at regular intervals. If the cap is too large, pull up on the bobbin thread at regular intervals until you get the right amount of ease.

Stitch and press the sleeve underarm seam, and pin the sleeve into the armscye, matching up the construction marks. Hold the ease in position by placing pins every ½" (13mm) to ¾" (19mm) around the sleeve-cap. Insert the pins right at the seamline. This is important for good ease control.

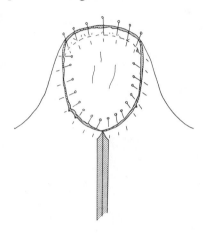

If you have a free arm machine, place the sleeve over the free arm so that the sleeve is on the bottom and the garment is on the top. If your machine doesn't have a free arm, stitch with the sleeve on top and the garment on the bottom.

Start the stitching at one notch; go all around the sleeve, past the starting point, and end at the second notch. This will give you a double line of stitching in the underarm area for strength. Trim the seam allowance to ¼" (6mm) between the notches, and to ⅜" (9mm) around the top of the sleeve.

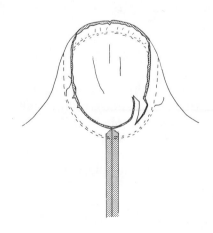

Optional Method

There is another method of setting in sleeves that can be used for sleeves with the minimum amount of ease. The sleeve is sewn to the armscye before any of the underarm seams are stitched.

Easestitch the sleeve-cap and pin the sleeve in the armscye, matching up construction marks. Start stitching at the notch and go around the sleeve to the other notch. Stitch and press the underarm seam of the garment and sleeve.

Complete the seam in the underarm area. Trim the seam allowance to ¼" (6mm) and zigzag or double stitch.

This method of stitching the underarm seam of the sleeve and garment is better than stitching the seam in one operation. It is less apt to pull out and gives a better fit because it follows the body contour.

Sleeve Width

Patterns are designed for an average sized figure. If you have extra thin or heavy arms you may find that you have to alter the sleeve width. Sleeves that are too wide will sag and wrinkle, while sleeves that are too narrow will bind and pull. If you suspect any of the sleeve problems found below, it is advisable to make up a muslin to check the pattern fit. Some of the following alterations cannot be made once the fashion fabric is cut.

Thin Arm: Determine how much should be re-

moved by pinning a lengthwise fold down the length of the sleeve. Allow enough ease for wearing comfort and to allow your hand to slip through the bottom of the sleeve.

Make the same size tuck along the lengthwise grain of the paper pattern. Use this new pattern to re-cut the sleeve. This alteration will also reduce the sleeve cap ease. Compare the altered sleeve with the armscye measurement to make sure you have enough ease. Too little ease will cause binding in the upper sleeve.

Heavy Arm: Determine how much extra width is needed in the sleeve by cutting the muslin sleeve open along the length, as illustrated. Allow the cut to spread as much as necessary and fill in the gap with a scrap of fabric, pinned in place. Sometimes you will have to release the stitching at the sleeve-cap and add some extra fabric at the top of the sleeve, also.

Slash the paper pattern down the center of the sleeve and out to each underarm point. Spread as needed and patch the slash with paper. Use this new pattern to cut the sleeves.

Armscye Size

A very important part of a well-fitting garment is the correct armscye size. Many people do not realize just how critical this is for a perfect fit. Perhaps you have heard that you should select your pattern size by the armscye fit rather than by the bust measurements. There is a great deal of truth to this statement, but when there is a great discrepancy between the armscye size and the bust measurement, it is probably better to buy the pattern by the bust size and adjust the armscye size. An armscye that is too small will give an uncomfortably tight fit. Armscyes that are too large will cause the sleeve to bind and restrict movement. Test for and correct this problem in muslin.

The sleeve should finish 1″ (25mm) below the arm pit. A tight armscye will be higher than this and need to be cut down. Alter the paper pattern the required amount. Remember that you are concerned with the fit at the seamline, not the cut edge of the

garment. Note: Tennis players, or people engaged in similar sports sometimes need their serving arm's armscye cut lower in order to accommodate the extra muscle development in that arm.

Large armscyes should have the underarm filled up with the needed amount. Add this to the paper pattern.

Sleeve Hang

Various problems will affect the hang of the sleeve. Many of them will be solved if the sleeve is eased and stitched correctly. Some will be caused by posture or figure shape and require the repositioning of the sleeve in the armscye or some pattern alteration.

Too Much Sleeve-Cap Height: This problem will make the sleeve wrinkle just below the shoulder. It is solved by pinching out the excess fabric in a fold across the top of the sleeve. Do the same thing to the paper pattern, and then re-cut and stitch the sleeve.

Too Little Sleeve-Cap Height: This problem causes the sleeve to pull and develop vertical wrinkles. Measure both armscye and sleeve seamline to see how much more ease is needed. Make the pattern adjustment by slashing the pattern apart in the upper portion of the sleeve cap, spreading it the amount needed to give the required ease, and then filling in the gap with an extra piece of paper. Cut the sleeves from your fashion fabric with the altered pattern.

Improper Hang: Some figures will need to have the sleeve re-positioned in the armscye because of their posture or body build.

People with very erect figures, who tend to hold their arms toward the back will usually develop wrinkles at the back of the sleeve, as illustrated. This problem is solved by removing the sleeve from the armhole, rotating it toward the front, and then re-stitching it.

People with round posture, who tend to hold their arms toward the front will usually develop wrinkles at the front of the sleeve, as illustrated. This problem is solved by removing the sleeve from the armhole, rotating it toward the back, and then re-stitching it.

SLEEVES WITH A CUSTOM TOUCH

Sleeves that have the proper fit and are made with the correct sewing methods will give your clothes a custom look. Listed below are some other techniques that will contribute to that look and also add a few designer touches not usually found on commercial patterns.

The Lined Sleeve

A fully lined sleeve is a good technique to use with sheer or lightweight fabrics. It adds body to the sleeve and eliminates the need for a hem. Fully lined dresses can also use this method to line the sleeves.

The fabric that you use for the sleeve lining can be the fashion fabric or a color-matched lining fabric. The fashion fabric can be used only if it is of a lightweight and solid color. Sheer prints will show through the sleeve layers and look unattractive.

Allow just a seam rather than a hem width at the bottom of the pattern. Cut two sleeves of fashion fabric and two sleeves of lining fabric. Trim ⅛" (3mm) from the lower edge of each sleeve lining. This will allow the seam at the lower edge of the sleeve to roll to the inside after the sleeve has been constructed.

Stitch and press the underarm seam of each sleeve and sleeve lining. With right sides together, slip a sleeve lining down inside each sleeve and pin the edges together. Stitch around the sleeve edge with the given seam allowance and then trim the seam to ¼" (6mm).

Pull the two layers of sleeve apart and press open the seam.

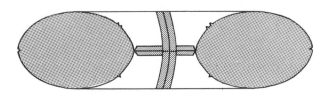

Tuck the lining up inside the sleeve, in the finished position, making sure the seam rolls to the inside. Press the edge of the sleeve with the point of the iron. Baste the upper edges of the sleeve together and you are ready to sew it into the armscye.

Making Short Sleeves

Patterns calling for long sleeves can easily be changed to short sleeves, if desired. First determine the short sleeve length by measuring from the shoulder to the level where you want the sleeve to end, or measure the length of a short sleeve on some finished garment.

Mark the sleeve length on the long sleeve pattern, measuring down from the seamline at the cap of the sleeve.

Now draw another line 1½″ (38mm) below the first. This allows for a hem. Trace the sleeve onto another piece of paper, making sure that you indicate

both lines. Trim away the excess paper along the lower line.

Fold the pattern up along the hemline. Trim the sides of the folded section so that they are even with the sides of the sleeve. Unfold the hemline and the finished pattern will look like this. Use this pattern to cut the sleeve from your fashion fabric.

Trimming Sleeve Seams

Sleeve seam allowances should be trimmed once the sleeve has been sewn into the armscye. The amount trimmed will be determined by the fabric.

* Trim the underarm area between the notches to ¼″ (6mm) for all fabrics. Double-stitch or zig-zag the trimmed area.

* Trim the seam allowance around the top of the sleeve to ⅜″ (9mm) for woven fabrics, and ¼″ (6mm) for knits.

* Armscye seam allowance for sheer fabrics should be stitched twice, ⅛″ (3mm) apart, and trimmed close to the stitching line. Press the seam allowance toward the garment so it won't show through the sheer fabric.

Designer Details

If you look at designer fashions in department stores and specialty stores, you will notice that they feature some unusual details not found on other clothes. This extra touch is one of the things that sets designer fashions apart. Very few of these details are difficult to make; they are mostly imaginative.

Make it a habit to look at designer fashions when you are shopping to see what's new. You can easily copy most of these special details. This is a good way to have a fashionable but inexpensive wardrobe. Some sleeve details found on designer fashions are sketched below along with suggested construction tips.

Short Sleeve with Fake Cuff and Tab: This design can be used for both men's and women's fashions. It looks great made up in interlock knits. Instructions for the fake cuff are given on page 194. Just add your own tab and hold it in place with a button.

Sleeve with Patch Pocket and Flap: This smart pocket detail can be applied to long or short sleeves of either knit or wove fabrics. Make your own pattern for the small patch pocket and flap.

Notched and Buttoned Cuff: This cuff treatment is a good finish for a sports shirt. Increase the hem width to 3″ (15mm).

Fold the hem up, right sides together, and draw a notch at the center of the sleeve that is ¾″ (19mm) deep and wide. Stitch along the notch lines; clip to the point of the V, and trim the seam allowances. Turn the hem to the right side.

Stitch and press the sleeve underarm seam. Turn the hem up in position and secure by hand or machine stitching. Topstitch the hem edge if desired, and hold the hem in position with a couple of small buttons.

SLEEVE VENTS

There are many ways of finishing off the vents of long sleeves. Since each method gives a slightly different look; your choice should be influenced by the overall style of the garment. Instructions are given below for the three basic vent finishes that are used on sleeves with cuffs. These vents are constructed before the underarm seam is sewn.

Most sleeve patterns will have vent markings on them. However, if you are making your own or adapting a sleeve pattern, the vent is located 2½″ (64mm) away from the underarm seam on the back part of the sleeve. Vent lengths are 2½″ (64mm) to 4″ (10cm) long.

THE PATCH VENT

This type of vent finish is probably the easiest to make and works well with knits because you don't have problems with fraying edges. It can be used with wovens also, but special care must be taken with the raw edges of the patch fabric. Directions for handling this problem will be given at the end of this section.

Vent Construction

Cut two pieces of fashion fabric that are 1" (25mm) longer than the vent length and 3" (76mm) wide. Indicate the length of the vent down the center of the wrong side of the patch with a chalk or pencil line.

Position the patch on the sleeve at the vent location, right side to right side. Start stitching ¼" (6mm) to the side of the vent line, taper to the end of the line, take one straight stitch across the end, and stitch along the other side ending ¼" (6mm) from the center line.

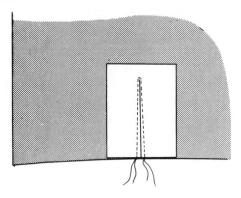

Slash to the point of the V, turn the patch to the underside and press, rolling the seam to the wrong side of the sleeve. The patch is held in position by *understitching*, which is done at this point, or with topstitching or fusible web, which is done after the cuff has been applied.

This patch technique can be used with woven fabrics, but care must be taken with the cut edges of the patch. If the fabric is firmly woven and does not fray easily, then zigzagging the cut edges is usually sufficient. However, if you are using a fabric which tends to fray, it is suggested that you face the patch with a lining type of fabric. Most lightweight, nonfusible interfacings can be used for this purpose.

Cut two patches from the fashion fabric and two patches from the lining fabric that are ¼" (6mm)

wide and longer than the measurements given above. These additional measurements will allow for seams. Place the right side of a fashion fabric patch against the right side of a lining patch and stitch around three edges with a ¼" (6mm) seam. Trim the corners, turn the patch to the right side and press.

Construct the vent by placing the faced patch in position on the right side of the sleeve. Stitch and finish as directed above.

Apply the cuffs to the sleeves using one of the methods described in the following section.

THE CONTINUOUS BOUND VENT

The continuous bound vent is probably the most common vent finish found on shirts. The strip of fabric used to bind the vent edges should be cut on the lengthwise grain of the fabric.

Vent Construction

Cut two strips of fashion fabric that are twice the length of the vent and 1½" (38mm) wide. Press over a ¼" (6mm) seam allowance along one long side of each strip.

With a short stitch length, staystitch around the vent line starting ¼" (6mm) from the line at the sleeve edge, tapering down to the end. Take one stitch across the end and then stitch along the other side of the vent line, as illustrated. Slash the vent line down to the stitching at the point of the V.

Place a vent strip against the slash, right sides together. The edges of the strip will be even with the edges of the slash except at the point of the V. Here, the strip will extend beyond the V about ¼" (6mm).

Working on the sleeve, stitch just outside the staystitching line, making a seam approximately ⅜" (9mm) wide. Make sure that you catch just a thread or two of the sleeve fabric at the point of the V.

Fold under the pressed ¼" (6mm) seam and then fold the binding strip over the vent seam allowance until the edge just covers the seam. Stitch along the edge by machine or hand.

MACHINE FINISH   HAND FINISH

Pull the two sides of the bound vent out away from the wrong side of the sleeve. Stitch the top of the vent at an angle as illustrated. This will help hold the vent in position after the cuff has been applied.

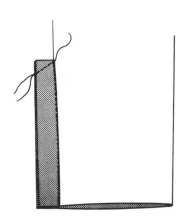

Note: When applying a standard cuff to a continuous bound vent, the upper part of the vent will be folded under, against the sleeve, and the under part of the vent will be pulled out away from the sleeve. If you are working with a French cuff, both vent sides will be folded under against the sleeve before the cuff is applied.

THE TAILORED PLACKET VENT

The tailored placket is the kind of sleeve vent found on men's and women's tailored shirts and jackets. This one is easy to do because it uses only one pattern piece for the placket rather than the two required by most patterns. You will find the pattern for the placket piece in the back of the book. It can be lengthened or shortened as needed, and it will work with any sleeve pattern. This piece can also be used for a neckline placket on a man's or woman's sport shirt. All you have to do is make it longer and put it on upside down.

It is suggested that you make a placket sample on some scrap fabric before you begin work on your actual garment. This will only take a few minutes and will help you decide if the length is correct. Once you see how easy this placket is to make, you will never again groan when faced with a tailored sleeve.

Placket Construction

Cut out two placket pieces and mark both foldlines with small clips. Transfer the stitching box to the wrong side of each placket piece.

Baste under a ¼" (6mm) seam allowance on both long sides of the placket pieces and press. Turn down both sides of the placket point ¼" (6mm), clipping at the one side as needed, baste and press. You can miter the three points at the top of the placket piece by following the instructions on page 110.

This will reduce the bulk at the top of the placket, which is especially important with heavy fabrics.

Fold over both sides of the placket along the foldlines, wrong sides together and press. The basted edges of the placket should just meet the sides of the stitching box.

Place the right sides of the placket pieces against the wrong sides of the sleeves so that the stitching box is centered over the sleeve vent line. The pointed side of the placket piece should be toward the front of the sleeve. Pin in place and stitch around the box with a short stitch length.

Slash down the center of the box to within ½" (13mm) of the end and then cut into the corners as illustrated. Do not cut the stitching.

Press each side of the placket toward the middle, along the seam line. Turn the sleeve to the right side and pull the placket piece through. Press again so that the sleeve seam allowances are pressed into the placket.

Fold over the narrow side of the placket and pin so that the basted edge just covers the stitching line. Stitch close to the edge, ending at the top of the opening. Make sure that you don't catch any of the other side of the placket in this stitching.

Pull the underneath part of the placket out to the side, and fold over the pointed section of the placket so that the basted edge just covers the seamline. Press and then stitch close to the folded edge, ending the stitching at the top of the opening. Pull the threads through to the wrong side and tie.

Now spread the sleeve out flat, right side up, and arrange the placket in the finished position. The basted edge should just cover the stitching line, and everything should be flat and smooth. Fold down the point of the placket and trim away some of the excess layers of fabric. Pin or baste the placket in place.

Finish stitching the placket as illustrated in the diagram. Pull the threads to the wrong side and tie them at the end of the stitching line at the top of the placket.

Press the placket well from the wrong side and finish the sleeves by stitching the underarm seam and then applying the cuffs.

CUFFS

Perfect cuffs are a sure test of the expert seamstress. If you can construct and apply them so that the points or curves are exact, the facings don't "peek-a-boo" around the edges, bumps don't form at the sleeve joining seam, and all edges are straight and crisp with even topstitching, then you are a success. This section should give you the help you need to make professional looking cuffs plus the patterns and instructions for some other cuff styles that you will find on designer and sport clothes.

TYPES OF CUFFS

There are two basic types of the standard cuff, one that involves 2 pieces of fashion fabric and one that uses just one piece of fabric which is folded back on itself. You may find that you prefer one type to the other, and it is a simple matter to change pattern pieces to the type you prefer.

The standard cuff is designed to be applied to a gathered, straight or pleated sleeve, with a vent opening. Because the lower sleeve edge is enclosed within the cuff, it can be rolled up the arm or turned back over a sweater or jacket sleeve without having visible raw edges.

The Two Piece Cuff

This type of cuff probably gives the finest finish, and it can have either square, angled or curved corners. The cuff consists of two identical pieces of fashion fabric, one of which is interfaced.

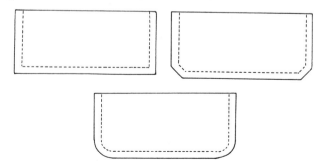

The One Piece Cuff

This cuff is made from one piece of fashion fabric which is folded back on itself. Interfacing is applied to just one half of the fabric piece, and the corners will always be square.

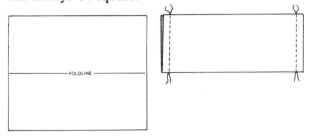

CUFF INTERFACING

Interfacing is applied to cuffs made from all types of fashion fabrics in order to add body and keep them looking crisp. Fusible interfacings, woven or non-woven, are ideal for cuffs because the interfacing seam allowances can be trimmed away, eliminating bulk in the seam areas.

The interfacing should always be applied to the upper cuff piece so that it lies between the visible part of the cuff and the seam allowances. This prevents the "shadowing through" of the seam allowances on lightweight fabrics.

One-piece cuffs should have interfacing applied to the upper half of the cuff piece only. The seam allowance of the interfacing should be trimmed from each side and the interfacing should end just short of the fold line.

CUFF CONSTRUCTION

Pin the right sides of the cuff together and pull the facing piece out beyond the upper cuff about ⅛″ (3mm) at the outside edges of the cuff. This will make the facing smaller than the upper cuff and enable you to roll the seam to the facing side when pressing the finished cuff. Stitch the cuff on the interfaced side, using the edge of the interfacing as a guide.

Always take at least one diagonal stitch across the points of square corners. This allows room for the fabric to turn smoothly in the corner and prevents "rabbit ears." One stitch of regular length is adequate for average weight fabrics while 2 stitches might be required for heavyweight woolens. Remember — the thicker the fabric, the more room needed at the point.

LIGHTWEIGHT   HEAVYWEIGHT

If you are working with a fabric that tends to fray quite easily, you will find it helpful to shorten the stitch length as you go around corners and points. You will probably have to take two or three of the shorter stitches across the diagonal in order to give you the needed turning room, but the shorter stitch length will prevent fraying at the points after the cuff has been trimmed and turned.

Shorten the stitch length when going around curves also, and keep the machine moving at all times for a smooth stitching line.

Once the cuff has been stitched, *grade* and trim the seam allowance. Turn the cuff to the right side and use a *point turner* or threaded needle to help you get the corners square. Thread a hand needle with a short, double thread. Insert the needle exactly at the cuff corner and pull on the thread to bring the point all the way out. Pull away the thread after the point is perfect. Press the cuff on the wrong side, rolling the seam so it doesn't show on the right side of the finished cuff.

CUFF APPLICATION

The two methods of applying the standard cuff are the wrap method and the topstitched method. Try each method to see which one you prefer. The topstitched method must be used when working with very narrow cuffs, since it is impossible to wrap these and still have stitching room.

The following things should be kept in mind when applying cuffs: make sure the sleeve ease is distributed evenly or pleated neatly into the cuff; don't let bumps form where the cuff ends join the sleeve; and make sure the topstitching is neat and even.

The Wrap Cuff

Prepare the cuff as directed above. The lower edge of the sleeve should be finished as indicated by the pattern, with a vent, pleats, gathers, or left plain. Apply the cuff using the following instructions.

With the sleeve inside out, pin the right side of the cuff to the right side of the prepared sleeve edge and stitch just the upper cuff layer to the sleeve edge with the given seam allowance.

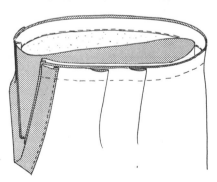

To insure a neat finish at the vent edge, wrap the cuff facing back around the cuff so that the right side of the cuff facing is to the wrong side of the sleeve, and the cuff seam allowance is pressed open. Stitch for about 2″ along the original seamline.

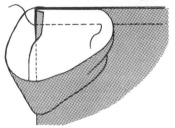

Trim and grade the seam allowance. Close the remaining part of the cuff facing by hand, or, if you are going to finish the cuff with topstitching, close it during that process.

Note: We have found that the seam allowance joining the cuff to the sleeve will be less bulky and visible on the right side if you make two rows of stitching about ⅛″ (3mm) apart when first joining the cuff to the sleeve. This is particularly important if you are working with a sleeve that has been gathered onto the cuff. The extra row of stitching helps control the thickness of the gathers. Trim the seam allowance close to the second stitching line.

The Topstitched Cuff

Prepare the cuff as directed above, except press down the seam allowance along the top edge of the interfaced cuff piece and trim it to ⅜″ (9mm) before you stitch the two cuff pieces together. Stitch, *grade* and trim the seam allowance; turn and press the cuff, rolling the seam to the facing side.

With the prepared sleeve right side out, pin the cuff facing to the sleeve edge, right side of facing to the wrong side of the sleeve. Extend each edge of the sleeve about ⅛" (3mm) beyond the edge of the cuff. This helps to eliminate bumps at the edge of the joining seam. The rest of the sleeve should just fit the top of the cuff. Adjust gathers, ease or pleats if necessary.

Stitch the cuff to the sleeve with the given seam allowance, starting and ending the seam ⅛" (3mm) narrower than the given width. Pull the folded edge of the upper cuff out of the way while stitching. Trim the seam allowance to ¼" (6mm).

⅛" (3mm) EXTENSION

Turn the sleeve right side out and arrange the cuff in the finished position so that the folded edge just covers the stitching on the right side of the sleeve. The seam allowances at the ends of the cuff should be pushed down into the cuff and carefully pinned so that no bump forms and all the stitching is completely covered. Edgestitch the upper cuff to the sleeve, holding the cuff taut in front of and behind the presser foot to eliminate puckers. A sewing machine with a free arm is excellent to use for this fi-

nal stitching. Topstitch the edges of the cuff if desired.

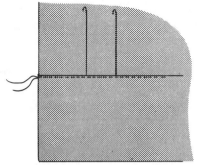

Note: If you want a cuff application that shows no topstitching, fold the seam allowance down on the facing part of the cuff instead of the upper cuff. Trim this folded seam allowance and then stitch the two cuff pieces together. Turn the sleeve inside out and apply the cuff to the sleeve with the right side of the upper cuff against the right side of the sleeve. Follow the above stitching instructions. Arrange the cuff in the finished position and *slipstitch* the facing edge of the cuff in place on the inside of the sleeve.

OTHER TYPES OF CUFFS

The following instructions are for other types of cuffs, some of which are found on designer clothes. Don't feel that you always have to use the cuff indicated on the pattern. Experiment a bit with these cuffs and do some designing of your own.

THE WING CUFF

This cuff is a good finish for blouse and dress sleeves. It can be used either with knits or woven fabrics that do not fray too easily. The turn-back feature is very feminine and attractive when worn with a long sleeved sweater or jacket. It is not the type of cuff that is meant to be rolled up the arm because of the raw seam at the sleeve edge.

The Sleeve Pattern

Use any long sleeve pattern, but first check the length and width before cutting the fashion fabric. The sleeve length should be long enough to reach the wrist bone. This will give wearing ease and allow the sleeve to puff a bit. The finished width a-round the bottom of the sleeve should be 4½″ (114mm) wider than the finished length of the cuff. Remember that seam allowances are not included in finished length or width measurements.

If you need to increase the width of the sleeve pattern, start adding about 2″ (50mm) below the armhole rather than directly at the underarm. This will give you a neater, smoother looking sleeve.

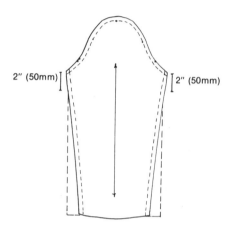

Mark two points on the lower back edge of the sleeve pattern as illustrated. These will be transferred to the sleeve fabric by making very small clips into the lower edge of the sleeve when cutting the fabric. If using knit fabric that runs, mark with pencil or soap.

Sleeve Construction

Cut two sleeves from your fashion fabric. Transfer the marks A and B by small clips. Stitch and press open the underarm seams.

Starting and ending at the clip marks, run two rows of machine basting around the lower edge of the sleeve. Make one row ¼″ (6mm) from the edge and the other row ⅝″ (16mm) from the edge.

The Cuff Pattern

Use the cuff pattern found in the back of the book. The pattern allows for the average wrist measurement. If you have a large wrist and need more length, cut the cuff in half in the middle and add an extra strip of paper to give you the needed size.

Cuff Construction

Cut four cuff pieces from your fashion fabric. If you are using a fabric with a pattern or plaid that needs to be matched, use special care in placing your cuff pattern on the fabric so that the two cuffs match and complement the pattern of the rest of the garment. Remember that the cuffs turn back on themselves, so take that into consideration also when you place the pattern on the fabric.

Cut two cuffs from fusible interfacing and trim away all the seam allowances. Since the cuffs turn back on themselves, you must fuse the interfacing to the cuff piece that will show when the garment is finished. This will be the under cuff rather than the upper cuff as on the standard cuff.

Pin the cuff and cuff facing right sides together. Pull the non-interfaced cuff out beyond the edge of the interfaced cuff about ⅛″ (3mm) in the wing section of the cuff. Reverse the procedure and pull the interfaced cuff about ⅛″ (3mm) out beyond the edge of the non-interfaced cuff in the lower section. Stitching the cuff when it is positioned and pinned in this manner will actually make the cuff facing smaller than the right side of the cuff, and it will be easier to roll the seam to the underside when pressing.

Stitch the cuffs together on the interfaced side with a ¼″ (6mm) seam allowance. Shorten the stitch length when sewing around the indentation to reinforce it. Take a diagonal stitch across each corner so that they will turn smoothly. Clip the indentation, trim the corners, turn, and press. Remember to roll the seam to the proper underside when pressing.

Fold the cuff back in the finished position and wrap it around a seam roll or a towel-wrapped soft drink bottle. Lightly press the fold. You will notice at this point that the cut edges of the cuff are not even. This is caused by the layers of fabric folding back over themselves. Pin the layers in this uneven position and then carefully trim them so that they are all even. This procedure will help the cuff stay in its turned back position when worn. Topstitch the cuff at this point if desired.

It is easier to work the buttonholes now rather than after the cuff has been attached to the sleeve. Using the illustration as a guide, use your button size to determine the buttonhole length. (See Closing The Gap, page 159). If you wear a lot of jewelry, you may prefer to use snaps at the cuff closing rather than buttons and buttonholes. Then your jewelry won't clash with or get caught in the buttons.

Cuff Application

With the sleeve inside out, pin the cuff to the bottom edge of the sleeve, right sides together. Make sure that the cut edges of the cuff and the sleeve stay even. The non-interfaced side of the cuff should be pinned against the right side of the sleeve. The cuff extension forms the under part of the cuff and is pinned to mark A. The straight side of the cuff overlaps the extension when finished and is pinned to mark B. Adjust the gathers so that the sleeve fits the cuff.

Make sure that you get the cuffs properly pinned to the correct sleeve. I have found it helpful to turn the sleeve right side out after the cuffs have been pinned in place and then slip them on my arms just to make sure that the right cuff has been pinned to the correct sleeve in the proper way. It is very easy to make a mistake at this point, so save yourself some time by double checking. Turn the sleeves inside out again for stitching.

Stitch the cuff to the sleeve with a ½″ (13mm) seam, stitching across the sleeve vent area. Use an overlock stitch or a combination of 2 rows of straight stitching ¼″ (6mm) apart, or one row of straight stitching with a row of wide zigzag right next to it. Trim the seam allowance close to the stitching.

105

Wrap the vent section of the sleeve edge snugly around the straight edge of the cuff (at the B mark). Stitch along the original seam about ⅝" (16mm), thus creating a pleat that will give a neat closure.

Turn the sleeves to the right side and finish them by sewing the buttons or snaps in place. The sleeves are now ready to be attached to the prepared garment. This cuff method gives a finished seam allowance that is turned up into the sleeve, leaving the cuff top smooth. No ridge will be made by a seam allowance on the right side of the cuff.

FRENCH CUFF FOR A KNIT SLEEVE

This mock French Cuff is designed to be used on knits only because you have to utilize the give of the fabric in order to slip the hand through the cuff. There is no sleeve vent, nor does the cuff unbutton.

The cuff can be used with a slim fitted sleeve or a fuller sleeve that has pleats or a few gathers. In any case, the finished sleeve width should measure 8" (20cm). The sleeve length should reach the wrist bone plus 1" (25mm).

Cut four cuffs from your fashion knit using the pattern found in the back of the book. Cut two pieces of fusible interfacing using the cuff pattern, and then trim away all the seam allowances. Fuse the interfacing to the upper cuff pieces.

Pin the cuffs together, right sides to right side, pulling the facings out approximately ⅛" (3mm) beyond the edge of the upper cuff pieces. Stitch them together on the interfaced side, taking a diagonal stitch across each corner. *Grade* the seam allowance, trim the corners, turn the cuff right side out, and press, rolling the seam to the facing side. *Understitch* the long top edge of the cuff if desired. The

outside edges of the cuff should also be topstitched at this point if you want that look.

Whip the ends of the cuffs together at the seamline, as illustrated. This will hold the cuff edges in place while stitching the cuff to the sleeve.

With the sleeve right side out, pin the right side of the cuff to the wrong side of the sleeve. Position the whipped ends of the cuff 3" (76mm) from the underarm seam on the back part of the sleeve. Stitch with a ⅜" (9mm) seam and then zigzag or overlock the seam edges.

For a nice finish, turn the cuff to the right side of the sleeve, rolling the cuff so that the seam is about ¼" (6mm) above the folded edge of the cuff, on the inside of the sleeve. Hand baste around the bottom of each sleeve about ½" (13mm) from the edge.

Now unfold the cuff and *slipstitch* the cuff facing to the sleeve so that the seam allowance is concealed. Remove the hand basting.

Catch the two edges of the cuff together, as invisibly as possible, about ½″ (13mm) above the folded edge. This helps keep the finished cuff up in the right position. Secure 2 buttons to each cuff as marked, one on the front and one on the back. Stitch both buttons in place at the same time so that they hold the cuff edges together.

The pattern for this cuff can be changed so that the edges of the cuff are square or rounded rather than pointed. Modify your pattern for these other styles before you cut the fabric. These cuffs are constructed the same way as the one described above.

PICK A POCKET

Pockets make sewing fun. There are so many kinds they seem to stimulate your creativity. A basic garment can assume many different looks by just using various pocket styles and or placements.

Kids love pockets, and you can please them with brightly colored applique or hole pockets, or put them in unusual places, such as on sleeves or the back of the lower leg. Ask for their suggestions. We're sure they can give you some interesting ones.

Tailored garments require more traditional pockets and the challenge here is making them perfect. Our construction techniques will make these pockets easy, so you need no longer hesitate about making them.

PATCH POCKETS

Some version of the patch pocket is the most common type of pocket found on garments. It is easy to do and can assume many looks, depending upon the design used. Instructions are given for a basic patch pocket plus some fun variations.

Basic Patch Pocket

The basic patch pocket consists of a pocket piece that has a round, squared off, or angled bottom. The top edge can have a narrow or wide hem. The pocket is usually topstitched to the garment, but it can also be hand or invisibly stitched in place.

Patch pockets cut from fabrics that need to be matched should be cut so they exactly match the garment fabric, or else they should be cut on the bias or opposite grain for effect. All-over printed

fabrics should also be cut so the pocket matches the garment. This is a custom touch you see on many designer clothes. See page 17 for more cutting information.

Patch pockets are usually interfaced to add more body, and fusible interfacing is a good choice. Cut the interfacing from the pocket pattern and trim away all the seam allowances before fusing it in place. Trim the interfacing along the foldline at the top of the pocket also.

The top edge of the patch pocket can be handled in two different ways. The topstitched edge gives a sporty look while the hemmed edge gives a more tailored look.

The topstitched finish requires a ¾″ (19mm) hem allowance for woven fabrics, and a ½″ (13mm) hem allowance for knits. *Clean finish* the edge of the hem for woven fabrics. Press over the hem and finish with two rows of topstitching.

Use the following instructions for a patch pocket with a hemmed edge. Fold the hem back along the foldline, right sides together, pulling the hem edge ⅛″ (3mm) beyond the pocket edge, as shown. Stitch the given seam width. Trim the corner and seam allowance and turn the hem to the finished position.

Press the pocket hem from the wrong side, rolling the seam to the wrong side. Press over the rest of the pocket seam allowances.

Square or angled corners should be mitered for a neat finish. Rounded corners should be *ease-stitched* to help them turn smoothly.

Miter square or angled corners by pressing a diagonal fold across the corner, just where the seamlines meet. Trim the folded section to a scant ¼″ (6mm), Fig. 1. Press over the other seam allowances; the fold should miter neatly in the corner, Fig. 2. Whip the folds together with a few hand stitches. Trim the entire pocket seam allowance to ¼″ (6mm).

Miters can also be stitched rather than folded, if you prefer. This reduces thickness in the corner area and is the preferred method for thick or bulky fabrics. Follow the instructions below for a stitched miter.

Press over both seam allowances and mark the point where they meet with small clips, Fig. 1. Refold the corner on the diagonal, right sides together. Match up the clips and stitch from them to the point where the creaselines meet, Fig. 2. Trim the seam allowance, finger press open the seam and turn the corner to the right side.

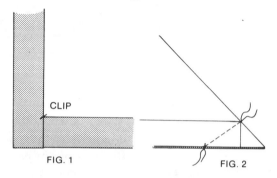

Easestitch rounded corners just slightly less than the given seam width. Trim the pocket seam allowance to ¼″ (6mm) and notch the curves so they lie flat. Pinking shears are good for trimming this type of curve. Press over the seam allowance, rolling the stitching to the underside.

Press under the top corners of topstitched pockets, as shown. This keeps the raw edges from showing.

Stuffing a Kleenex between the pocket and garment while pinning or basting in place will allow for needed wearing ease. This procedure is not necessary on children's or work clothes, but it does give a custom look to your nicer garments. Pin the pocket in place, using just enough pins to keep it from shifting while stitching. Some fabrics may need to be hand basted in place.

Machine stitch the pocket to the garment using the desired stitching pattern. Reinforce the pocket corners by stitching one of the following patterns. Note: An extra piece of fabric placed behind the pocket corner on the wrong side of the garment will add reinforcement.

The pocket can be hand stitched to the garment for a more tailored look. It is suggested that you first baste the pocket to the garment along the edge, so you have a guideline to follow on the wrong side.

Always work from the wrong side when you hand-stitch a patch pocket in place. This makes your stitches invisible. Catch just the pocket edge with small *backstitches*. Occasionally check the right side to make sure the stitches aren't showing.

Instructions for invisibly stitching a patch pocket in place are given on page 114.

Lined Patch Pockets

Many patch pockets require a lining. This gives them a nice inside finish. Interface the wrong side of the upper pocket piece, as described above. Use a lightweight fabric for the pocket lining. Cut the pocket lining from the pocket pattern, using the instructions below.

Fold the pattern over along the hemline. Measure up ½" (13mm) from the lower edge of the hem and draw a line. This is the lining cutting line. Trace off the lining pattern onto a piece of tissue or pattern paper.

Stitch the lining and pocket along the top edge with a ¼" (6mm) seam, right sides together. Leave 1" (25mm) unstitched in the middle. Press open the seam allowance.

Pin the lining and pocket, as shown, pulling the lining out beyond the pocket edge ⅛" (3mm). This will make the lining slightly smaller than the pocket when it is finished. Stitch around the pocket. *Grade* the seam allowance, trimming the corner or notching the curves as needed. Turn the pocket to the right side through the opening in the seam.

Press the pocket from the wrong side, rolling the seam to the underside. Close the open seam with a few hand stitches. You are now ready to stitch a perfectly lined patch pocket to your garment.

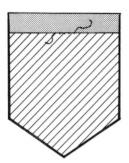

Self-Lined Patch Pocket

The technique of self-lining a patch pocket can be used for medium and lightweight fabrics. It makes the lining process quick and easy because you don't have to cut and handle a separate lining fabric.

Fold down the hem at the top of the pocket pattern. Place the folded edge on a fabric fold, and cut out a double pocket.

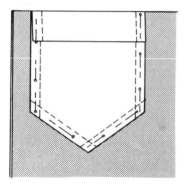

Interface one half of the pocket piece, using fusible interfacing, as directed above.

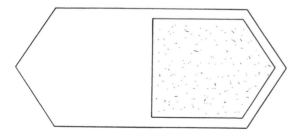

Fold the pocket piece in half, right sides together, and pin. Position one layer so that it extends ⅛″ (3mm) beyond the other layer. This will be the pocket lining. Stitch as indicated, with the given seam width. *Grade*, trim and notch the seam allowance as necessary.

Cut a small slit in the lower part of the pocket lining. Cut woven fabric on the bias so the cut edge won't fray. Turn the pocket to the right side, through the slit.

With the lining side up, press the pocket, rolling the seam to the lining side. Whip the slit closed, or patch it with a small piece of iron-on interfacing. The pocket is now ready to be stitched to the garment.

The self-lined technique can also be used for novelty shaped pockets, such as the ones illustrated below. Use your imagination to come up with unusual shapes. Combine the pocket with appliqued details for a special look. These pockets are fun to use on children's clothes.

Cut the pocket from a double layer of fabric, and stitch the two layers, right sides together. Trim and clip the seam allowance as necessary. Cut the slit, turn the pocket to the right side and press. Stitch in place on the garment.

A big mitten is a cute shape to use on a child's jacket. Cut the pattern larger than the child's hand, allowing for seam allowances. Cut the lining piece from fleece for extra warmth. Construct the pocket as directed above and topstitch to the garment.

Patch Pocket With Self-Flap

This attractive pocket is seen on many designer clothes. It is basically a patch pocket, but it has an unusual self-flap. It can be topstitched or invisibly stitched to the garment. The pattern for the pocket is found in the back of the book.

Cut the pocket and flap facing from your fashion fabric. Use the upper part of the pattern for the facing. Interface the pocket piece up to the fold line with a fusible interfacing, remembering to trim away the seam allowances first. Interface the facing just to the foldline also. In this pocket, the flap facing will become the visible part of the flap. This is

why the interfacing is divided between the two pieces.

Stitch the facing to the pocket with a ½" (13mm) seam. Extend the pocket ⅛" (3mm) so that the seam will roll to the underside. Trim and clip the seam allowance as necessary. Turn the facing to the finished position. Press from the wrong side, rolling the seam so that it won't show on the finished flap.

Using a contrasting thread, machine stitch a scant ⅛" (3mm) from the seamline, within the pocket seam allowance, *easestitching* the curves. Trim the curves with pinking shears. Press over the seam allowance, rolling the stitching line just slightly to the underside. Make sure the curves turn smoothly. Trim the entire pocket seam allowance to ¼" (6mm).

Use one of the following methods for stitching the pocket to the garment. The topstitched method looks more sporty than the invisibly-stitched method.

Topstitch around the flap portion of the pocket. Pin the pocket to the garment, position the Kleenex as previously described, and topstitch in place. Backstitch at the ends of the stitching line for strength.

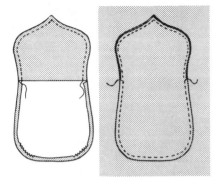

Press the flap down in position, using a pressing-cloth to protect the right side of the fabric. A button can be added to the pocket if desired.

The invisibly-stitched pocket may look difficult, but it is quite easy. It will really impress your friends and give them something to think about. The flap is usually not topstitched when you use the invisible stitching method.

Machine baste the pocket to the garment using a zigzag stitch made with the longest stitch length and the narrowest stitch width. Don't forget the Kleenex. Stitch on the edge of the pocket so that one side of the zigzag just bites into the pocket edge.

Using a regular straight stitch, sew the pocket from the inside, starting at the foldline of the flap. You will have to separate the facing and seam allowance from the pocket to get started. Stitch along the first stitching line, on the inside of the seam allowance. Work around the entire pocket, ending at the opposite foldline. Backstitch each end of the stitching line for strength. See page 126.

A larger version of this pocket can be made from the companion pattern found in the back of the book. Use the two pockets in combination on a jacket, the smaller one for the breast pocket and the larger one for the lower pocket.

The large pocket will have to be made as a separate pocket and flap. It will gap open if it is made like the self-flap pocket. The pocket can be topstitched or invisibly-stitched in place. Construct and apply the flap as instructed below.

Patch Pocket With Flap

Many patch pockets have flap coverings. They add a different look, and also make the pocket more secure if the flap is closed with a button or snap.

Always make the flap after the pocket has been stitched to the garment. This enables you to make the flap ¼" (6mm) wider than the finished pocket, which prevents the corners of the pocket from sticking out beyond the edges of the flap.

The flap can be faced with a lining fabric or self-fabric. Choose whatever works best with your fashion fabric. Use fusible interfacing on the wrong side of the flap to add body, if necessary. Pin the flap and facing together, positioning the facing so it extends ⅛" (3mm) beyond the flap edge. Stitch with the given seam width, trim and clip the seam allowance as necessary. Turn the flap to the right side and press, rolling the seam to the facing side. Topstitch if desired.

Position the flap so that the seamline is ½" (13mm) above the pocket with the flap extending ⅛" (3mm) on each side of the pocket. Stitch the flap, backstitching at both edges for strength. Trim the seam to a scant ¼″ (6mm).

Fold the flap down and press, using a pressing-cloth to protect the fabric. Topstitch ¼″ (6mm) away from the fold. Do not backstitch at the seam ends. Pull the thread ends through to the wrong side and tie them with a square knot. This gives a much nicer finish.

Patch Pocket with Fake Band

This patch pocket variation is suitable for both men's and women's fashions. It looks as if a separate band has been applied to the top of the pocket. Adjust the pocket pattern so that the hem is 2″ wide. Interface the pocket as previously instructed.

Fold the hem over in the finished position and then fold it over again. Stitch ¼″ (6mm) from the fold, catching the hem edge in the fold.

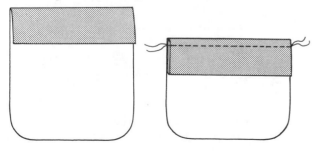

Unfold the hem and press from the wrong side. Topstitch across the pocket top if desired.

Press under the pocket seam allowances, mitering the corners or *easestitching* the curves. Trim and notch as necessary. Pin the pocket to the garment and topstitch in place. A pocket with round corners can be invisibly-stitched in place.

Machine baste the pocket to the garment using a zigzag stitch made with the longest stitch length and the narrowest stitch width. Don't forget the Kleenex, and stitch on the edge of the pocket so that one side of the zigzag just bites into the pocket edge.

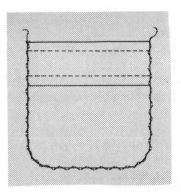

Using a regular length straight stitch, sew the pocket from the inside, starting at the top right hand corner of the pocket. Stitch on the first stitching line, on the inside of the seam allowance. Work around the entire pocket, ending at the opposite corner. Backstitch each end of the stitching line for strength. Fold down the ends of the seam allowance at the pocket corner so they won't show and catch in place on the wrong side by hand.

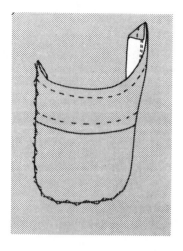

ZIPPER POCKETS

Zipper pockets are quite useful as well as decorative. They are ideal for sports clothes and outerwear, but are also used on other types of clothing. A zipper pocket requires a 5″ (13cm) or 7″ (18cm) zipper. Heavy, decorative zippers are now on the market. These are especially suitable for pockets in outer-wear. Regular zippers can also be used for pockets. Attach a ring or some sort of zipper pull to the slide, for convenience.

Two-Way Zipper Pocket

This pocket is ideal for outer-wear because it provides both the security of a closed pocket and the ready access of a hand-warmer pocket. The pocket lining can be cut from a fleece fabric for extra warmth.

Cut the pieces shown for each pocket. Use matching or contrasting fabric, as desired. You will also need a 7″ zipper for each pocket.

Sandwich the zipper between the two upper pocket pieces, with the right sides together and the edges even with the zipper tape. There should be ⅜″ (9mm) of fabric extending beyond each end of the zipper teeth. Stitch this unit together with a ¼″ (6mm) seam, Fig. 1. Separate the two fabric pieces and press so the zipper extends below, as shown. Edgestitch along the fabric fold, Fig. 2.

FIG. 1

FIG. 2

Repeat the above process with the two large fabric pieces, so that the other side of the zipper is enclosed.

Pin the pocket lining against the zipper unit, right sides together. The lining should extend ⅛″ (3mm)

beyond the zipper unit edges. Using a zipper foot, stitch around the pocket with a ¼″ (6mm) seam.

Note: Be careful as you stitch across the ends of the zipper. You need to stitch as closely as you can without hitting the zipper with your machine needle, which could break or damage your needle.

Trim the pocket corners and cut a slit in the lower portion of the pocket lining. Pull the pocket through to the right side and press. Close the slit with a few hand stitches or a small piece of fusible interfacing.

Pin the pocket to the garment in the proper position. Topstitch, as illustrated, leave an opening on one side of the pocket that is wide enough for the hand. Backstitch or bar tack both ends of the stitching for strength. The edge of the pocket opening can be topstitched before applying the pocket to the garment, if desired.

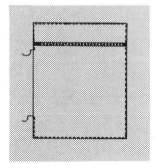

Patch Pocket with Exposed Zipper

Patch pockets with exposed zippers can be used on sport clothes. This technique is also useful for some novelty pockets. Cut the desired pocket shape, making sure it is large enough to accommodate the chosen zipper. Interface the wrong side of the pocket with non-woven fusible interfacing to help control any fraying.

Mark the zipper opening on the wrong side of the pocket piece. The opening should be ¼″ (6mm) wide and ⅛″ (3mm) longer than the zipper. Using a short stitch, sew around the marked box, Fig. 1. Cut the box open, as shown, making sure you make a large wedge; clip all the way into each corner, Fig. 2.

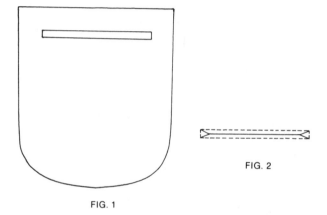

FIG. 2

FIG. 1

Working on the wrong side, press back the edges of the opening, rolling the fabric so the stitches are on the wrong side. Baste around the seam allowance to hold it in place.

Position the zipper under the opening. Baste in place. Using a zipper foot, secure the zipper by edgestitching around the box on the right side of pocket. Do another row of stitching ¼″ (6mm)

from edge. This helps control the zipper tapes, and makes the opening strong.

Finish the pocket by pressing under the seam allowances as described in the basic patch pocket section. Pin the pocket to the garment and topstitch in place.

Covered Zipper Pocket

In this version of the zipper pocket the zipper is covered and has a more tailored look. The construction is similar to a bound buttonhole, except a zipper is stitched under the opening. This pocket can be made as a patch pocket to be topstitched to the garment, or as a set-in pocket.

The pocket pattern should measure 7″ (18cm) by 8″ (20cm) for a 5″ (13cm) zipper pocket, and 9″ (23cm) by 8″ (20cm) for a 7″ (18cm) zipper pocket. Cut one pocket piece for the patch pocket, and two for the set-in pocket.

Cut two strips of fabric 1″ (25mm) longer than the zipper and 1″ (25mm) wide, for each pocket. Press these strips lengthwise, down the middle, with the wrong sides together.

Patch Pocket: Mark the zipper position with a line that is 2″ (5cm) longer than the zipper. Indicate the exact length with two vertical lines, as shown. Draw these lines on the wrong side of the pocket, and

transfer them through to the right side by machine basting.

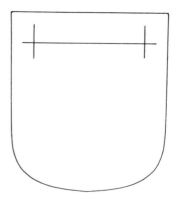

Working on the right side of the pocket pieces, position one fabric strip so that the cut edges are even with the pocket mark, and the ends extend ½″ (13mm) beyond the vertical lines. Stitch down the exact center of the strip, starting and ending exactly on the vertical lines. Position and stitch the other strip the same way.

Turn the pocket to the wrong side and cut an opening as shown, making good sized wedges in each corner. Make sure you cut just the garment fabric not the welts.

Turn both strips through the opening and adjust them so they fill the opening. Whip the opening closed and press from the wrong side. Remove the machine basting. You have just made a big buttonhole.

Center the zipper under the prepared opening, baste in place. *Stitch-in-the-ditch* around the pocket opening to hold the zipper in place or fold back the top and bottom sections of the pocket and stitch along the original seamlines. Use a zipper foot and a short stitch length for best results. Run the machine slowly as you stitch across the ends of the zipper — you don't want to hit the zipper with the needle.

Finish the pocket by pressing under the seam allowance as described in the basic patch pocket instructions. Pin the pocket to the garment and topstitch in place.

Set-In Pocket: The set-in zipper pocket follows the same construction steps as above except the pocket opening is constructed in the garment fabric, rather than the pocket piece. After the zipper has been completed, the pocket piece is positioned behind the opening and stitched in place. This is a good pocket for a warm-up suit. You can also make an extra large pocket by cutting the pocket piece the same size as the lower half of the garment and catching the pocket edges in the side seam, center front and bottom edges of the garment.

If you don't want the pocket stitching to show, use two pocket pieces, placing one on the wrong side of the garment before you construct the opening. After the zipper has been stitched in place, pin the two pocket pieces together and edgestitch around all four sides.

ONE-PIECE WELT POCKET

This welt pocket is easy to make and has many applications. It was originally designed for sweaters, but is equally good for sports shirts, pants, jackets, and even dresses. A word of caution: use a regular patch pocket on sports shirts made of lightweight fabric. This welt pocket would shadow through to the right side.

The welt and pocket are made of one piece of fashion fabric. It can be used with knits and medium to lightweight woven fabrics. Use the welt pocket technique given on page 126, for thick or bulky fabrics.

The measurements given in the diagram below are for the average size shirt pocket. You can change the width of the pocket or welt by changing the distance between the vertical or horizontal lines. The back pocket on men's pants should be 5½″ (13cm) wide, to allow for the hand. We will refer to the diagram below as the pocket grid.

Cut a pocket piece 2″ (50mm) wider than the pocket opening and 10½″ (27cm) long. This makes a pocket with a finished depth of about 4″ (10cm). Adjust the length of the pocket piece if you want a deeper or more shallow pocket.

Cut a piece of stay fabric for each pocket that is 2″ (50mm) longer and wider than the grid. Use a non-fusible, woven interfacing for the stay fabric. Trace the grid onto the pocket stay with a pencil or marking pen. Be accurate with your lines and mark them as indicated on the above diagram.

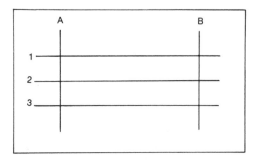

Position the pocket stay on the wrong side of the garment so that line 2 is centered over the pocket location marks. If you are working with a horizontally striped fabric, make sure the pocket location mark is on or parallel to a stripe. Using a contrasting thread and a long stitch, machine baste along the grid lines so they are tranferred to the right side of the garment. Stitch the vertical and horizontal lines from the same direction so the grid will stay square. Change back to a matching thread and adjust your machine to the normal stitch length.

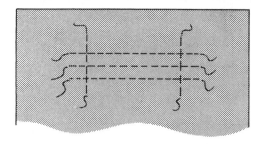

Working on the right side of the garment, pin the bottom edge of the pocket piece ⅛″ (3mm) above line 2. The piece should be centered over the hori-

zontal grid lines, with the right sides of the fabric together.

Turn the garment to the wrong side and stitch along line 1. Start and end the stitching line where line 1 crosses A and B. Backstitch at each end for strength.

Again, working on the right side, fold over and press 1″ (25mm) of the free end of the pocket piece, and bring the fold down to line 3. Pin in place. Turn the garment to the wrong side, and stitch along line 2 between lines A and B, backstitching at each end.

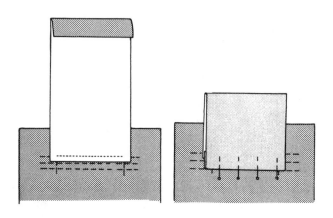

Cut the pocket open between lines 1 and 2. Make a good sized wedge at each corner. Do not cut through the pocket fabric. Hold it out of the way and cut just the garment and interfacing fabric.

Pull the pocket through the opening to the inside, and arrange the welt so that it completely fills in the opening. Whip the pocket closed with a few hand stitches or hold it closed with a strip of transparent tape.

Fold back the side of the garment until you see the wedge on top of the pocket fabric. Stitch across the base of the wedge through all fabric layers. Make this stitching line slightly convex. This helps square the pocket corners. Continue stitching down the side of the pocket. Do another row of stitching to the side of the first, using either a straight or zigzag stitch. Trim the seam allowance. Note: A stretch-overlock stitch is good for stitching the pocket sides because it is so strong.

A pencil slot can be made on a man's sport shirt pocket by making another line of stitching ¾" (19mm) from the front edge of the pocket.

Finish the other side of the pocket in the above manner. Press the pocket from the wrong side, remove the basting and whip stitches, and trim away the stay fabric close to the stitching lines. You can bar tack the pocket ends for extra strength.

The pocket welt can be made from a contrasting fabric if desired. This looks very nice when you match the welt to pants or skirt fabric. Cut a contrasting welt 2" (50mm) wider than the pocket opening and 2½" (64mm) long for woven fabrics, or 2" (50mm) long for knits or Ultra Suede® fabric. Follow these instructions for stitching the contrasting welt to the pocket piece.

Trim 2" (50mm) from one end of the pocket piece and stitch the woven fabric welt to the end of the piece with a ¼" (6mm) seam. Press seam open, Fig. 1. Attach the knit or suede welt piece by overlapping the pocket edge ¼" (6mm); zigzag in place, Fig. 2.

FIG. 1   FIG. 2

THE EXPANDABLE POCKET

This expandable pocket is great for sports clothes used for golf, tennis, or hiking. Once you try it you'll find many other uses for it also. The pocket is very attractive if you add machine embroidered initials or a name to the pocket front. Edgestitch it in a contrasting color or apply an applique or sport motif, such as a golf tee or tennis racquet, for fun. The pattern for the pocket is found in the back of the book.

Cut a piece of fusible interfacing to fit within the inside fold lines of the pocket and fuse it in place on the wrong side.

Turn down the top of the pocket along the fold line, wrong sides together, and work a machine buttonhole, as indicated. Stitch across the bottom of the hem, if desired. Apply any applique or monogram.

Fold the lower corners of the pocket on the diagonal, right sides together, and stitch along the marked lines, Fig. 1. Use a short stitch length and take one stitch across the bottom point, as illustrated. Backstitch or tie the thread at each end. Trim the seam to a scant ¼" (6mm), cutting away excess fabric at the points; clip into the point of the V, Fig. 2.

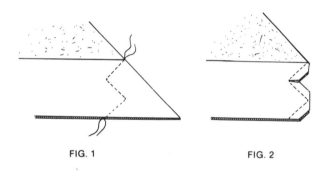

FIG. 1   FIG. 2

Press the pocket along the inside fold lines and edgestitch around all three sides.

Turn under a ½" (13mm) seam allowance around the outside edge of the pocket, and press.

Pin the pocket to the garment making sure that the back edges are directly under the front edges when the pocket is in the folded, closed position. Stitch the pocket to the garment.

Fold the sides of the pocket together at the top edge and stitch a small triangle in the corner. This will keep the pocket top from gapping open. Sew a button to the garment underneath the buttonhole.

A flap can be added to this pocket if desired. Cut it so that the finished measurement is ¼" (6mm) wider than the finished width of the pocket. Stitch the flap in place as previously directed.

FACED-HOLE POCKETS

The faced-hole pocket is decorative as well as functional. It is used mainly on children's clothes, but can also be applied to some adult sports clothes. Use a matching or contrasting fabric behind the pocket opening; topstitch with a matching or contrasting color; or combine the pocket with a large applique. It is fun to think up new designs for this pocket. Your imagination is your only limit.

First of all, determine the size and shape of the pocket opening. Make it large enough for the hand to slip through easily. If you are combining the pocket with an applique, stitch the applique to the garment before you begin the pocket construction.

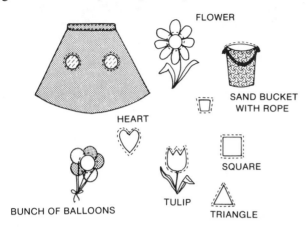

FLOWER

SAND BUCKET WITH ROPE

HEART

SQUARE

BUNCH OF BALLOONS

TULIP

TRIANGLE

Draw the pocket hole on a piece of paper and draw a pattern for the pocket piece around the hole, as illustrated. The pocket pattern should be 1″ (25mm) larger than the hole, around the top and sides, and long enough to give the desired pocket depth plus ¼″ (6mm) for a seam.

Cut an upper and under pocket piece from the pattern. The under pocket piece will be visible through the faced hole, so cut it from the fabric that you want to show.

Draw the hole design on the wrong side of the upper pocket and pin it in position on the right side of the garment. Stitch around the hole, using a short stitch length, Fig. 1. Cut out the hole, leaving a ¼″ (6mm) seam allowance. Clip the seam as necessary, Fig. 2.

FIG. 1

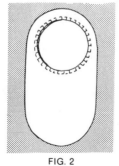

FIG. 2

Turn the upper pocket to the inside of the garment and press so the seam is on the edge. Topstitch around the opening with one or more rows of stitching. You now have a neatly faced hole in your garment.

Working on the wrong side, pin the under pocket to the upper pocket only. Stitch around the outside of the two pocket pieces with a ¼″ (6mm) seam. Do another row of stitching — regular or zigzag. Now how is that for a fun pocket?

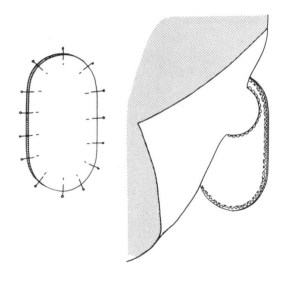

POCKET IN A SEAM

This pocket technique is used for small concealed pockets in a waistband seam, flap pockets in a waistline or yoke seam, or men's or boy's pants pockets in either the back yoke or waistline seam. It can be large or small, topstitched for emphasis, or left plain.

Instructions will be given for the small waistline pocket. Directions for other versions will be given at the end of this section.

Mark the desired pocket width and placement on the pattern seamline. Transfer these marks to your fashion fabric with small clip marks at the fabric edge.

123

Cut one pocket piece 1″ (25mm) wider than the pocket opening, and twice the desired pocket depth plus two seam widths. This pocket piece is usually cut from the fashion fabric. If a flap is being used with the pocket, the pocket piece can be cut from the lining fabric.

Position the pocket piece over the opening marks, right sides together. Stitch the pocket opening making the seam ⅛″ (3mm) wider along the lower edge. Trim and clip the seam allowance.

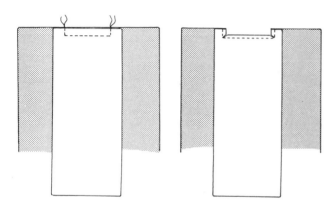

Turn the pocket to the wrong side of the garment, and press the edges. Bring the bottom edge of the pocket piece up behind the opening, and pin.

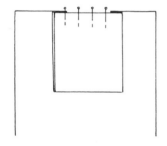

With the garment right side up, fold it back until you see the pocket seam allowance. Stitch along the seamline, continuing down the side of the pocket. Double stitch the seam, trim the seam allowance, and repeat the process on the other side of the pocket. Press from the wrong side.

Pin the waistband in position and stitch in place, making sure you don't catch the edge of the pocket opening. Backstitch at both ends of the pocket opening for strength. The pocket opening will now be barely visible below the waistband seam.

Flaps are added to this type of pocket when it is placed in a yoke seam. Construct the flaps according to the instructions previously given. Make the flaps ¼″ (6mm) wider than the finished pocket opening.

Pin the flap over the opening after the entire pocket has been finished. Stitch in place just above the given seamline.

You are now ready to sew the yoke to the garment. Just make sure you don't catch the edge of the pocket in the yoke seam.

Pockets that don't have flaps can be topstitched for emphasis. Topstitch the lower edge of the pocket, from corner to corner only, after the pocket piece has been turned to the wrong side and pressed. Pull the thread ends to the wrong side and tie, Fig. 1. Complete the topstitching after the pocket has been completed, exactly meeting the existing line of topstitching. Pull the thread ends to the wrong side and tie, Fig. 2.

FIG. 1   FIG. 2

TAILORED PATCH POCKET

The tailored patch pocket is the one used on men's and women's tailored coats and jackets. It is lined and invisibly-stitched in place. This isn't as difficult as it sounds, and it is very impressive when perfectly finished.

Many tailored garments are cut from patterned fabrics that have to be matched. Be extremely careful when cutting-out the patch pocket so it exactly matches the pattern of the garment. Being "off" a little bit can ruin an otherwise perfect garment.

Interface the wrong side of the patch pocket. Use a fusible interfacing and trim away the hem and seam allowances before fusing in place. This preserves the pocket's shape, and keeps it from becoming baggy.

Leave the hem at the top edge of pocket unstitched at the sides. Stitch the sides of the pocket a scant ⅛″ (3mm) from the seamline, within the seam allowance, *easestitching* around the corners. This is a guideline for the final stitching. Note: Use a lighter color thread for the seam allowance stitching if you have a dark fashion fabric. This will make it easier to see when you work inside the pocket.

Press the pocket from the wrong side, rolling the seam allowance so that the stitching line is ⅛″ (3mm) from the folded edge. Notch the pocket corners as necessary.

Cut the lining to match the finished size of the pocket and trim ⅛″ (3mm) from the three outside edges. Fold down 1″ (25mm) at the top edge of the lining and press. This slightly smaller lining supports the pocket and keeps it from becoming baggy.

Pin the lining to the garment in the proper place, right sides together, remembering to insert the Kleenex to give wearing ease. Stitch the lining in place using a zigzag stitch. Note: The lining is finished slightly smaller than the pocket. This prevents the pocket from stretching out of shape.

Position the pocket over the lining; the pocket edges should extend ⅛″ (3mm) beyond the lining. Machine baste the pocket in place, using a zigzag made from the longest stitch length and the narrowest stitch width. Start the stitching at the hem foldline and adjust the stitch so that the zigzag just bites into the edge of the pocket.

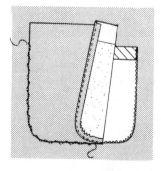

Adjust your machine to a regular, straight stitch. Working inside the pocket, start at the hem foldline and stitch on top of the first stitching line you made around the seam allowance, backstitching at each end for strength. As you stitch around the bottom of the pocket check to make sure you don't catch any unwanted fabric in the stitching.

Finish the top corner by wrapping the hem, so that the hem seam allowance is against the pocket seam allowance. Stitch next to the existing seamline, making sure you don't catch any garment fabric. Turn the facing to the inside. If you don't topstitch, reinforce the pocket corners from the back with invisible hand stitching.

Slipstitch the lining to the pocket hem. Topstitch around the pocket if desired. This pocket technique gives a neater, more finished looking pocket, than one that is separately lined and then topstitched in place.

Unlined Tailored Patch Pocket

An unlined patch pocket, with rounded corners, can also be invisibly-stitched in place. Prepare the pocket as described above except eliminate the pocket lining. Stitch the pocket to the garment with the long, narrow zigzag stitch. Start and end the stitching at the hem foldline.

Working on the inside, stitch the pocket to the garment with a regular, straight stitch; use the seam allowance stitching as a guideline. Start and end the stitching at the hem foldline, backstitching for strength.

Finish the top corner by wrapping the hem so that the hem seam allowance is against the pocket seam allowance. Stitch next to the existing seamline, making sure you don't catch any garment fabric in the stitching. Turn the hem to the inside; topstitch the pocket edge if desired, or secure the corners with several invisible stitches from the wrong side.

WELT POCKETS

Welt pockets, with or without flaps, are used extensively on tailored garments. They should be carefully constructed so that companion pockets are identical in size and placement, and they exactly match or artistically contrast with the garment fabric. The welt pocket can have a single or double welt. Look at fine ready-to-wear to see how the two types are used.

All pocket openings should have a woven stay placed in them if the garment front is not completely interfaced. Use a piece of lining fabric or lightweight, non-fusible interfacing for the stay. This adds support to the pocket opening.

Single Welt Pocket With Flap

Transfer the pocket opening marks to the right side of the garment with hand or machine stitching, using a contrasting thread.

Cut two pocket pieces, 7½" (19cm) by 18" (46cm) from lining fabric or pocket drill. Use lining fabric for women's garments and pocket drill for men's garments. Cut two welt pieces 2½" (63mm) by 7½" (19cm), from the fashion fabric. Match the welt pieces to the garment if you are working with a patterned fabric.

Construct the flap as previously described and position it on the garment, right sides together, with the edge of the flap on the pocket opening line. Stitch the flap with a ¼" (6mm) seam, backstitching at each end. Trim the seam allowance to ⅛" (3mm).

126

Prepare the pocket lining by stitching the welt piece to the top of the lining piece. Press the seam allowance down into the lining, Fig. 1. If you are using pocket drill, applique a 3" (75mm) wide strip of lining fabric to the bottom end of the pocket drill, Fig. 2. This lining strip will back the pocket opening and be more attractive than plain drill.

FIG. 1   FIG. 2

Center the welt piece over the flap. The welt edge should be at the flap seam. Pin in place. Draw a line ½" (13mm) below the flap stitching line and machine baste along this line through all layers. Be sure this measuring and stitching is accurate.

Press the pocket welt up along the basted line and pin.

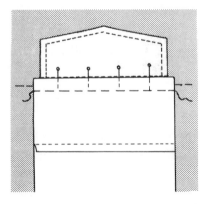

Working on the wrong side of the garment, stitch ¼" (6mm) below the flap stitching line, using a regular, straight stitch. Start and end the stitching 1/16" (1.5mm) short of the flap stitching line. This makes the pocket opening slightly narrower than the flap and makes sure the opening is completely covered by the flap when the pocket is finished.

1 STITCH SHORT   1 STITCH SHORT

Remove the welt basting stitches, unpin the lining and cut the pocket open, as indicated. Cut just the garment and interfacing fabric, making a good-sized wedge in each corner.

Pull the pocket lining through the slash and arrange the welt so it completely fills the opening under the flap. Whip the pocket closed, and press from the wrong side.

Working on the right side, fold back the garment until you see the wedge lying on top of the welt. Machine stitch across the base of the wedge, catching it to the welt fabric. Make the stitching line curve slightly toward the pocket. This helps square the pocket opening. Repeat this procedure on the other side of the pocket.

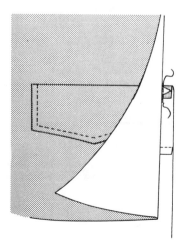

Pin the free end of the pocket lining in position behind the pocket. Turn the garment to the right side, and fold down the top of the garment until the flap seam is exposed. Stitch along the flap seamline, catching the pocket lining.

Stitch down the sides of the pocket with a double row of stitching. Trim the seam allowance and press from the wrong side.

Double Welt Pocket With Flap

Do not construct the pocket flaps for this type of pocket until the double welt opening has been finished. Carefully measure the opening and then make the flaps 1/16″ (1.5mm) wider. The flaps are then squeezed into the opening which prevents having unfilled gaps at the pocket corners.

Each pocket needs two welt pieces. The top welt should be cut 1″ (25mm) wide and 2″ (50mm) longer than the pocket opening. The bottom welt should be cut 3″ (76mm) wide and 2″ (50mm) longer than the opening. Cut the pocket lining 7½″ (19cm) by 18″ (46cm). Use lining fabric for women's garments and pocket drill for men's garments.

Cut two strips of ½″ (13mm) wide fusible interfacing and apply them to each welt strip as shown.

NARROW WELT

WIDE WELT

Press the narrow welt piece in half lengthwise, wrong sides together. Position it on the right side of the garment with the cut edges along the pocket opening line. Stitch in place down the exact center of the welt, backstitching at each end. Make sure the stitching starts and stops on the vertical lines marking the ends of the pocket.

Stitch the wide welt piece to the top of the pocket lining with a ½″ (13mm) seam. Press the seam down into the pocket lining.

If you are using pocket drill, applique a 3″ (76mm) wide strip of lining to the lower edge. When the pocket is opened, the lining rather than the pocket drill will show.

Working on the right side of the garment, center the lower welt over the pocket marks with the edge of the welt on the pocket opening line. Machine baste exactly ½″ (13mm) below the top of the welt. Press up the welt and lining along this line and pin in place.

Turn the garment to the wrong side; stitch exactly ¼″ (6mm) below the pocket opening line, starting and ending 1/16″ (1.5mm) short of the vertical lines. Backstitch each end. Be sure the stitching lines are parallel and exactly ½″ (13mm) apart.

Remove the welt basting and cut the pocket open as shown, making a good sized wedge in each corner. Cut through just the garment fabric and interfacing. Don't cut through any pocket or welt pieces.

Turn the welt and pocket lining through to the inside. Adjust the welts so they meet in the center of the opening. Whip the welts closed and press from the wrong side.

Working on the right side, fold back the garment until the wedge is exposed. Stitch across the base of the wedge, catching it to the welt fabric. Make the stitching curve slightly toward the pocket. This helps square the pocket corners. Repeat the process on the other side of the pocket.

Remove the whip stitches across the pocket opening. Construct the flap so it is 1/16″ (1.5mm) wider than the opening.

Mark the line where the top welt falls on the flap with a strip of drafting tape. This tape should be positioned a welt width down from the seamline at the top of the flap. Check to make sure the distance from the bottom of the tape and flap edge is equal on both sides. This is important.

Slip the flap into the opening so that at least 1/4″ (6mm) extends above the upper welt seam; pin and baste in place. Fold down the top of the garment until the welt seam is exposed. Stitch along the seam catching the flap in the process.

Bring the free end of the pocket lining up into position and pin. Stitch again along the welt seam, catching the pocket lining. Backstitch at each end for strength.

Finish the pocket by stitching the edges with a double row of stitching. Trim the seam allowance. Press the pocket from the wrong side.

The width of the upper welt can be made smaller by cutting the welt piece 1/2″ (13mm) rather than 1″ (25mm) wide. This makes the finished welt 1/8″ (3mm) wide.

Double Welt Pocket Without Flap

The double welt pocket is sometimes made without flaps. Just follow the instructions above, except leave out the flap. The corners of this type of pocket can be finished with an *arrowhead* if desired. Make the arrowhead by hand or cut one from leather or Ultra Suede® fabric for a different look.

TAILORED BREAST POCKET

This is the pocket used on tailored suit coats and sports jackets. It is used for both men's and women's clothes, and is always placed on the left side of the garment.

Cut the welt from the fashion fabric, matching it to the garment if the fabric is plaid or striped. Cut the pocket lining 5½″ (14cm) by 12″ (30cm) long. Interface the upper half of the welt piece with fusible interfacing. Construct the welt as given in the pattern instructions. It can be topstitched if you wish. Transfer the pocket marks to the right side of the garment with machine basting, using a contrasting thread.

Position the welt on the right side of the garment, centering it between the pocket marks, as shown. The cut edge should be along the center line. Pin and stitch with a ¼″ (6mm) seam, backstitching at each end.

FIG. 1

Center the pocket lining over the welt, right sides together, and pin in place.

Working on the wrong side of the garment, stitch ¼″ (6mm) above the center line and restitch on the first welt stitching line being sure not to overstitch at the ends. Make the top line 1/16″ (1.5mm) short of the vertical lines on both sides. Backstitch at the ends of both stitching lines, Fig. 1. Cut the pocket open as indicated, making large wedges in each cor-

ner. Cut through the garment and lining fabric, Fig. 2.

FIG. 1   FIG. 2

Pull the lining through to the inside, and press the opening. The welt should be pressed up in the finished position, Fig. 1. Fold down the top half of the lining and pin to the lower half. The bottom edges will not meet exactly; just pin them as they fall, Fig. 2.

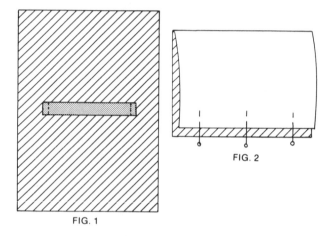

FIG. 1   FIG. 2

Working on the right side, fold back the garment until you see the wedge. Stitch across the base of the wedge, catching it to the pocket lining. Make the stitching line curve slightly toward the pocket. This helps square the pocket corners. Backstitch for strength, continue stitching down around the pocket lining and up the other side, making sure you stitch along the base of the other wedge. Do another row of stitching and trim the seam allowance.

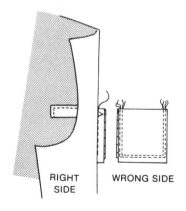

RIGHT SIDE   WRONG SIDE

Hand stitch the edges of the welt to the garment from the wrong side.

INSIDE BREAST POCKET

Men's suit coats and sport coats have one or more inside breast pockets. The pocket is placed on the left side of the garment for a right-handed man, and on the right side of the garment for a left-handed man, if just one pocket is being used. Some men like lots of inside pockets — just don't let them get carried away.

The breast pocket usually extends into both the facing and lining fabric. We would like to give you a method for making this pocket that has a facing extension for the entire pocket and gives an elegant, custom touch to a man's coat.

Add an extension to the pocket area of the coat facing that measures 2½" (6.5cm) by 4" (10cm). The top of the extension should fall at least 1" (25mm) below the armhole seam, in order to prevent bulki-

ness in that area. Center the extension on the existing pocket line on the facing pattern.

Fuse a 1" (25mm) by 6" (15cm) strip of non-stretch, fusible interfacing to the wrong side of the pocket extension. This prevents the pocket opening from stretching out of shape. Mark a 5" (13cm) long pocket opening line on the wrong side of the pocket extension. The end of the line should be ¾" (19mm) in from the end of the extension. Machine baste the mark through to the right side of the fabric.

Cut the garment lining as directed in the pattern. Cut about 2½ yards (228cm) of 1" (25mm) bias strips from the fabric scraps. Join these bias strips as necessary to bind the jacket-facing edge with a *Hong Kong* finish.

Pin a bias strip to the facing edge, right sides together, and stitch with a ⅛" (3mm) seam. Stretch the bias at "inside" corners and ease it around "outside" corners, Fig 1. Wrap the bias strip around the seam allowance and hand baste in place, Fig. 2.

Cut a pocket lining piece that measures 6" (15cm) by 14" (35cm). If you are short of lining fabric, or if the man is hard on pockets, cut the lining from *pocket drill*. Cut two pieces of lining fabric 3" (7.5cm) by 6" (15cm). Topstitch these to the pocket drill piece as shown.

Press over 1½" (13mm) at the top of the pocket lining piece. With right sides together, center the lining over the pocket line, with the foldline directly on the pocket line; pin in place. Working on the wrong side, stitch ¼" (6mm) above and below the pocket line and across each end. Count the stitches across the ends so they are of equal length.

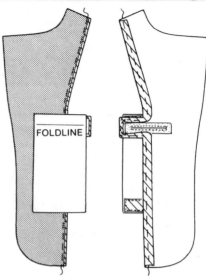

Note: Start the stitching line on one side of the box, never in a corner. This prevents a buildup of stitches in the corner that will interfere with a smooth turn.

Cut the pocket opening along the center line, making a good sized wedge in each corner. Cut all the way to the corner stitching so the corner will turn neatly.

Turn the pocket lining through to the wrong side, wrapping the lining around each ¼" (6mm) seam allowance. This forms two pocket welts. Baste the top welt in position. Pin the lower welt and catch in place by *stitching-in-the-ditch*. The pocket opening will now look like a big bound buttonhole.

Working on the wrong side, form a box pleat at each end of the pocket. Make sure each side of the pleat is the same width. Hand stitch across each pleat for a precise pocket corner. Press from the wrong side.

Bring the bottom edge of the pocket lining up into position behind the opening. Pin in place and secure by *stitching-in-the-ditch* along the top welt.

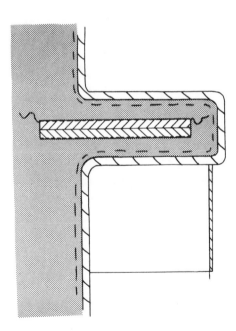

Fold over the extension until you see the wedge. Stitch along the base of the wedge to secure the pocket corner. Continue stitching down the side of the pocket. Do another row of stitching and trim

the seam allowance. Repeat the process for the other side of the pocket.

Make a handy, pencil slot in the pocket by stitching ¾″ (19mm) in from the front edge of the pocket lining. Now a pen or pencil will always stay upright and easy to reach.

Construct the garment lining as directed and attach it to the facing.

Lap the *Hong Kong* finished facing over the lining edge, twice the given seam width. This is because you haven't taken a seam from the facing edge. Pin in place. Pull the finished pocket through the opening to the right side, so it won't get in the way of the final stitching. Catch the facing to the lining by *stitching-in-the-ditch* along the edge of the *Hong*

133

Kong finish. Stitch just to the dot at the bottom of the facing.

Trim the excess seam allowance from the wrong side of the lining. Trim the lining away from the pocket opening so the pocket can be tucked back through the opening to the finished position. Push the pocket back through to the inside, and you have an elegantly finished pocket.

Make a matching pocket on the other facing or just finish its edge with the *Hong Kong* finish. Lap the facing over the lining twice the given seam width, and secure as directed above.

ZIPPING ALONG

Have you ever wished you knew better ways of putting zippers in garments so that you ended up with a custom look rather than the home-sewn look you get when using regular zipper instructions? Well, help is right here because the following zipper techniques are not the ones found in ordinary sewing directions. These methods will help you obtain the professional results you want, and they are just as easy, or easier, than the procedures you have been using.

First, a few words about zippers in general. There are various types of zippers on the market today, and you should know about them so that you can choose the right one for the garment and fabric with which you are working. Lightweight fabrics need lightweight, flexible zippers. Heavyweight sport and outer-wear will require heavy-duty zippers. Zippers are made from both metal and synthetic material, the most common of which is polyester. You can now purchase lightweight metal zippers as well as heavy-duty polyester zippers. The material no longer governs the strength of the zipper as it once did. Your choice can be made on the color and look of the finished product.

Invisible zippers have given the home-sewer an alternative to the traditional zipper closing. These are great for printed fabrics that don't need the "busyness" of extra rows of stitching. They offer the ideal solution to the problem of zipper color when making a garment from more than one color. A lightweight, polyester coil, invisible zipper is a must for Qiana® knits and other thin fabrics. Regular zipper application on these fabrics can leave a puckered appearance along the zipper seams.

Invisible zippers do have some disadvantages though, of which you should be aware. They are not very attractive when put in center front seams of fitted or semi-fitted garments. Unless you sit or stand very straight at all times, they will bulge out, giving your figure an unattractive line. This does not happen in loose, flowing garments such as robes or caftans, so invisible zippers can be used in these garments without any problems. Stitching an invisible zipper into a striped or plaid fabric requires very careful sewing so that the design matches up across the zipper opening. The metal pull of the zipper is painted, which means that its color will chip off during the life of the garment. This can be slowed down by painting the pull with several coats of clear fingernail polish before the zipper is sewn into the garment.

ZIPPER KNOW HOW

Pre-shrink all zippers before sewing them into the garment. This prevents zipper seams from puckering after repeated washings, due to shrinkage of the zipper tape. It is still possible to get some shrinkage of the new synthetic zipper tapes.

For best results, stitch both sides of the zipper in the same direction — bottom to top — for regular zippers, and top to bottom for invisible zippers. Stitching one side in the opposite direction makes for matching problems and uneven ends at the top of the zipper.

Center a ½" (13mm) wide strip of drafting tape down the zipper seam, on the right side of the garment, when doing a center slot zipper. The edges of the tape will be guidelines for the final machine or hand stitching. Just be careful that you don't stitch into the tape with your needle. This will coat the needle with a sticky substance and interfere with your stitching.

Stabilize the seam area of a knit garment with strips of tape before you stitch an invisible zipper in place. Place long tape strips down each side of the opening so that they are about ¾″ (19mm) from the cut edge. This will keep the fabric from stretching and make sure that the seam edges are even when you get to the end of the zipper and lower garment edge.

Garments that have collars or some sort of binding at the neckline should have the zipper positioned so that the top of the teeth end at the neckline seam.

Garments with faced necklines should have the zipper positioned so that the top of the teeth end ⅜″ (9mm) below the finished edge. This gives room for the hook and eye closure that keeps the edges neat.

Did you know that you can shorten both metal and polyester zippers? Now you can use up all those odd zippers in your sewing drawer that always seem to be the right color but the wrong size. Shorten the zipper by hand stitching across the teeth at the desired length. Trim away the excess zipper ½″ (13mm) below the bar tack. Long zippers can be used for fly applications without having to shorten them first because the excess zipper will be cut off at the top once the waistband has been stitched in place. Unfortunately we haven't figured out a way to use zippers that are too short.

Insert zippers into the garment before you do any other sewing. It is easier to work on flat pieces of the garment rather than waiting until after the shoulder and side seams have been sewn. This works only if the pattern has been adjusted for fit so that no fitting has to be done in the finished zipper seam. Of course, garments with yoke and waistline seams in the zipper area should have those seams stitched and pressed first.

To the right is a diagram of a zipper with the parts labeled as we refer to them in the following instructions.

CORDED EDGE

ZIPPER PULL

ZIPPER TAPE

ZIPPER STOP

CENTER SLOT ZIPPERS

The center slot zipper is used in the back and front of the garments. Occasionally you see it at a side seam, but the lapped zipper is really the preferred zipper application there. There should be a ⅝″ (16mm) seam allowance when doing a center slot zipper.

Center Slot Zipper With A Facing

Pin the garment pieces together, right side to right side, and mark the bottom of the zipper opening with a pin. Allow a seam allowance plus ⅜″ (9mm) above the top of the zipper teeth when measuring the length of the zipper opening. Machine baste from the top down to the pin, change to a normal stitch length, back-tack to secure, and finish sewing the seam. Snip the basting threads on both sides just above the pin mark. Now snip the bobbin threads at one inch intervals for easy removal later. Press the seam open.

Place a strip of drafting tape along one edge of the wrong side of the zipper, overlapping the zipper by just ⅛″ (3mm). Position the right side of the zipper to the wrong side of the garment so that the zipper teeth run right down the seamline. Finger-press the tape firmly against the fabric. Using a zipper foot, edgestitch along the untaped side of the zipper, catching the zipper tape just to the seam allowance. Stitch from top to bottom, Fig. 1. Remove the tape and edgestitch the other side of the zipper to the other seam allowance. Make sure that the seam stays pressed open flat and stitch from top to bottom, Fig. 2.

FIG. 1   FIG. 2

Remove the basting from the top 2″ (50mm) of the center seam and open the zipper to that point. Clip the neck edge of the garment ⅝″ (16mm) from the edge of the seam allowance on both sides of the neck opening.

CLIP

Stitch the shoulder seams of the garment together and press. Prepare the facing by stitching the shoulder seams together, pressing them open and *clean-finishing* the outside edge of the fabric. Trim ½″ (13mm) from both ends of the facing.

Stitch the ends of the facing to the edge of the garment seam allowance, right sides together, with a ¼″ (6mm) seam. Make sure you catch the edge of the zipper tape in this stitching. The zipper is sandwiched in between the facing and garment at this point.

Pin the facing in place at the garment edge, matching up construction marks and seamlines, and fold the garment fabric at the ⅝″ (16mm) clip so that the facing fold is a scant ¼″ (6mm) short of the garment fold. Stitch the facing to the garment with the

139

given seam width, making sure the seams are the same width on each side of the zipper.

Grade and clip the neckline seam, trimming away excess fabric at the top corner of each side of the zipper. Turn the facing to the right side, *under-stitch* and press.

Machine Finish: On the right side, mark the bottom of the zipper with a pin so that you won't hit it with the machine needle. Using a zipper foot, start stitching at the seamline just below the zipper stop. Sew for about ¼" (6mm), pivot the fabric under the needle and stitch up the side of the zipper. When you get to within 1" (25mm) of the top edge, raise the presser foot and needle until it is just barely in the fabric. Carefully slide the zipper down below the needle, removing a few more basting stitches if necessary, and then continue stitching to the top of the opening. Make sure that the seam fold just covers the zipper teeth in the open section of the seam. Stitch the other side of the zipper in the same manner, from the center bottom of the zipper to the top. Pull the threads through to the wrong side at the bottom of the zipper and tie. Remove the basting stitches and lightly steam press the zipper from the wrong side. Sew a hook and eye in place at the top edge.

Hand Finish: Doing the final stitching of the zipper by hand is well worth the extra time because it gives a custom look to the finished garment. The stitching process is called *hand-pricking* and is done with a small backstitch. This is the easiest finishing technique for stripes or plaids.

Hand baste around the zipper opening about ¼" (6mm) from the seam. Using the basting stitches or a strip of tape as a guide, hand-prick around the zipper with small, even backstitches, using a single thread. Remove the basting stitches and steam press lightly from the wrong side. Sew a hook and eye in place at the neck edge.

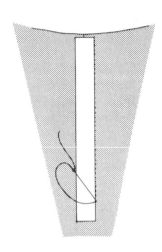

Center Slot Zipper With A Lining

The neckline facing can be eliminated on garments that are fully lined, letting the lining take the place of the facings. Use the following instructions for applying the center slot zipper in this situation.

Follow the instructions in the previous zipper section up until the edgestitching of the zipper has been completed. Trim ½" (13mm) from the center back edge of the lining pieces. Stitch the trimmed edge of the lining pieces to each side of the zipper tape. The zipper will be sandwiched between the garment and the lining seam allowance. Do this stitching with a zipper foot so that you can get right next to the zipper teeth.

Remove the basting from the center seam for about 1½" (38mm). At the neckline edge, fold over the zipper along the corded edge so that right sides are together. The garment fabric should extend a little beyond the lining fabric. Pin the lining in place around the neckline and stitch the neckline seam to within 1½" (38mm) of the shoulder seam. *Grade,* clip and trim the neckline seam and *understitch.* Turn the lining to the wrong side of the garment and carefully press the edge.

When attaching the lining to the sleeve edge, push or "crowd" the lining into the armhole so that it extends ⅛" (3mm) beyond the garment edge. This allows the neckline and armhole seams to roll to the underside. There is no need for topstitching or hand-pricking the zipper. Sew a hook and eye at the neck edge, and now you have a truly invisible zipper finish.

Center Slot Zipper with a Waistband

Apply the zipper to the garment the same as for the first center slot zipper except position the zipper so that the top of the teeth are just a seam width below the cut edge of the garment. The top edges of the zipper tape will be enclosed in the waistband.

LAPPED ZIPPERS

The lapped zipper is used in the back of a dress or top, or on a skirt or pants at the side or center back. It is never used in the front of a garment. A ⅝" (16mm) wide seam must be allowed for this zipper application.

Because this type of zipper can be used at both the center back and side seams, we will refer to the garment sections as right and left, rather than right back and left back or back and front. Make sure the garment fits before inserting the zipper so you won't have to do any alterations. The zipper is applied to each of the garment pieces before they are sewn together.

Lapped Zipper With A Facing

Place the right side of the closed zipper down on the right side of the right seam allowance so that ⅛" (3mm) of the fashion fabric extends beyond the edge of the zipper tape. The top of the zipper teeth should be a seam width plus ½" (13mm) down from the top edge of the garment. Using a zipper foot, stitch from the bottom of the zipper stop to the top of the zipper as close to the teeth as possible. Pivot and stitch across the top of the zipper tape and then down the outside edge to the bottom of the stop.

Stitch the facing pieces together, press the seams open and *clean-finish* the outside edge.

<u>Unzip</u> <u>the</u> <u>zipper</u>. Insert a pin from the wrong side of the garment so that it comes through the zipper tape right at the seamline and is on the tape side of the corded edge of the zipper. This will be the pivot pin.

Pin the right facing in place along the top edge of the garment, right sides together. Push the pivot pin through the facing so that it comes out at the seamline. Pull the lower edge of the facing ½″ (13mm) out beyond the edge of the seam allowance. This will distort the facing a bit but it makes it lie flat when the garment is completed. Sew from the bottom of the facing, starting in the center of the zipper tape, and stitch up to the pivot pin. Remove the pin and take one diagonal stitch across the corner and stitch along the top edge of the facing to within 1½″ (35mm) of the facing seam. Remember, the garment pieces have not been joined at this point. *Grade,* clip and trim the seam allowance. Turn the facing right side out and press the faced edge and zipper area. The underside of the

zipper is now finished without any stitching visible on the right side.

Note: When working with heavy fabrics, angle the stitching up into the seam allowance a tiny bit after turning the corner and then gradually come back to the given seamline. This will give a smoother line to the finished edge.

Position the free side of the zipper on the seam allowance of the left garment piece, right sides together, so that the edge of the zipper tape is even with the seam edge. The top of the zipper teeth should be a seam width plus ½″ (13mm) down from the top edge of the garment. Note: It is very important that this side of the zipper be positioned on the garment exactly as the first side so that the top edges of the finished zipper will meet exactly. Edgestitch the zipper to the seam allowance as shown.

Close the zipper and sew the garment seam below the zipper, starting just slightly above and to the left of the zipper stop. This stitching should be approximately ⅛" (3mm) to the left of the visible stitching. Stitch all the way to the bottom of the garment taking a ⅝" (16mm) seam. Press the seam open, forming a little pleat at the bottom of the zipper on the right seam allowance. This allows for the finished zipper overlap.

Note: If the zipper is in the pants center back seam you should stitch the crotch seam to within 1" (25mm) of the inseam and then backstitch. This is to allow for the continuous stitching of the crotch seam after the inseam has been completed.

Make a clip into the top edge of the left garment piece ¾" (19mm) from the seam edge. Trim the free end of the facing ⅞" (21mm) and stitch the edge of the facing to the edge of the garment seam allowance with a ¼" (6mm) seam. Make sure you catch the zipper tape in this stitching line.

CLIP

Fold the garment back on the ¾" (19mm) clip so that the facing and zipper are sandwiched in between the garment layers. The garment should extend a good ¼" (6mm) beyond the corded edge of the zipper. Stitch the facing in place with the given seam width ending 1½" (38mm) short of the garment seam (shoulder or side seam). Turn the facing to the right side and close the zipper to see if the finished edges meet exactly at the top of the garment. Adjust the seam width if necessary. Grade, clip, trim and turn the facing to the finished position. Press lightly from the wrong side.

Close the zipper and pin the lap in place making sure that the right side is covered by ⅛" (3mm). This lap is important so that the zipper doesn't show when the garment is worn.

Machine Finish: Place a pin at the zipper stop so that you know where it is and won't hit it with your machine needle. Place a ½" (13mm) wide strip of drafting tape along the folded edge of the zipper lap to act as a guide for the final stitching. Using a zipper foot, stitch the left side of the zipper, starting just below the zipper stop and continuing up the side, making a ½" (13mm) wide seam. Pull the thread ends through to the wrong side at the bottom of the zipper and tie.

Sew a hook and eye at the top of the opening.

Hand Finish: For the professional touch, *hand-prick* the side of the zipper with small even backstitches. Mark the stitching line with a line of hand-basting or a strip of ½″ (13mm) wide drafting tape.

Hand finishing the zipper is the best method to use when working with stripes or plaids. This makes it so much easier to match up stripes across the zipper opening, and really doesn't take much more time than machine stitching. Sew a hook and eye at the top of the opening.

Join the garment seams (shoulder or side seam) and complete the faced edge. *Understitch* the entire faced edge for a perfect finish.

Lapped Zipper with a Collar or Waistband

Follow the instructions for the lapped zipper with facings, except position the zipper on the seam allowance so that the top of the teeth are just a seam width down from the top edge. Of course, you won't be using facings, so just ignore those instructions. Lap the left side of the zipper over the right side ⅛″ (3mm) and finish with machine or hand stitching.

INVISIBLE ZIPPERS

Pre-shrink invisible zippers before inserting them into a garment, and make sure that you have the special zipper foot that should be used with your brand of zipper.

The zipper is applied to each side of the seam before the two pieces of garment are stitched together. Stabilize the seam area of stretchy fabrics by placing a strip of tape down the seam about ¾″ (19mm) in from the cut edge.

Unroll the zipper coil by pressing lightly with the steam iron or do it with your fingers. Check the zip-

per package instructions for this information. Position the zipper face down on the seam allowance so that the top of the zipper teeth is 1″ (25mm) down from the top edge of the garment if you are using a facing finish, and a seam width down from the top edge if you are applying a collar or waistband. The teeth of the zipper should run right along the seamline.

Backstitch at the top of the zipper tape and hold the zipper in position with your fingers or pins while stitching with the special zipper foot. The coil of the zipper should run through the groove on the left side of the zipper foot, and the needle should be positioned in the center of the foot. Stitch as far down the zipper as you can and then backstitch.

Note: You will get better results on heavy or bulky fabrics if the needle is positioned a little to the left of center. This allows for the thicker fabric and will let the zipper work more smoothly. Stitch thin fabrics close to the zipper teeth and thick fabrics farther away from the teeth. When the zipper is closed, you should not be able to see any of the zipper in the opening. If you do, that means that you didn't stitch close enough to the teeth. This problem can be corrected easily by re-stitching both sides of the zipper.

Close the zipper and position the unstitched side of the zipper on the other seam allowance, with the zipper face down. It is important that both sides of the zipper be positioned identically so that patterned fabrics match across the zipper opening and the garment edges meet after the rest of the seam has been closed. Matching plaids, stripes or patterned fabrics across the zipper opening can be done quite easily if you make some light pencil marks across the wrong side of the zipper at key matching points. Match these zipper tape marks to corresponding points on the other seam allowance. Pin in place.

Open the zipper, position the coil in the groove on the right side of the foot and stitch the other side of the zipper for a perfect match.

Close the zipper and complete the garment seam by pushing the special zipper foot all the way to the left, pull the end of the zipper out away from the seam area and start sewing about ⅜″ (9mm) above the end of the zipper stitching and a scant ⅛″ (3mm) to the side. Backstitch at the beginning and close the remainder of the seam, making sure the edges are even at the bottom.

Pull each seam allowance out away from the garment and stitch the ends of the zipper tape to the seam allowance only. This will control the ends of the tape and keep them flat after repeated washings.

Clip a mark at the top edge of the garment ⅝″ (16mm) from the open edge. Trim ½″ (13mm) from the back edge of both ends of the facing. Stitch this trimmed edge to the garment edge. Make sure the stitching catches the zipper tape — the zipper will be sandwiched in between the garment and facing.

Pin the facing in place at the neck edge, folding at the ⅝″ (16mm) clip mark. There will be a ⅛″ (3mm) extension of the folded garment beyond the folded edge of the facing. Stitch the neckline seam with the given seam width. *Grade,* clip and trim the seam allowance and turn the facing to the finished position.

ZIPPER IN A SLASH

The zipper in a slash is used only on knit fabrics. This is because you will be working with a very narrow seam allowance, ⅛″ (3mm). Most woven fabrics ravel too much to handle this narrow a seam. The slash zipper leaves one less seam to sew and match, which is especialy welcome when working with striped or patterned knits.

A polyester rather than a metal zipper is the better choice for this application. First of all, it is lightweight and more flexible than a metal zipper. This is important when working with many knit fabrics. Second, polyester zippers are more attractive because they look more delicate and don't have the paint-chipping problems of metal zippers.

It is important that the zipper be pre-shrunk before inserting it in the garment. This helps prevent the buckling that you see so often on many ready-to-wear knits. The zipper tape shrinks in the first washing and pulls the knit fabric into unsightly bumps, making the zipper look like a roller coaster.

You must decide what type of neckline finish you are going to use on the garment. If you are just going to turn under and topstitch the neck edge or bind it with *Chanel Trim*, then insert the zipper before the neck edge is finished. If you choose to apply a mock or full turtleneck collar, insert the zipper after the collar has been stitched to the neck edge.

Garment Preparation

Sew the garment shoulder seams and press. The neckline seam allowance should be left intact if you are topstitching or binding the neck edge. Trim the seam allowance to ¼″ (6mm) if you are applying a turtleneck collar.

Turtleneck Collar Preparation

There are three types of turtleneck collars you can apply to your garment. Follow the instructions below for cutting each type of collar.

A mock turtleneck stands up around the neck but does not fold over on itself. Cut a 5″ (13cm) wide

collar piece across the stretch of the fabric and about 16″ (61cm) long.

A full turtleneck or a pre-folded turtleneck collar folds down around the neck. They look the same in front but the zipper treatment in back is somewhat different. The zipper in the full turtleneck goes all the way up through the collar and turns back down on itself when the collar is worn. The zipper is applied to the pre-folded collar after the collar has been folded into the finished wearing position. The zipper goes just to the fold of the collar, and it does not turn back down on itself. This makes for a less bulky finish at the back of the neck. Cut the full or pre-folded turtleneck collar 10″ (25cm) wide across the stretch of the fabric and about 16″ (41cm) long.

Determine the finished length of the collar by folding the collar strip as it will be when it is worn, once for the mock turtleneck and twice for the full or pre-folded turtleneck. Wrap it around the neck until it looks good and feels comfortable. You will find that soft, stretchy knits need less length than firm, heavy knits. Cut the collar so that the ends just meet at the center back. Do not allow for a seam allowance. Collar length should never be more than the neckline measurement. *Clean-finish* one long edge of the collar piece with wide zigzag stitching.

Collar Application

Fold the garment in half and press a crease down the center back the approximate length of the zipper less the finished width of the collar. Cut down the exact center back of the garment for about 1″ (25mm). Stitch the unfinished edge of the collar to the neck edge of the garment with a ¼″ (6mm) seam. The collar will usually be smaller than the neck edge so you will have to distribute the collar evenly around the neckline. This will be an easy matter if you first divide the collar edge and neck edge into four equal sections and then stitch just a section at a time, stretching the collar to fit the neck edge.

The finished top fold of the collar should be marked with a pin. Find the top fold of a mock turtleneck by folding the collar piece back down on itself, wrong sides together, so that the edges meet. Place a pin at the fold.

The first fold of the full turtleneck is found in the same way; however, the width of each folded section will be approximately twice that of the mock turtleneck. Mark the fold with a pin.

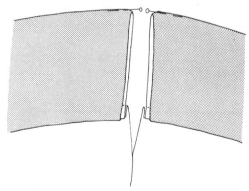

The finished top fold of the pre-folded turtleneck is found by folding the collar in half so that the

cut edges are even, wrong sides together. Now bring the fold down so that it covers the neckline seam by about ½″ (13mm). Put a pin in just the top layer of fabric at the top fold line. Pull the back section of the collar out away from the rest of the turtleneck and pin the three sections of collar in the finished position at the neckline seam; baste along the edges to hold everything in position. The pin marks the top folded edge of the collar, while the back section that is free will act as a facing for the turtleneck and will be stitched in place after the zipper has been applied. The reason for folding the collar down below the neckline seam is so that the seam will be covered all around the neckline when the garment is worn. It is important that you don't make the turtleneck collar too tight when you measure it around the neck. Tight turtlenecks tend to ride up and expose the neckline seam.

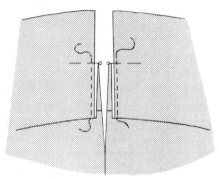

Zipper Application

Measure the length of the zipper from the top of the pull to the top of the stop at the bottom. If you measure to the bottom of the stop it will be exposed in the finished garment and become unsightly after the paint chips. Mark the zipper length on the crease with a pin, measuring down from the neckline seam if no collar is used, or from the fold pin if a turtleneck collar is used.

Place strips of tape down both sides and across the bottom of the center crease as illustrated. Keep the edges of the tape ½″ (13mm) from the crease. This is a stay tape, not a stitching guideline. It prevents stretching the cut edges of the knit while stitching the zipper in place. Stretched edges will add to the unsightly bumps along the zipper after the garment has been washed.

Staystitch a box around the center back crease that is exactly ¼″ (6mm) wide. The stitching line is ⅛″ (3mm) to each side of the crease line. You can draw stitching guidelines on the wrong side of the garment if desired. Use a zipper foot when stitching along these lines for greater visibility, or you can swing your needle all the way to the right and run the edge of the zigzag foot along the center crease. This will give you a box ¼″ (6mm) wide. The bottom of the box is at the pin mark. Slash down the center back line to within ¾″ (19mm) of the bottom pin, then cut into each corner to the stitching, forming a good sized wedge.

Position the zipper as shown so that the right side of the zipper is against the right side of the garment. The stop at the bottom of the zipper should be completely above the bottom of the stitched box. Secure the zipper to the garment by *stab-stitching* across the zipper teeth to the corners of the box. Make sure that this stitching is done between the teeth and the stop so that the stop doesn't show after the zipper is completed.

Bring the zipper up along the slash edge into the finished position. Pin the right side of the garment to the right side of the zipper so that the staystitching line is next to the teeth of the zipper. Using a zipper foot, stitch from the bottom up along the staystitching so that you don't end up with an unsightly pucker at the bottom of the zipper. Stitch to the top of the pull only, not to the end of the tape.

through the collar section on the first stitching line. Trim away the excess tape at the top of the zipper.

Be sure that the neckline seam is turned up into the collar as you stitch across it. The top of the zipper teeth should end at the pin that marks the top fold of the collar if you have measured and stitched everything correctly. If you are not using a collar, the top of the teeth will end at the neckline seam.

Note: When you come to within 1″ (25mm) of the top of the zipper, you must lift the presser foot, raise the needle and hold the zipper tape in position while you unzip the zipper with the other hand. It is impossible to stitch neatly around the zipper pull if you don't do this. Move the garment back two stitches (do not backstitch) so as to take up the excess loop of thread that forms when you pull the needle out of the fabric. This loop would catch easily in the zipper and eventually break. Finish stitching just to the top of the pull.

Unzip the zipper all the way. With the zipper tape flat, turn down the excess tape at the top, at right angles to the garment as shown. Wrap the back or facing half of the collar over the zipper, right sides together. The teeth of the zipper should extend into the collar at this point, and the cut edges of the collar should extend approximately ¼″ (6mm) below the neckline seam. Stitch down

Close the zipper and pin the other side of the slash to the zipper tape, right sides together, making sure that the stitching line is right along the zipper teeth and the neckline seam matches exactly across the zipper. It is suggested that you hand-tack the zipper to the garment at the neck seam to make sure it doesn't shift in the final stitching process. Mismatched seams at the neckline are a sure way to achieve that "loving hands at home" look.

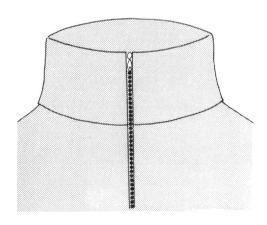

Finish stitching this side of the zipper as you did the first side, from bottom to top. If you are using a collar, you will finish the inside neck edge by hand stitching the edge of the collar to the neckline seam, or you can catch it in place by *stitching-in-the-ditch* on the right side of the garment. Collarless necklines are finished by binding the edge with bias or *Chanel Trim*, or just turning under the seam allowance and topstitching in place.

THE FLY ZIPPER

Putting a fly zipper in a pair of pants is really a simple procedure. You will find various methods in pattern instructions, but the one found below is the easiest and can be adapted to any pattern.

The Pattern

First of all, examine your pattern to see what pieces are used in the fly construction. Some patterns will have the fly facing cut as one with the pants front pattern. That is what you want.

If your pattern has a separate fly-facing you must make it into a cut-on-facing by overlapping the facing pattern and the front pattern so that the seamlines match. Pin the pattern pieces together and use this new pattern to cut your fashion fabric.

Zipper Construction

Before removing the pattern from the cut garment pieces, mark the center front stitching line with a small clip and the dot at the bottom of the zipper seam with a small pencil mark on the wrong side of the fabric.

Apply some fusible interfacing to the wrong side of the left fly facing, as shown. This interfacing stabilizes the fly area and keeps it looking neat. This is especially important when working with knit fabrics. Mark the center front stitching line on the wrong side of the fly-facing.

It is also advisable to edgestitch a piece of pre-shrunk twill tape to the left fly facing, next to the foldline, on knit garments. This stabilizes the fold of the fly and keeps it neat.

The fly zipper is completed after any front pocket detail is sewn, but before any other sewing is done on the pants.

With the right sides of the pants front together, machine baste down to the dot at the bottom of the zipper. Clip the bobbin threads at 1″ (25mm) intervals for easy removal of the basting after the zipper has been completed. Stitch the seam below the dot with a regular or straight stretch-stitch, stopping 1″

(25mm) before the end of the seam. If you are using just a plain straight stitch, double stitch this lower seam for strength. This seam area is very difficult to repair if it pulls out later in the wearing process. Clip to the seamline at the bottom of the fly facings as indicated.

The fly always opens from the right on men's pants. You will see it opening from both the right or left on women's pants. There doesn't seem to be a consistent rule in ready-to-wear about this. Right-handed women will probably find a right-opening fly more convenient while left-handed women might prefer the left-opening fly. Since the majority of people are right-handed, we will give instructions for the right-opening fly. If you prefer a left-opening fly then just follow the instructions below, substituting left for right.

With the right sides of the fabric together, pull the right fly facing out away from the garment front and press the seam open.

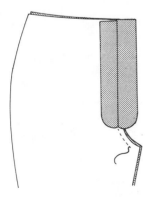

Use a zipper that is at least as long as the distance from the dot to the waistline seam. If the zipper is longer, it can be easily cut off after the waistband has been stitched in place. Metal trouser zippers are good for heavy-duty use, but most polyester zippers will serve just as well in everyday clothes, and the color selection is greater.

Place the zipper face down on the right fly facing so that the bottom of the stop is ¼" (6mm) above the dot. If you want the narrow fly finish that some patterns call for, you should place the edge of the zipper teeth right along the center seamline. Make the regular width fly finish by placing the left edge of the zipper tape along the center seam. Using a zipper foot, stitch down the right zipper tape close to the teeth. Stitch again along the outside of the tape.

Turn the zipper over, right side up, and pull it out to the side so that it faces up. Press.

Now, rearrange the pants fronts so that the left fly facing is pulled out to one side. Position the zipper face down on that facing, making sure that the zipper is pulled over as far as it can go. Secure with a few pins and stitch down the left zipper tape just to the side of the teeth. Stitch again along the edge of the zipper tape. Both sides of the zipper should be stitched from top to bottom.

Open up the pants fronts and place them right side down on a table. Fold over the fly facings onto the left pants front, making sure they are pulled over as far as they can go, and pin in place. If all your zipper stitching up to this point is straight, and your machine's bobbin stitching is perfect, it is best to do the final stitching from the wrong side. Stitch along the edge of the zipper tape, curving smoothly over to the center front line, or pivot the fabric under the needle at a point just above the end of the zipper teeth and then stitch down to the dot at an angle. Backstitch at the end of this stitching line for strength.

Press the whole zipper assembly from the wrong side using a steam iron, and then remove the center front basting.

The Zipper Guard

The zipper guard is a layer of fabric stitched in place behind the zipper. It protects your skin or shirts and blouses when the zipper is zipped up. While you won't always see a zipper guard on ready-to-wear garments, it is a nice custom touch and is an absolute must for snug-fitting pants in order to prevent painful pinches.

The guard is easily made from a piece of fabric cut 2" (50mm) longer than the zipper and 3" (76mm) wide. Use your fashion fabric or cut it from a matching lightweight fabric if you prefer. Fold over 1½" (31mm) along one long side and press with the wrong sides together.

Open the zipper and position the guard so that the top edge is even with the top edge of the pants and approximately ¾" (19mm) extends beyond the edge of the zipper teeth. Stitch in place down the fold of the fabric to the left of the teeth. If you don't use a zipper guard, edgestitch this fold to hold the zipper in the proper position.

The final stitching can also be done from the right side of the garment, if you prefer. First, machine baste along the edge of the zipper tape from the wrong side. This holds the fabric layers firmly so they don't drag against each other during the final topstitching. Mark the stitching line with a sliver of soap, 1¼" (31mm) from the fold for the wide fly finish, or ¾" (9mm) from the fold for the narrow finish. Topstitch down the side of the zipper, curve or angle the bottom of the fly to the center front.

Close the zipper, turn the pants to the wrong side and trim the right fly facing so that it is even with the edge of the zipper guard. Trim the cut edges of the guard close to the edge of the zipper tape underneath it.

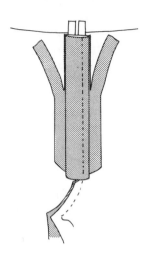

Make a small bar tack at the end of the zipper stitching on the right side of the pants front.

Fold over the left pants front until you expose the edge of the left fly facing, which should be directly on top of the folded edge of the zipper guard. Make a small bar tack through all these layers of fabric about ¼″ (6mm) above the zipper stop. This bar tack prevents you from tearing out the bottom of

the zipper. It is especially important on snug-fitting pants.

Trim away any excess guard fabric at the bottom of the zipper and your fly zipper is finished. If the zipper you used was longer than the fly opening, just trim away the excess <u>after</u> the waistband has been stitched in place. Don't do it now; otherwise the zipper slide might just slip off the cut end, leaving you in a real fix.

Zipper Guard Variation

You can cut down on bulkiness in the zipper area by making the zipper guard from a single rather than a double layer of fabric. This works only if your fashion fabric is firm enough to hold its shape and does not fray badly. This is a great technique for most double knits because you don't have to worry about the cut edges. Woven fabrics should have the cut edge zigzagged in order to prevent fraying.

The single layer zipper guard is made by adjusting the fly extension of the pattern so that it is at least 1¾″ (44mm) wide.

Construct the fly zipper as described above, except when you get to the zipper guard instructions just wrap around the right fly facing along the edge of the zipper tape so that it forms the guard. Open the zipper and stitch through this fly facing close to the edge of the fabric fold so that the facing is held in the guard position.

Trim the left fly facing close to the edge of the zipper tape. Close the zipper and trim the guard even with the left fly facing.

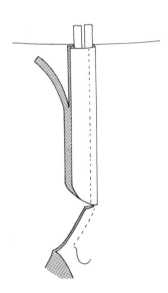

Bar tack the zipper as described above and trim away excess facing fabric at the bottom of the zipper.

THE FAKE FLY

Many times you will want the look of a fly zipper on knit pants but want to eliminate the bulk that it creates. The solution is a fake fly. Of course, it will work only on pants that can be pulled on over the hips without an opening of any kind. It is a great fly to use on men's and boys' swim trunks.

The pattern should have a cut-on-facing at the fly instead of a separate facing. Adjust your pattern according to the instructions in the fly zipper, if necessary.

Baste and permanently stitch the center front seam as described in the fly zipper, and clip to the seam line just below the dot, Fig. 1. Using a regular straight stitch, make a new seam ½″ (13mm) from the basted center front seam, stitch all the way down to the clip, Fig. 2.

FIG. 1   FIG. 2

Press the fly facings over onto the left pants front and pin in place. Turn the garment to the right side and topstitch approximately 1¼″ (31mm) from the fold, curving down to the dot at the bottom of the fly opening. Steam press from the wrong side, trim away any excess fly facing and remove the center front basting.

EXPOSED ZIPPER WITH DECORATIVE TRIM

It's fun to spice up your wardrobe with fancy trimmed zippers. There are so many beautiful ribbons and trims available, you will find it difficult to make a choice. The techniques for applying trimmed zippers are easy to do and the result is great. They can be put in a seam or slash opening.

Buy enough ribbon-type trim to go down both sides and across the bottom of the zipper. Pre-shrink both the trim and the zipper.

Stitch the trim to both sides of the zipper tape, mitering or creating a point at the bottom. The edge of the trim should be as close to the zipper teeth as possible without interfering with the zipper slide.

Zipper In A Seam

Stitch the seam closed below the zipper opening and clip to the end of the stitching line on the diagonal. Press the seam open.

Bring the seam allowance in the open section through to the right side and press along each seam line so that the fabric is right side to right side. Trim the seam allowances if they are going to extend beyond the edge of the zipper trim.

Position the trimmed zipper on the right side of the garment so that the top of the zipper teeth is a seam width down from the top edge of the garment. Sew the zipper in place by edge stitching along the trim.

Turn the garment over and *slipstitch* the edge of the seam allowance to the zipper tape.

Zipper In A Slash

On the center of the garment, press a crease that is the length of the zipper plus a seam width. Stitch a long box around the crease so that it is exactly ¼″ (6mm) wide.

Position the trimmed zipper on the right side of the garment so that it is centered over the box. The zipper stop should be at the bottom of the box. Edge stitch the trim to the garment.

Turn the garment to the wrong side and slash down the center of the box to within ¾″ (19mm) of the bottom. Clip into the corners forming a wedge.

Turn under the cut edges along the machine stitching line and slipstitch to the zipper tape. This technique can also be used with the zipper that has its own wide decorative tape.

NOTES

CLOSING THE GAP

Have you ever given much thought to the how's and why's of buttons and buttonholes? Have you ever wondered how fashion designers figure out where to place the buttonholes on a new creation so that the buttons complement the design and fit of the garment? Surely they must have some guidelines, but what are they?

Since most of us usually follow a commercial pattern, which gives buttonhole locations and button size, we don't run into too many problems. However, as soon as we start to do "our own thing," we then need the knowledge that designers have so the result is a custom, rather than a home-made look.

You might now be thinking, "Why would anyone need to change the button and buttonhole information on a pattern?" Well, for starters, the pattern might require some alteration that would affect button placement; maybe the fabric selected has such a design that the buttonholes have to be adjusted to complement it, or perhaps you want to use groups of two small buttons in place of large ones.

Button and buttonhole guidelines are also necessary if you are designing your own pattern or using one that doesn't contain button and buttonhole information.

Well then, what has to be considered when working with buttons and buttonholes? Some of the things to be taken into account are: the style lines of the garment, whether the garment is fitted or loose, the selected fabric, and the size of the buttons.

BUTTON SELECTION

Let's start with the basics of button choice. Buttons should be interesting design features as well as functional. Give some careful thought to your choice of buttons. Many times the "right" button can turn an ordinary garment into a fashion statement. The "wrong" button can make an otherwise fashionable garment look home-made.

Most patterns come with a suggested button size, and as long as you follow this guide you will not have any problems. However, if you decide to use a larger size than recommended, you must change the distance between the closing line and the edge of the garment to accommodate the larger button. The width of the facing must also be changed the same amount. Failure to do this will place the buttons too close to the edge of the garment when it is closed. Refer to #2 in the buttonhole placement section.

Think about groups of buttons rather than a single button. Two or more small buttons placed close together can take the place of one large button and add interest to the garment.

Consider unusual types of buttons, such as wooden toggle buttons with string or leather thongs serving as buttonholes, Chinese ball buttons or frogs made from matching or contrasting tubing, or don't use buttons at all; instead, apply some of the decorative gripper snaps that are now available.

Select small lightweight buttons for fabrics that are thin or soft. Large or heavy buttons can be used on crisp or thick fabrics.

Buttons should be compatible with the cleaning method used for the finished garment. While most buttons are machine washable, you will find some that should not be washed or even dry-cleaned. These types of buttons are best used on garments that don't require frequent cleaning and can be attached with button-pins instead of being sewn in place.

Always keep buttons ½″ (13mm) or smaller for blouses or tailored shirts. Larger buttons are sure to give a home-made look.

Select non-shank buttons for double breasted garments that do not have two rows of buttonholes. The buttons will lie flatter against the garment if this is done. Shank buttons droop if they are not supported by a buttonhole.

Contrasting buttons up the front of a garment will establish a strong vertical line which is good for short or heavy figures. The reverse is true for tall or thin figures.

Take a scrap of garment fabric to the store when you buy your buttons. Make a buttonhole-size slit in it and place this over various buttons to see how they look on that particular fabric. If you can't find just what you want, then consider covered buttons. They are a snap to make when you buy one of those covered button packets and follow the instructions.

BUTTONHOLE PLACEMENT

Most of the patterns that you will be working with will contain complete buttonhole placement information. If you have to make some pattern alterations or are designing your own pattern, you will need the following information to help you place the buttonholes correctly.

1. Buttonholes should start ⅛″ (3mm) beyond the closing line of the garment in order to accommodate the shank of the button. The shank can be either a part of the button or one formed by thread. See Fig. 1.

2. The distance between the closing line and the edge of the garment is equal to the width of the button, for an average size button, and equal to one half the button width plus ½″ (13mm) for large buttons. These measurements make sure that the buttons do not come too close to the edge of the garment when it is buttoned. See Fig. 1.

3. The top button on garments that close all the way up should be positioned so that it is the same distance down from the finished edge as it is in from the front edge of the garment.

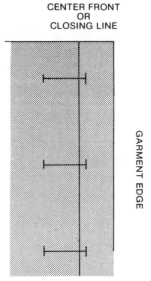

4. The button is always sewn to the closing line of the garment whether it is the center front or some other line.

5. Buttonhole length is equal to the width of the button plus ⅛″ (3mm). The length for an extra thick, round or bulky button can be determined by wrapping a narrow strip of paper around the biggest part of the button and then using one half that measure. Add an extra ⅛″ (6mm) for thick coating-type fabrics.

6. Vertical buttonholes are placed directly along the closing line. Button location for vertical buttonholes is ⅛″ (3mm) down from the top edge of the buttonhole rather than the center

of the buttonhole. This makes the closing less apt to pull open.

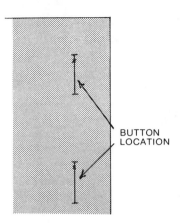

BUTTON LOCATION

7. Buttonholes in plackets or tab-fronts should be made vertical, otherwise the button will pull to the edge of the buttonhole and will not be on the center front line. This includes false plackets that are made by topstitching only. Some designer fashions will take exception to this rule.

8. The buttonhole underlap must be wide enough to extend beyond the buttonhole opening when the garment is closed. If you follow the above rules for button and buttonhole placement this will not be a problem. However, if you try to make a garment a little larger by moving buttons out, you will run into this situation.

9. Fitted garments should have a button at the bustline in order to prevent gapping. This is especially important for large busted figures. If it is impossible to place a button there because of fabric or pattern design, then secure the area with a concealed snap.

10. Fitted garments should also have a button or hook and eye placed at the waistline. If a belt is worn with the garment, use the hook and eye rather than the button in order to reduce bulk at the waistline. Make sure the buttons are spaced equally above and below the belt and are of sufficient distance away so they don't interfere with it.

11. A button should also be placed at the widest point of the hips.

12. Never place buttonholes in the hem area of a garment. The last button on a dress or shirt should be placed 4" (10cm) to 5" (12cm) above the hemline.

13. Loose fitting garments can have buttons placed almost anywhere for design purposes. However, if they are widely spaced, it might be a good idea to place snaps between them to make for a perfect closure.

14. Patterns for short heavy figures usually need more buttons than those for tall thin figures. Small to average size buttons are suitable for short figures, while larger buttons can be used for taller figures.

15. Buttonholes are placed on the right side of the garment for women and the left side of the garment for men. If you ever goof and set women's buttonholes on the left, don't worry, you're in good company. Many European designers place all their buttonholes on the left side. If you place men's buttonholes on the right side, you are going to have to think up your own excuse.

BUTTONHOLE TYPES

The type of buttonholes you use on your garment is pretty much up to you. Machine buttonholes can be used on any type of apparel, but the beautiful bound buttonhole is essential for the custom look on your nicer clothes. Bound buttonholes are not used on men's clothes except for leather jackets and coats or corduroy jackets that use a bound buttonhole made of leather. Believe it or not, bound buttonholes are not difficult to make. The method given below is easy to master and makes gorgeous buttonholes.

Buttonholes don't always have to look the same. They can be varied by placing them on the diagonal, or in the case of bound buttonholes, make the lips of a contrasting fabric or a fabric cut on the bias or lengthwise grain. An entirely different fabric such as silk or real or synthetic leather can also be used for the lips of the buttonhole. Some garment styles will require buttonholes in seamlines at a yoke or waistline. These are also easy to make following the instructions given below.

The buttonhole area on garments made from fabrics cut on the bias should be well interfaced in order to keep the buttonhole firm and neat. Machine buttonholes on bias cuts tend to ripple if not interfaced adequately. This problem can be easily prevented by placing the buttonholes on the straight grain so that the buttonholes run at an angle to the edge of the garment. This makes for neater buttonholes and also adds a fashion touch.

It is a good idea to make a complete machine or bound buttonhole sample on a fabric scrap before you begin to make them on the garment. This is important even if you have made lots of buttonholes before because it lets you double check the buttonhole size, and it also shows you how the fabric will handle the type of buttonhole you have chosen. Make the buttonhole scrap from the same types and numbers of layers of fabric that make up the actual garment. This will give you a true picture of the finished buttonhole.

MACHINE BUTTONHOLES

Machine buttonholes are made after the garment has been completely assembled. Marking the placement of the buttonholes is done at this time if the tape method is used, or it can be done just after the garment has been cut out if you use the basting method.

Most zigzag machines have the ability to make a good machine buttonhole. This is done by man-

ually turning the fabric under the presser foot in order to make both sides of the buttonhole, or the machine utilizes a built-in mechanism which will automatically stitch both sides of the buttonhole without having to turn the fabric. Follow the directions included in your machine instruction book for perfect buttonholes.

A buttonhole attachment can be purchased to fit most straight stitch machines that will enable you to make professional buttonholes. The attachment automatically measures each buttonhole so that they are all identical in size. It can make both regular and keyhole type buttonholes. Keyhole buttonholes are used on men's wear and children's and women's coats and jackets.

Many home-sewers use the buttonhole attachment for making machine buttonholes even though their zigzag machine has the ability to do so without the special attachment. This is desirable because all the buttonholes will come out the same length, and it is the only way of making a machine-made keyhole buttonhole.

Machine buttonholes should be reinforced with some type of interfacing. If possible, color match the interfacing to the fashion fabric. This eliminates the problem of having white interfacing threads showing in the buttonhole slash. If you have no choice as to interfacing color, camouflage the white line with a colored pencil or felt tip pen.

Marking Buttonholes

Even buttonholes are the sign of an expert seamstress. Buttonholes of unequal length and separation will detract from the overall look and can ruin an otherwise perfect garment. There are several ways of marking the garment for machine buttonholes, but the easiest one makes use of ½″ (12mm) wide strips of drafting tape. Drafting tape is preferable to transparent tape because it is visible on all types of fabrics. Note: Test a piece of tape on a fabric scrap before placing it on the garment to see if it pulls off the fabric without leaving a mark. Tape cannot be used on napped fabrics because of this problem. Mark these fabrics with machine or hand basting. Never leave the tape on the garment for an extended period of time. It is possible for a sticky residue to transfer to the fabric.

Note: Some machines may have difficulty feeding when tape is used to make buttonholes. The presser foot gets hung up when it runs along the tape. Use machine or hand basting to mark buttonholes if your machine exhibits this problem when making a test buttonhole.

Tape Marking: Place the paper pattern in position over the completed garment and stick pins through both ends of the buttonhole lines. Make sure the pattern is positioned so that the <u>seamline</u> rather than the cut edge is along the finished edge of the garment. Carefully pull the pattern away from the fabric, leaving the pins in place. A cardboard cutting board will give you something to stick your pins into, making this marking process easier. Double check the pins with a ruler to make sure they are accurately placed. You don't want drunken buttonholes.

Place long strips of tape down along the outside edge of each row of pins. Place short strips of tape (cut approximately ½″ (13mm) wider than the buttonhole length) across the two long strips. The short strips should be placed above, rather than below the pins.

Start the buttonhole by putting the needle into the fabric where the two strips of tape cross. Start at the

front edge of the buttonhole when using a machine that moves forward when stitching the first side of the buttonhole. If your machine backstitches the first side, then place the needle in the fabric at the other end of the buttonhole. It is important that you adjust the position of the needle in the fabric so that it never sews into the tape. This will put a sticky coating on the needle causing it to skip stitches.

Complete the buttonhole according to your machine's procedure, using the tape strips as guides for equal lengths.

Thread Marking: Transfer the buttonhole marks to the wrong side of the cut-out garment piece. Use the pattern and pin technique described above, except mark each pin with a pencil dot rather than tape strips. Using a ruler, connect the dots, and then hand or machine baste the lines through to the right side.

The only mark necessary when using a buttonhole attachment is the one at the front edge of the garment. A tailor's tack or light pencil mark is an easy way to transfer this mark to the fabric. The buttonhole attachment automatically measures the length of the buttonhole. Just make sure that the buttonholer moves in a straight line, perpendicular to the edge of the garment.

Many times you can utilize the lines on regularly striped or checked fabrics as guides for buttonholes. Use tape strips as needed, or just make a light pencil mark at the beginning and end of each buttonhole. If the last stitch at each end of the buttonhole just covers these marks, you will never see them.

Buttonhole Thread

Garments made from fabrics other than lightweight wovens and knits look best if the buttonholes are stitched with buttonhole thread instead of regular thread. There are two types of buttonhole thread on the market today. One is made from silk and the other from polyester. Polyester thread has a greater color selection and is usually easier to find since most fabric stores now carry it. It is great to use for topstitching and for sewing buttons in place. Silk buttonhole thread looks elegant on the finished garment but is somewhat difficult to find.

You will need a larger machine needle when stitching with the thicker buttonhole thread. (See machine needles page 34). Thread both the top and bobbin of your machine with buttonhole thread, and then try a sample buttonhole on a scrap of fabric, to see if any machine adjustments are necessary. Some machines will need to have the upper thread tension increased. If you still have problems, then try using regular thread on the bobbin and the buttonhole thread on the top.

If buttonhole thread is not available, you can get the same thick-looking buttonhole by using two strands of regular thread on the top. Thread the two strands through the machine and needle just as though they were one threads. This technique makes the buttonhole strong, and it will stand out from the fabric. This is especially important when the buttonholes contrast with the fabric.

Corded Machine Buttonholes

Corded machine buttonholes really add a professional touch to your garments. A soft piece of pearl cotton or carpet thread is placed under the buttonhole foot and covered by the zigzag of each side of the buttonhole. This type of buttonhole is very good on knit fabrics because it stabilizes the buttonhole edges so that they don't stretch out of shape and ripple. Check your machine instruction book for special helps when making corded machine buttonholes.

BOUND BUTTONHOLES

Bound buttonholes are made on a garment before any other sewing is done. The buttonholes are worked through both the fashion fabric and the interfacing if they are both fairly lightweight. If you are using a heavyweight fashion fabric or hair canvas for the interfacing, the buttonholes should be worked before the interfacing is applied. Once the buttonholes are finished, windows are cut in the interfacing at the appropriate places to allow for each buttonhole, and then the interfacing is applied to the garment.

Fashion fabrics that fray easily should always have the buttonhole area backed with fusible interfacing in order to keep the narrow, buttonhole seams from fraying away. Fusing interfacing to the whole garment front will take care of this, or use just a lightweight patch of fusible interfacing for each buttonhole if the fashion fabric is very heavy or if a hair canvas is used for the interfacing.

The backs of bound buttonholes, which are in the garment facing, are finished after the facing has been permanently stitched in place. Various ways of finishing the backs of bound buttonholes are given below.

Marking Buttonholes

Precise marking of the buttonhole location and length is very important. Unequal spacing and length of the buttonholes can ruin the look of a garment no matter how professional your actual buttonhole technique.

The easiest way to transfer buttonhole lines to the garment piece is to use a buttonhole grid. This grid is drawn directly on the wrong side of the garment piece before applying the interfacing, if the fashion fabric is heavy or you are using hair canvas for the interfacing. Draw the buttonhole grid on the wrong side of the garment piece of lightweight fabrics, using lightweight or fusible interfacing, after the interfacing has been applied. Follow the instructions below for making the grid.

Place the paper pattern over the wrong side of the garment piece. Stick pins through each end of the buttonhole marks. Starting at the bottom edge, carefully lift the paper pattern and put a small pencil dot where each pin pierces the fabric. Remove the first two pins and work on up the buttonhole line. Remove the pattern and double check your pencil dot spacing with a ruler.

Connect the vertical rows of dots with a pencil line, extending the lines approximately 1″ (25mm) beyond the top and bottom dots. Draw the horizontal buttonhole lines, from dot to dot, extending them approximately 1″ (25mm) beyond the vertical lines Check to make sure they are parallel.

Transfer the grid marks to the right side of the garment by machine basting along each line with a contrasting thread. Stitch both vertical lines and all horizontal lines from the same direction so that the grid stays square. Double check the grid at this point to make sure every line is in the proper place. Make any necessary corrections.

A single, bound buttonhole should be accurately marked with hand basting. Insert a pin straight through the fabric at the exact ends of the buttonhole mark. Using the needle and thread, secure the thread at one pin with a few stitches. Wrap the thread around the opposite pin, bring it back to the first pin and then take small stitches between the pins, using the loose thread as a guide. Secure the end with a few stitches.

Buttonhole Construction

It is recommended that you do the same step on all the buttonholes at the same time rather than make one complete buttonhole and then go on to the next one. This speeds up the sewing process and also makes it much easier for you to catch a sewing or size mistake before it is too late.

The buttonhole method given below is what we consider the ultimate bound buttonhole. It isn't harder than any other method, in fact, we think it is the easiest, and it makes the nicest looking buttonhole.

Cut a strip of fabric 1″ (25mm) wide and long enough to give you two pieces for each buttonhole that are 1″ (25mm) longer than the finished buttonhole length. Cut these strips on the bias, unless the bias cut isn't attractive when working with patterned fabrics. Bias cuts are easier to handle because the edges don't fray easily. Knits can be cut on the bias or the lengthwise grain.

Fold the strip lengthwise down the middle with wrong sides together and press. Stitch the length of the strip ⅛″ (3mm) from the folded edge. It is important that this stitching line be accurate because this is what determines the evenness of the buttonhole lips. If the fabric tends to fray, do several more rows of stitching as illustrated. Note: Garments made of bulky fabrics such as coatings should have ¼" (6mm) rather than ⅛" (3mm) allowed for the lip width. Cut the buttonhole strip 1½" (38mm) wide to allow for this extra width.

Staystitch a box around the horizontal buttonhole mark. The stitching should be ⅛" (3mm) on each side of the basting line and directly on the vertical lines. Count the stitches as you sew across the ends of the box so the narrow sides will be equal.

Cut the long prepared buttonhole strip into equal pieces that are at least 1" (25mm) longer than the buttonhole width. Position one strip on the right side of the garment so that the strip stitching line meets the bottom stitching line of the buttonhole. Hand baste the strip in position, and then secure the strip by machine stitching just below the first stitching line, beginning and ending exactly on the verticals.

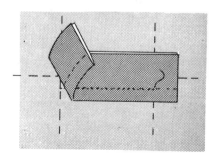

Pull the strip down out of the way and position another buttonhole strip along the upper line with the folded edge up. Hand baste and secure this strip by stitching just along the first stitching line, beginning and ending exactly at the verticals.

These two lines of stitching have to be accurate for perfect buttonholes. Count the stitches as you sew to make sure each stitching line is the same length. Do not backstitch at the beginning or ending of each line. Pull the threads through to the wrong side and tie them in a square knot.

Cut between the stitching lines, as shown, being careful not to cut into the buttonhole strips. Leave a good sized wedge at each end of the buttonhole.

Turn ...ips through to the wrong side and you will ...ne lips of the buttonhole begin to take shape. Straighten everything out, making sure that the little wedges in each corner are tucked to the wrong side. Baste the lips of the buttonhole closed and steam press from the wrong side.

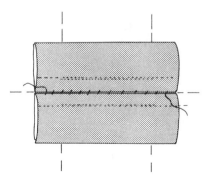

Fold back the right side of the garment along one edge of the buttonhole until the wedge is exposed. Machine stitch across the base of each wedge catching it to the lips of the buttonhole. This stitching line should curve slightly in toward the center of the buttonhole for a neater finish on the right side. Backstitch to make sure this stitching is strong.

Fold back the other side of the garment along the edge of the buttonhole and stitch across the other wedge as directed above. Steam press from the wrong side.

Trim the excess strips to about ¼″ (6mm) from the wedge stitching. Hold the scissors at an angle so that they *grade* the edge of the strips rather than make a blunt cut.

The front side of the bound buttonholes is now finished. Construct the rest of the garment and finish the back of the buttonholes after the facing has been sewn in place. Use one of the methods given below.

Method #1: Baste the facing in place between the buttonholes and stick pins through to the wrong side at each end of the buttonholes. Slash the facing

open between the pins. Turn under the raw edges, forming a curve, and hem in place to the wrong side of the buttonholes.

Method #2: Baste the facing in place between the buttonholes and stick pins through all four corners of each buttonhole.

Slash open as illustrated. Turn under the raw edges, forming a box and *slipstitch* in place to the wrong side of the buttonholes.

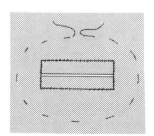

Method #3: Use this method for fabrics that fray. Pin the facing in place between the buttonholes and stick pins through the ends of the buttonholes.

Transfer these marks to the right side of the facing with light pencil marks.

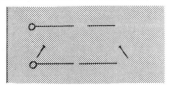

Pull the facing away from the garment, and make a clean-faced buttonhole opening using a lightweight non-ravelly fabric, such as sheer tricot. Stitch as illustrated and cut open the length of the stitching. You have now faced the facing.

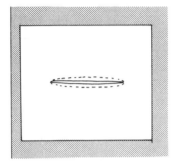

Turn the facing patch to the wrong side of the facing and press, rolling the facing patch under so that it doesn't show on the right side. Catch the faced opening to the wrong side of the bound buttonhole.

Method #4: Use this method for knits. Baste the facing in place around the buttonhole. Working on the right side, *stitch-in-the-ditch* all around the buttonhole. Use a short stitch length so that the machine will feed slowly and bury the stitches in the fabric. On the facing side, cut the buttonhole open just inside the stitched box.

Corded Buttonholes

Corded bound buttonholes are an elegant touch to any garment. Not only does the cording give a nice raised appearance but it adds strength and stability to the buttonhole lips. Corded rather than regular bound buttonholes are a good choice for knit fabrics because they control the fabric stretch across the buttonhole opening.

Use a #9 cotton cord or a heavy string for the filler. Place the cord along the fold of the buttonhole strip and stitch with a zipper foot. The distance between the folded edge and the stitching line should be about ⅛″ (3mm). Use this corded strip for the buttonhole lips following the instructions given above.

SEAM BUTTONHOLES

This type of buttonhole is found at waist and yoke seams of garments. It is very simple to do and looks nicer than trying to work a machine buttonhole close to a seamline. The front and back of the buttonholes are worked the same if the facing has a seam in the same place as the garment. Otherwise, the back of the buttonhole is worked as for the back of a bound buttonhole. (See methods above).

Mark the buttonhole width on the seamline and leave this area unsewn when stitching the seam. Backstitch at both ends of the opening for added strength.

Reinforce the sides of the buttonhole by stitching on a strip of seam binding to each seam allowance above and below the opening. Extend this strip a-about ¼" (6mm) on both sides of the buttonhole opening.

Press open the seam and secure each end of the buttonhole with a small bar-tack made by machine or hand.

BAR TACK

BUTTON LOOPS

Some fashions call for button loops instead of machine or bound buttonholes. These are fun to make and you get quite a sense of accomplishment when you complete a perfect line of button loops down a bridal dress or some other fine creation.

Select a ball or half-round button when using button loops. Why not go all the way and make your own Chinese Ball Buttons with matching tubing? Instructions for these are given below.

If you decide to put button loops on a pattern that has been designed for conventional buttonholes, you must make a few pattern changes to accommodate the different closure. The side of the garment to which loops are sewn will need to be altered. The button loops will be sewn to the closing line, which is usually the center front or center back line. Adjust the garment and facing pieces so that there is only a seam width to the side of this closing line. Note: Button loops require the pattern to have a separate facing.

Make either self-filled or corded tubing for the button loops. Lightweight fabrics should be corded, while heavier fabrics can use the self-filled technique. Cut bias strips long enough for the amount of tubing that you need and six times as wide as the desired finished width. Trim one end of the strip into a sharp point.

Self-Filled Tubing

Securely stitch a string or narrow cord to the pointed end of the strip. The string should be a couple of inches longer than the bias strip. Fold the bias strip in half, right sides together, and position the string down in the fold so that at least 1" (25mm) extends beyond the end of the strip. Start stitching a little bit wider than the desired seam width and then taper back, as illustrated so that the tubing will have some extra room to start the turning process. Stretch the fabric slightly as you sew or use a small zigzag rather than a straight stitch. The seam will then have some give so that you won't break stitches when you turn the tubing. Trim the seam allowance so that it is the same width as the distance from the fold to the seamline, for average weight fabrics. Sheer fabrics can have a much wider seam allowance in order to fully stuff the tubing. Carefully turn the tubing by pulling the string and working the tubing back over it.

Corded Tubing

Proceed as for the self-filled tubing except use a piece of cording of the desired size in place of the string. The cording should be twice the length of the bias strip. Position it along the fold of the strip so that half its length extends beyond the end of the strip. Secure the cord to the strip. Stitch as directed above and then trim the seam allowance close to the stitching. Turn the cording by pulling on one end of the cording and work the tubing back over the other section of cording. Using a zipper foot during the stitching will allow you to stitch quite close to the cording. Remember to stretch the fabric slightly as you sew.

Bias Tubing

Bias tubing in various fabrics is available, by the yard, and you can use this tubing for your button loops if you can find some that matches or complements your garment fabric.

Button Loop Construction

Draw a button loop grid on a piece of paper that is as long as the closure area and about 3" (76mm) wide. Line A is the seam line. The distance between lines A and B is approximately one half the button diameter plus the width of the cord. The distance between the horizontal lines is the button diameter plus twice the width of the cord.

Pin the loops within the guide lines on the grid, adjusting them so that the seams of the loops are up. The loops can be placed separately or as a continuous series.

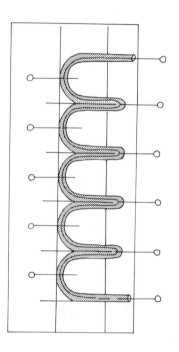

Hold the loops in place with a strip of drafting tape and stitch them to the paper just outside the seamline.

Remove the tape and pin the loop grid in place on the garment, (paper side up) lining up the edge of the paper with the edge of the garment. Stitch the loops to the garment along the seamline. Remove the paper. Trim the open ends of the loops on an angle in order to reduce bulk.

fasten the ends to the underside of the button with a hand needle and thread.

Finish the button loop area by applying the garment facing. Adjust the button location by pinning the garment together along the closing lines and then marking the buttons at the ends of the loops.

FROGS

Frogs are another type of closing that can be made from tubing. They look the nicest when made with corded tubing. Two basic frog designs are given below, but you can make your own if you wish. Attach Chinese ball buttons to one or both sides of the frog.

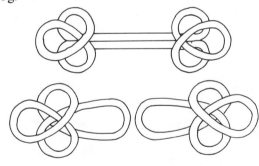

CHINESE BALL BUTTONS

The Chinese ball button, made from the same tubing as the button loop, is an elegant touch to any garment. The size of the button is determined by the thickness of the tubing. Tubing made from lightweight to medium-weight fabrics should be corded, as shown above. Each button will take approximately 10″ (25cm) of tubing.

Form the button following the diagrams at the right. Keep the tubing seam up while forming the button so that it won't be visible on the right side of the finished button. Make sure the tubing does not twist. Carefully tighten and mold the button until it is round. Trim away the excess tubing and

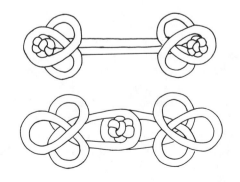

Draw the frog design on a piece of very thick card-board or styrofoam. Lay the tubing along the lines, holding it in place with pins. Tack the tubing together where it meets and/or laps. Remember to keep the tubing seam up so that it won't show on the right side of the frog. Tack the finished frog and ball buttons in position on the garment.

SEWING ON BUTTONS

Proper technique is just as important when sewing a button to the garment as it is when making the buttonholes. The button should be correctly positioned with a long enough shank so that the garment will close smoothly. Use the information below to help you sew your buttons correctly.

Buttons are sewn to the closing line of the garment. This is usually the center front or center back line, but not always. Check your pattern to be sure. Lap the garment in its closed position and mark the first button by sticking a pin through the buttonhole end closest to the edge of the garment. Carefully lift the top layer of garment and mark where the pin enters the fabric. Sew the first button to this mark. Button the garment after the first button has been sewn in place and then mark the next button position with a pin. Stitch the second button in place and follow this procedure for the rest of the buttons.

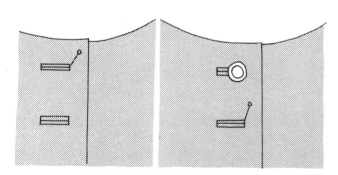

All buttons should have a shank that is the same thickness as the garment at the buttonhole area. This makes for a smooth closing. Many buttons come with a built-on shank. Other buttons should have shanks created for them from thread. This is done while the button is being sewn in place. If the built-on shank of a button is not long enough to accommodate the thickness of the garment, it should be made longer with thread.

Buttons without built-on shanks or with very short shanks are the best choice for lightweight fabrics. Long shanked buttons will droop when the garment is buttoned because the fabric is not thick enough to hold the button in position.

Sew buttons to the garment with buttonhole thread or doubled, regular thread. Run the thread through *beeswax* before sewing in order to strengthen the thread and keep it from tangling. Waxed dental-floss can be used to sew buttons in place. It is very strong because it is made of nylon, and is recommended for metal shanked buttons that tend to cut ordinary thread.

Create a thread shank for flat buttons by stitching over a toothpick or match stick. Remove the stick and wrap the thread around the shank threads a couple of times and then fasten to the garment.

Create a longer shank on a button that already has a built-on shank by placing the stick between the garment and the button and then stitching over it.

Sometimes a jeweled button on a dressy garment will tend to snag the fabric when it is buttoned. Avoid this problem by stitching the button to the top side of the buttonhole and then placing a snap underneath each buttonhole to close the garment. Do not cut open machine buttonholes, and do not finish off the back of bound buttonholes when using this procedure.

Tuck-in shirts and blouses should always have flat buttons placed below the waistline.

COVERED SNAPS

Covered snaps make a custom finishing touch on your dresses, jackets and coats. They will require a #3 or #4 snap, which is fairly large, so don't try to use them on lightweight garments. Un-covered snaps do just fine here.

The fabric used to cover the snaps should be a matching piece of lining or some other lightweight fabric. Cut two circles of fabric which measure about twice the diameter of the snap. Make a series of small stitches around the very edge of each fabric circle with a hand needle and thread. Keeping the threaded needle attached to the fabric, center the snap piece, wrong side up, on the circle and pull the fabric up tightly around the snap. Secure the fabric in position by taking some stitches across the snap, flattening the fabric.

Cover each half of the snap by using the same method. Sew the snaps in place by carefully feeling for the stitching holes with the needle. Holes will soon wear in the fabric in the proper place when the snap is closed.

TAILORING TACTICS

For years the tailored coat or jacket has been the ultimate test of the home-sewer. Many hours of construction steps, including lots of detailed hand work, were required. Now the tailored garment is a much quicker and simpler project, thanks to all the recently developed sewing aids.

The biggest tailoring time-saver is realized with fusible interfacings. How much easier it is to fuse the interfacing to the garment front, the undercollar, and the hem areas. Applying interfacing this way will cut your construction time in half.

Because you can use the above, time-saving technique, don't feel you are making a less-than-first-quality garment. Examine the designer suits, in both men's and women's fashions; you will see that the majority use fusible interfacings. You are in good company, so take advantage of this help.

Occasionally you will need to use non-fusible interfacing or hair-canvas on a tailored garment. For example, velvet would require hand applied interfacing because fusing an interfacing in place would ruin the nap. However, fusible interfacing is ideal for velveteen and corduroy.

It is possible to purchase pre-formed coat interfacing that can be hand-stitched into the garment front. This product is called a canvas front, or coat hymo and is available at tailor's supply houses. You will have to trim the hymo to fit your particular garment, but it will save much handwork.

Pattern instructions seem to be better written than the ones we used years ago, and they use many new construction techniques that simplify the whole process. A tailored garment is now an enjoyable undertaking, rather than something to be endured and overcome.

While we don't plan to guide you, step by step, through the construction of a tailored jacket, we do want to give you the tailoring tips and alternate construction methods that we use in our own sewing.

PATTERN NOTES

Look at the ready-made, tailored jackets, suits, and sport coats you have hanging in the closets at home. The men's garments will have the undercollar applied by hand, and the back lining will go all the way up to the collar, thus eliminating the back neck facing. Some women's garments will be made the same way, while others will have a stitched and turned collar, with or without a back neck facing.

Since you are making your own clothes, you have the choice of construction methods. We would like to recommend that you use the man-tailored way of applying the under collar for both men's and women's garments. This method can be used with any jacket or coat pattern, except heavy outerwear, and we feel that it gives the nicest rolling collar and lapel, with the flattest finish. It also gives you very good control of the under collar, so that you get an accurate roll and identical collar points.

A hand-applied under collar should have all the seam allowances trimmed away, and should be interfaced with a fusible, non-woven interfacing. Trim the interfacing slightly smaller than the under collar, so that it will not "peek" out around the finished edge. An extra layer of interfacing applied below the collar roll line will add extra support to the collar stand.

If your pattern calls for a back neck facing and you are going to use the man-tailored method, eliminate the facing by pinning it to the back lining pattern. Overlap the back facing and lining pattern pieces until the seamlines meet. Add extra width at the center back of the facing to allow for the back pleat. Cut the lining fabric from this altered pattern.

Whether you use the man-tailored collar method or some other collar application method, we still suggest that you eliminate the back neck facing from tailored garment patterns. This reduces bulk at the back of the neck and prevents a facing line from showing through on the right side of the garment.

In this section you will find two methods of handling the sleeve vents. One involves a change in the shape of the pattern at the lower edge. Read through the sleeve vent instructions before cutting the fabric, so you can decide which method you want to use. Make the necessary pattern alterations required by your choice.

FITTING

Test your pattern in muslin or some other fabric (i.e. denim or corduroy) before cutting into expensive fabrics. This lets you work out any fitting problems in a cheaper fabric.

The garment should be tried on periodically during the construction process to check the fit. Baste the main garment pieces together after the front interfacing has been applied. Baste the shoulder pads in position and the under collar in place, but omit the sleeves at this point. Check the fit and length; make any necessary adjustments.

Do another fitting just before you stitch the sleeves in place. Baste the sleeves in position and check the fit and sleeve hang. Make any necessary adjustments and then permanently stitch the sleeves in place.

INTERFACINGS

Use a fusible interfacing of a woven, non-woven, or hair-canvas type. Choose the weight that gives the desired, finished look to your fashion fabric. Thin fabrics will need heavier interfacings than bulky fabrics.

Apply interfacing to the entire garment front, collar, pocket flaps, and sleeve hems. Thin fabrics can also have interfacing applied to the front facing. Sometimes the entire garment will benefit from fusible interfacing. Certain fabrics, such as cotton velveteen, will always look unpressed unless you add some extra support.

Trim away all seam allowances from interfacing pieces before fusing. Apply interfacing to the wrong side of upper pocket flap pieces, and to the under, rather than upper collar piece, when the man-tailored method is used. Interfacing can also be applied to the upper collar if a thin fashion fabric is used.

The use of fusible interfacing makes it easy to reduce bulk in the dart area. Fuse the interfacing to the garment piece, except for the dart area. Transfer the dart marks to the interfacing, using the paper pattern as a guide. Cut away the interfacing along the dart lines, and complete the fusing process.

Stitch the dart, using the cut edges of the interfacing as a guide.

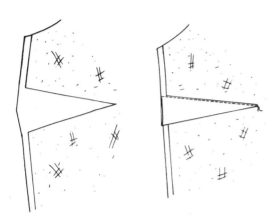

An extra piece of interfacing applied to the lapel point of the garment front will add firmness and help the lapel lie flat.

Construction marks, such as pocket locations, should be transferred to the wrong side of the garment piece after the interfacing has been fused in place.

Interfacing should be applied to sleeve hems. Use either a fusible or non-fusible type.

Cut fusible interfacing the same width and shape as the hem allowance, and fuse it in place before stitching the sleeve seams.

Cut non-fusible interfacing ½" (13mm) wider than the hem, and stitch it to the hem edge with a straight or zigzag stitch. Hand baste along the hemline. If you are using a woven interfacing, cut it on the bias. Non-woven interfacing should be cut the same shape as the hem edge.

POCKETS

Pockets add interest to your tailored garment as well as serve a functional purpose. There are many pocket styles from which to choose, and you can substitute one pocket style for another on any given pattern.

Directions for various types of pockets are found on page 109. Just remember, as you construct the pockets, that they should match in size and shape. If the pocket calls for flaps, make the flaps first, and

177

then construct the pocket opening to fit the flaps. This makes sure there are no gaps between the flap and the end of the pocket opening. Make sure each set of pockets and flaps are the same size.

If you are using a patterned fabric for your garment, make sure the pocket or flaps match the pattern perfectly, or cut them on the bias for a contrast.

TWILL TAPE APPLICATION

Twill tape is used in tailored garments to stabilize certain areas. It keeps things from stretching out of shape, and adds strength. Use ¼" (6mm) or ½" (13mm) twill tape that has been pre-shrunk. Apply it to the following areas. (A new product, STAY-TAPE, requires no pre-shrinking as it is nylon. It is thin, thus eliminating bulk.)

Lapel Roll Line

Twill tape is applied just behind the roll line of the lapel in order to keep it firm and help the lapel roll properly. It is pulled taut as it is applied, so that the lapel assumes a slight curve. Apply the tape after the front interfacing has been fused in place.

Start the twill tape at the neckline seam, about ⅛" (3mm) behind the roll line. Pull the tape taut as you machine baste down the middle. End the tape 1½" (38mm) above the front edge. Hand catch both edges of the tape to the interfacing. Remove the machine basting.

To set the roll line, position the garment front over a *tailor's ham* and firmly press the lapel in the finished position.

Back of the Neck

Twill tape should be applied to the neckline seam allowance of the garment back. This stabilizes the area and adds strength. Apply the tape after the center back seam has been sewn and pressed, but before the shoulder seams are stitched.

Measure the distance between the shoulder and center back seam on the paper pattern. Cut a strip of twill tape twice this length.

Position the twill tape on the wrong side of the neck seam allowance, so that the lower edge is just slightly above the seamline, and the edges of the tape end at the shoulder seam. Machine stitch along the center of the tape with a regular stitch length.

When you finish the neck edge of the garment, be careful not to catch the tape in the seamline. This would add unnecessary bulk.

Pockets

Garments that have set-in, rather than patch pockets, should have the back corner of the pocket supported with a strip of twill tape that has the other end attached to the armscye seam allowance. This keeps the pocket area from becoming baggy.

Stitch one end of the tape to the pocket seam allowance at the inside back corner. Affix the other end of the tape to the armscye seam allowance, as shown. Be careful that the tape is long enough so that it doesn't create a pull on the garment.

BACK VENTS

Most tailored garments have either a center back or two side back vents. There are two ways of finishing the corner of the upper vent. We would like to give directions for both methods, and you can choose the one which works best for you.

Apply a 1½″ (38mm) wide piece of fusible interfacing to the facing portion of the upper vent. This adds support and keeps it neat.

It is a good idea to check the lower edge of the vent before you begin the finishing process. A little trimming done at this point will make for an even line across the finished vent edges.

Lay the garment, wrong side up, on a flat surface, and arrange the vent layers in the finished position. Trim all the layers of the vent so that they are even with the garment edge. Then trim the under vent slightly shorter so it doesn't "peek" out.

Miter the corner of the upper vent, or do a simple faced finish. Either method gives a neat, flat vent.

The Mitered Vent

Press the vent facing over in its finished position, and then press up the hem allowance. Clip the two layers of fabric where they meet. Mark the corner with a pin.

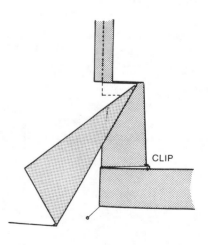

Now refold the vent along the diagonal, with right sides together, matching the clip marks. Stitch from the clips to the corner pin.

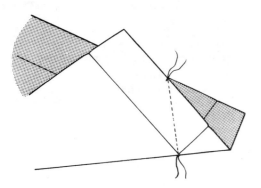

Trim the seam, turn and press from the wrong side. Slip an envelope in between the layers of fabric so that seam impressions won't show on the right side.

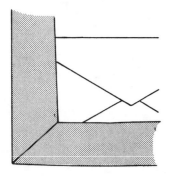

The Faced Vent

Fold the vent facing against the garment back, right sides together. Position the facing so that a scant 1/8″ (3mm) extends below the edge of the garment. Stitch across the bottom of the vent, along the hemline.

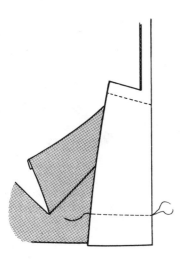

Trim the seam allowance, as shown. Turn the vent to the right side, and press. Roll the seam to the inside and use an envelope as a shield between the fabric layers.

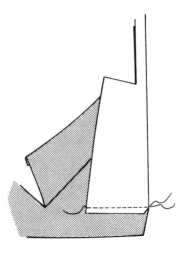

Fuse the upper vent facing to the jacket with fusible web to keep it from drooping

SLEEVE VENTS

Some jacket and coat patterns are now using a new construction technique for the sleeve vent. It consists of an extension below the hem allowance on both the upper and under sleeve pattern pieces. This extension acts as a facing for the vent and gives a smooth, flat finish.

You can modify any sleeve pattern to take advantage of this technique. The modified patterns will require a few extra inches of fabric to accommodate the length of the extensions. If you are short of fabric, then use the sleeve pattern as given, and follow the instructions for the mitered vent.

Sleeve Vent with Extended Facings

Measure the length of the vent extension on the upper sleeve pattern from the hemline to the top of the extension. Make note of this measurement and then trim away the extension as indicated.

TRIM

Add an extension at the bottom of the sleeve pattern that is 3″ (76mm) wide. The distance from the hemline to the bottom of the extension should be the same as the measurement of the vent extension you have already taken.

Now, add the same size extension to the vent area of the under sleeve. Leave the side extension intact on this pattern piece.

Cut the fashion fabric using these new sleeve pattern pieces. Apply interfacing to the hem allowance, as previously described. Stitch and press the front sleeve seam.

Turn up the sleeve hem, right sides together, pulling the sides of the vent out a little beyond the sleeve edges. Stitch along both vents with the given seam allowance. Trim the seam, turn and press, rolling the seam to the inside, for a neat finish. Remember to slip an envelope in between the layers of fabric when you press.

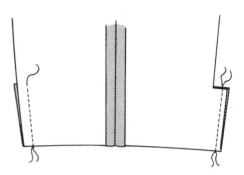

Stitch the upper sleeve seam with the given seam allowance. The upper vent extension should be opened up and pulled out of the way during this stitching process. End the stitching ½″ (13mm) below the top edge of the vent extension.

Clip the under vent extension to the seamline and press open the upper sleeve vent. Secure the sleeve hem with a loose *catchstitch*, or *fusible web*.

Mitered Vent

Use this finishing technique on sleeve vents that don't have the lower extensions.

Interface the sleeve hem as previously described. Stitch and press open the front sleeve seam. Fold the hem up in its finished position and press.

Press over the upper sleeve vent extension along the seamline. Clip into the vent and hem edge where they meet. Mark the corner with a pin.

Refold the vent along the diagonal, right sides together, lining up the clip marks. Stitch from the clips to the corner pin. Trim the seam, turn to the right side and press, using an envelope as a shield.

Finish the other side of the vent by folding the hem up, right sides together. Pull out the hem edge just slightly beyond the sleeve edge. Stitch the length of the extension with a ¼" (6mm) seam. Trim, turn and press. Secure the sleeve hem with a loose *catch-stitch*, or *fusible web*.

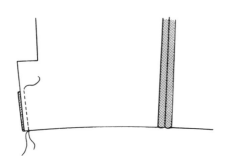

Note: If you anticipate any sleeve length adjustment on the garment at a later date don't trim away the excess fabric at the mitered corner. Just squash it out flat with your fingers, and turn it to the inside of the sleeve hem. The sleeve length can now be adjusted without any danger of your running out of fabric.

THE TAILORED SLEEVE

Set-in sleeves, in the tailored garment, require absolute control of the sleeve-cap ease, with no tucks, gathers, or puckers along the seamline.

Easestitch the sleeve-cap before pinning the sleeve into the armscye. Match up all construction marks and pin, making sure the pins enter the fabric right at the seamline. Stitch with the given seam allowance. Trim the sleeve seam to ⅜" (9mm) around the top, and ¼" (6mm) between the notches. Do not press the seam.

Shoulder Pads

Tailored garments usually require padding in the shoulder area. Some garments will need thicker padding than others, depending on the style and the person's figure and posture.

Men's suits and coats and women's outer coats need more padding than lightweight jackets. Padding is sometimes added to the shoulder area of a tailored dress.

The pad may consist of one or many layers of padding material. Whatever the thickness, padding helps the garment hang better and gives a professional look.

Shoulder pads can be purchased ready-made in various sizes and thicknesses. Pads for men's wear are usually thicker and bigger than pads for women's wear. The thickness of purchased shoulder pads can be reduced by pulling out some of the middle layers of padding before placing the pad in the garment. The outside edges of many pads can be trimmed, if you find them too large for your purpose.

You can make your own shoulder pads, so that you get just the right size and thickness that you need. This will save quite a bit of money as well. Purchase a yard of polyester fleece, and keep it handy in your sewing supplies for pad making.

The pattern for the pad is made from the garment pattern. Overlap the front and back pattern pieces at the shoulder seam. Draw a pad outline on the paper pattern. The sleeve edge of the pad should extend ¼″ (6mm) into the seam allowance for dresses and lightweight jackets, and ⅜″ (9mm) into the seam allowance for suits and coats. The back of the pad should be longer than the front. Mark a notch on both edges of the pad pattern at the shoulder seam.

Construct the pad by cutting the number of layers of polyester fleece needed to build up the desired thickness. Cut them all the same size and mark the notches with a small clip.

Pads made of multiple layers should have the inner layers trimmed in order to reduce bulk at the outer edges. Trim as indicated.

Stack the padding layers so that the sleeve edges and notches are even. Roll the pad over your fist

and pin the layers together as they fall. You will notice that the outside edges are now uneven. Secure the padding layers in this rolled position with hand stitches.

Holding your scissors at an acute angle, trim the edges of the pad so that you make a beveled edge. Do this so that the top layer of the pad is longest.

Shoulder pads are inserted after the sleeve is permanently stitched into the armscye. Trim the sleeve allowance to either ¼″ (6mm) or ⅜″ (9mm), as directed above.

With the sleeve seam allowance turned out into the sleeve, position the pad so that the pad edge is even with the trimmed sleeve seam. The garment should be turned right side out when positioning the pad so it will assume the proper curve. Placing the pad and garment over your knee during this process gives the desired curve.

Remember that the longest part of the pad is placed toward the back of the garment. Match up the notches with the shoulder seam, and pin in place. Secure the pad by *stabstitching* through the pad edge and sleeve seam allowance. Do not pull the stitches tight. Secure the free edge of the pad to the shoulder seam allowance.

Sleeve Padding

Sleeve padding is used in tailored dresses, jackets and coats, to support the top of the sleeve. It prevents the seam allowance from showing through to the right side and gives a soft roll to the sleeve-cap. Used alone or in combination with shoulder pads, sleeve padding is added to the sleeve after any shoulder padding has been stitched in place.

Sleeve padding is made of a bias strip of soft material that is cut long enough to go around the top half of the sleeve. Lambs wool makes excellent padding for garments that are going to be dry-cleaned. Polyester fleece or other similar fabrics can be used for garments that are to be washed. Sometimes it is possible to buy pre-formed sleeve padding at tailor's supply houses. These are referred to as sleeve-heads. They are usually quite thick and should be used for tailored coats and jackets, rather than lighterweight garments.

Cut a bias strip of padding fabric 3″ (7.5 cm) wide, and about 8″ (20cm) long. Fold over 1″ (25mm), and baste as shown.

Permanently stitch the sleeve into the armscye and trim the seam allowance to ¼″ (6mm) or ⅜″ (9mm), as directed above. With the sleeve seam allowances turned out into the sleeve, position the sleeve padding so that the fold goes along the seamline. *Slip-stitch* the fold to the seamline of the sleeve-cap.

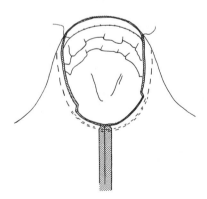

Turn the garment to the right side and mold the sleeve-cap over the padding for a smooth look. Holding a steaming iron a couple of inches away from the sleeve-cap will help in the molding process. Do not touch the garment with the iron.

LININGS

Always select a slick finished lining fabric for your tailored garments. This makes it easy to slip the garment on and off. Choose either a solid color or a patterned fabric. Make a co-ordinated outfit by using the lining fabric for a blouse or matching tie.

Linings should have a pleat at the center back, to allow for wearing ease. The pleat should be ¾″ (19mm) to 1″ (25mm) deep. Hand stitch the fold of the pleat, with a cross-stitch for a professional touch.

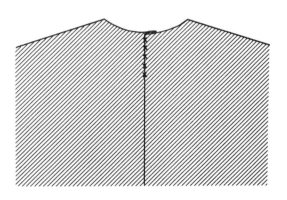

Cut the sleeve lining ½″ (13mm) higher in the underarm area. This allows for the extra fabric needed to go up and over the underarm seam allowance.

Hand baste the lining to the garment's armscye seam allowance before you sew the sleeve lining in place. Place the basting stitches in the seam allowance, next to the seamline.

Easestitch the cap of the sleeve lining and regular stitch the rest of the sleeve along the seamline before stitching the sleeve lining in place. Use the stitching line as a guide for turning under and basting the seam allowance. Transfer the construction marks to the folded edge with a chalk or soap mark. Trim and clip the seam allowance in the underarm area to release the curve.

Turn the sleeve lining inside out and pin to the garment, matching up construction marks. The folded edge of the lining should just cover the basting stitches. Hand stitch the lining in place, using small stitches, for strength.

THE FRONT FACING

The front facing should always be cut slightly wider and longer than the garment front at the top corner of the lapel. This provides ease at the lapel point so that it will roll toward the body and lie flat. Thick fabrics will require more ease than thin fabrics. Since patterns are designed with average fabrics in mind, you may find that you will have to increase or decrease this ease when working with certain fabrics.

The lapel ease must be preserved when stitching the facing to the garment front. Control it by folding the facing corner along the diagonal, right sides together, and then weaving a long pin or needle along the fold. Leave the pin in position while stitching around the lapel point.

The lower edge of the front facing should be cut slightly shorter than the garment front. This makes it easier to roll the seam to the inside when pressing the garment front. Thick fabrics will require more shortening than thin fabrics.

Well designed patterns will allow for the above size differences between the garment front and the front facing. However, it is always a good idea to compare the two pattern pieces, lining up the notches on the front edge before you cut your fashion fabric, to see just how much has been allowed. Adjust the differences if you don't think they are right for your fabric. If you do any pattern designing or changing, this knowledge is necessary, for a professional finish.

Think about the curve, rather than a straight line, when stitching across the top of the lapel. The finished lapel will then have a straight, top edge, rather than the slight, downward curve it so often gets.

Garments requiring two or more bound button holes should have the buttonhole side of the garment left about ¼" (6mm) longer than the button side. This will allow for the slight drawing-up that occurs when buttonholes are made. This makes sure the underlap doesn't extend below the garment front when the garment is buttoned.

Press open the front edge seam allowances before they are graded. This pressing makes it easier to turn and press the front edge.

Use a *point presser* to help you press the seams open, or press them open as described on page 46.

Understitch the lapel area if you are not going to topstitch the garment edges. This will give a hard edge on which to turn and press, and also keeps the lapel facing from "peeking" to the right side.

COLLAR APPLICATION

The diagram below identifies the various parts of the collar and lapel area. Seam allowances are always trimmed and pressed open in the gorgeline, no matter what application method you use. The seam allowances around the back of the neck are pressed up into the collar to add support to the stand.

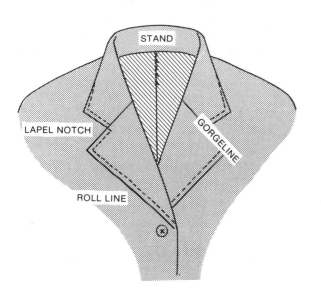

We advise you to follow your pattern instructions for applying collars, since they are usually quite complete. However, we would like to introduce a new way of applying the man-tailored collar. It gives you very good control of the upper and under collar and is easy to do.

Interface and construct the garm... directs. Construct the lining, ex... Stitch the lining to the front f... the front facing to the garme...

Stitch the facing as instruct... ing all the way around the... t, so that the whole neck edge is... rim, clip and grade the seam... them open, and turn the facir... e right side.

Press the ne... garment sid... side aroun... e seam rolls to the ... on, and to the lining ...ck.

Press und... ance along the outside edge of t'... ter the corners for a flat finish a... ⊃ ¼" (6mm).

...ges from the wrong side, using ... that you get a flat finish. Use a *clapper*... or resilient fabrics.

Position the right side of the upper collar against the inside of the garment so that the edges of the

CLOTILDE HAS DEVELOPED A NEW METHOD WITH BETTER RESULTS — SEE PAGES 28-30 OF THE "SEW SMART" SUPPLEMENT", FOR THE FLATTEST COLLAR NOTCH.

collar are at the lapel dot and the seam allowance extends above the neck edge. Pin in place after you have made sure the lapels extend an equal amount beyond each side of the collar. Check to make sure that the ends of the collar are of equal length too. This is very important!

Wrap the under collar around a *tailor's ham* and steam the roll line in order to establish the collar's shape.

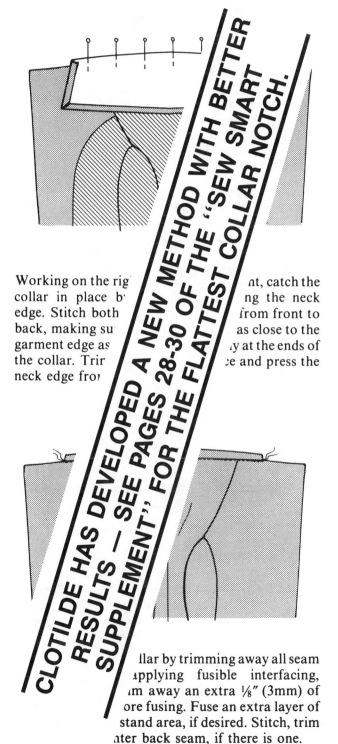

Working on the rig   nt, catch the
collar in place b   ng the neck
edge. Stitch both   from front to
back, making su   as close to the
garment edge as   y at the ends of
the collar. Trir   e and press the
neck edge fro

Pin the under collar in place, making sure the edges are all slightly short of the upper collar edges. The lower edge of the collar should just cover the neckline seam. Try on the garment to make sure the collar is smooth and flat. Adjust the under collar if necessary. Hand stitch the under collar in place, around all four edges, using a *felling stitch*.

llar by trimming away all seam
applying fusible interfacing,
m away an extra ⅛" (3mm) of
ore fusing. Fuse an extra layer of
stand area, if desired. Stitch, trim
nter back seam, if there is one.

Note: Most fashion fabrics can handle the raw edges of the trimmed under collar, if you use a nonwoven, fusible interfacing. If you are working with a fabric that frays badly, then we suggest that you use wool melton for the under collar. This is now available at most notion counters in collar-size pieces. Cut it on the straight grain and eliminate the seam at the center back of the collar.

FINISHING TIPS

Press up the hem of the garment and secure in place by hand, or use a *fusible web*. We like to use the fusible web because it is so quick and adds a little bit of firmness to the garment edge. Cut the web slightly narrower than the hem width and fuse in place, following the manufacturer's instructions, so that you get a perfect bond.

The Lining

The lining should be attached to the garment hem so there is a free fold at the bottom to provide wearing ease. Make sure the lining is long enough at the top of the center back vent so it doesn't pull. Check the length of the lining, and trim it so that it is even with the hemmed edge of the garment. Press up a lining hem that is one half the width of the garment hem.

Baste the fold of the lining hem where it falls against the garment hem.

Working through the vent opening, hand or machine stitch the lining edge to the garment hem, using small stitches. Remove the basting and hand stitch the lining to the garment on both sides of the vent.

Use a fine *catchstitch* over the raw edge of the facing that extends below the lining hem. This will hold the edge in place and keep it from fraying. Never turn this edge under.

Garments that do not have vent openings will require a slightly different technique of finishing the hem. Trim and press up the lining hem allowance, as described above.

Hand baste the lining to the garment about ½″ (13mm) above the lining edge. Fold back the edge of the lining and catch only the turned-under section to the garment hem. Remove the basting.

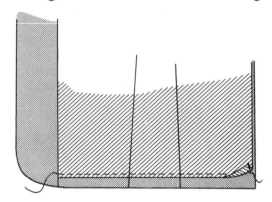

The Sleeve Lining

Trim the sleeve lining so that it is even with the edge of the sleeve, and press under a ¼″ (6mm) hem. Position the folded edge 1″ (25mm) above the sleeve edge, matching up the sleeve and lining seams. *Slipstitch* in place. This will allow a ⅜″ (9mm) free fold of lining around the sleeve edge when the garment is worn.

Pressing

The finished lapel is never hard pressed further than 1″ below the gorgeline. It should have a soft roll. The roll line of the collar can be steamed and pressed to set it. Place a *tailor's ham* in the neckline of the garment and use it as a body form during the pressing process.

Top Stitching

Topstitching is an attractive detail on many tailored garments. Not only does it add interest, but it keeps the garment edges flat, and facings in their proper position. Use topstitching thread or two strands of regular thread, so that it will show up well. See page 34 for more topstitching helps.

Buttons and Buttonholes

Machine buttonholes are used on men's garments. The keyhole style is preferred. Use a buttonhole attachment for this type of buttonhole, or take the finished garment to a tailor's shop to have them made. A regular machine buttonhole can also be used, if the keyhole is not available, but it should be made with buttonhole thread or with two strands of regular thread on the top. Insert both threads through the needle's eye.

Women's tailored garments are nicest when the bound buttonhole is used. Machine buttonholes can be used, if desired. Heavy fabric garments, such as coats, need a keyhole type buttonhole. See page 159 for more button and buttonhole helps.

TAILORED STYLES

The cut and style of tailored garments changes with the current fashion, just like other types of clothes. Lapels get wide or narrow, jacket lengths go up and down, waists go in and out. You can follow the current fashion, but this tends to date our clothes, and sometimes the current style is not what looks good on your figure.

Women with wide hips look better if the jacket is longer than the length a slim person might choose. A heavy, mature figure will find a princess line, minus the center back seam and vent, a good choice for the larger figure. This is also a good pattern for a person with a sway-back and large hips.

A good length for both men's and women's jackets and coats is found by standing erect, with the arms hanging in a relaxed position, and cupping the fingers. The fingers should cup right around the hem of the garment without causing it to wrinkle.

The sleeve length for both men's and women's garments is a matter of choice. However, a recommended length is determined by letting the arm fall in a relaxed position, and then extending the thumb up and out, as far as it will go. Adjust the sleeve length until no break occurs in the fabric. A sleeve that will be worn with French cuffs should be cut ½" (13mm) shorter, so that more of the cuff will show below the sleeve edge.

Of course, your personal preference will take precedence over the above suggestions, but we feel you should consider them when making your tailored garments.

SEWING TIPS

Fold up the lining that extends below the dot at the bottom of the facing before you stitch the lining and facing together. This makes it easier to finish the lower edge of the lining.

Before cutting the lining away from the left side of the vent, lay the lining against the garment in the finished position to make sure you are trimming the correct side.

Topstitch the collar, as shown. Shorten the stitch length as you stitch in the seam well of the gorgeline so the stitches bury down in the fabric. This short line of stitching flattens the gorgeline and makes the collar notch neat.

THE FINISHING TOUCH

Hems and edge finishes add the final touch to your garments. Hems should never show on the right side unless you are making a decorative finish. Various fabrics and garment styles require different hem techniques. Edge finishes can be used instead of conventional hems on many garments, especially those made of knit fabrics. Some of the edge finishes given in this section can also be used around sleeveless armholes, necklines, and the front edges of coats and jackets.

HEM WIDTHS

The first thing to consider once you have marked the proper hem length is the hem width. Suggested widths are given in the chart below. Trim your garment accordingly.

Dress or skirt	Straight	2½"-3" (64mm-76mm)
	A-line	1½"-2" (38mm-50mm)
	Full	½"-1" (13mm-25mm)
Pants		1½"-2" (38mm-50mm)
Shirts and Tops	Tuck-in	¼"-½" (6mm-13mm)
	Pull over	1"-1½" (25mm-38mm)
Sleeves		1"-1½" (25mm-38mm)
Jackets and Coats	Lightweight	1½"-2" (38mm-50mm)
	Heavyweight	2"-3" (50mm-76mm)

THE BASIC HEM

After determining the proper length, trim the hem to the desired width. Trim the seam allowances below the hem fold to ¼" (6mm). This will reduce bulk in the hem area.

Fold the hem up in position, basting along the fold.

Press from the fold up, placing a strip of paper or large envelope between the fabric layers to prevent impressions on the right side.

Small amounts of fullness at the top edge of the hem can usually be steamed out. The fullness found on A-line or flared hems should be controlled with a line of *easestitching* ¼" (6mm) from the hem edge.

Do the proper hem finish for your particular fabric and garment, and secure the hem using one of the techniques given below.

Hem Finishes

Pinked and Stitched: Use this hem finish on fabrics that don't ravel very much. Straight stitch ¼" (6mm) below the top of the hem and then pink the edge.

Turned and Stitched: Use this finish only on light-weight, woven fabrics. It is too bulky for most other fabrics. This finish is commonly used on washable cottons. Turn under ¼″ (6mm) of the hem edge and edgestitch. If you are working with a sheer fabric, you can eliminate the edgestitching and just baste the fold in place.

Overcast: This finish is used for fabrics that tend to ravel. Straight stitch ¼″ (6mm) from the edge and then overcast by hand or machine.

Bound Hem Finish: Seam binding is used for loosely woven fabrics and washable garments that would be too bulky if the hem edge is turned and stitched. Use ribbon seam binding or stretch lace for straight hems and bias seam binding for flared or curved hems. Pre-shrink the seam binding if you are going to wash the garment or finish with SEAMS GREAT® which is nylon sheer cut on the bias. This gives a soft, flat finish to all hem edges.

Hong Kong Finish: Bulky fabrics that tend to fray can be finished with the elegant Hong Kong finish. This finish is used on elegant silk dresses made in Hong Kong — hence its name. This is a good method to use if the garment is unlined. Cut ¾″ (19mm) wide bias strips of lightweight lining fabric to use

for the binding. Stitch the bias strip to the hem edge with a ⅛″ (3mm) seam, right sides together. Turn the strip over the hem edge to the wrong side. Secure the bias strip by hand or *stitching-in-the-ditch.*

Hem Techniques

There are two basic hemming techniques, the flat finish and the inside hem. The flat finish has the hem edge sewn flat to the garment. The hem is stitched in place with a *blindstitch, catchstitch,* or *slipstitch,* depending on the hem finish.

The other hem technique is referred to as an inside finish. The hem stitches are done between the garment and hem fabric, using either a *catchstitch* or *blindstitch.* This is the method to use with your fine knits and wovens. Because the garment and hem are lightly layered together the hem will never show a ridge on the right side of the garment, and will be invisible on the wrong side.

First of all, let's see how the various flat finishes are done and then go on to the inside finish. Whatever technique used, never pull the hem threads tightly, or else the hem will show on the right side. This is your one chance to get away with sloppy sewing!

Hemming Stitch: Working from right to left, take a stitch in the hem edge and then just catch a thread of the garment, as shown.

Catchstitch: This hem is very strong and is a good choice for children's clothes. It is also quite flexible and can be used on very lightweight, ravelly knits.

Work from left to right, catching just a thread or two of the garment and hem edge.

Slipstitch: This technique is used only on a flat finished hem that has been turned and stitched. Work from right to left. The needle runs along the hem fold, coming out periodically to catch a thread of garment fabric.

Tailor's Hem: The tailor's hem is the inside hem that is used on fine knits and wovens. It makes an invisible hem finish on both sides of the garment.

Pin the top edge of the hem about ½″ (13mm) from the hem edge; place the pins parallel to the hem edge. Fold the hem back as illustrated. Working from left to right, do a catchstitch between the hem and the garment fabric. Insert the needle into the fabric opposite to the direction you are hemming and the threads will cross over each other, locking each stitch. If one stitch breaks, the others will stay in place until you can make repairs.

You can also use a locked, *blindstitch* for the tailor's hem. Pin the hem in place, as directed above, and roll back the hem edge ¼″ (6mm). Working from right to left, catch several threads of the rolled-back hem. Next, insert the needle just behind the thread and take a small stitch that won't show

on the right side of the garment; cross over the thread and insert the needle in the hem fold about ½″ (13mm) to the left.

Double Hem: The double hem is another version of the inside hem. It is used on wide hems of garments that are made of knits or heavy fabrics, wherever a regular hem would sag and pull on the garment. It is also used on wide hems of lightweight fabrics to keep them from spiraling and ballooning out.

Fold up and baste the hem edge, and finish with the proper edge finish. Baste down the center of the hem; turn back the hem along this basting line and *catchstitch* the hem to the garment, as shown. Turn up the rest of the hem and secure as directed for the tailor's hem.

Machine Hems

Hems on fine garments are always done by hand; however, a machine hem is useful for children's or non-dress-up clothes. Machine hems can be done with the machine blind-hem or by topstitching.

Each machine has different settings for the blind-hem. Check your machine manual for blind-hem instructions.

The topstitched hem is quick to do, and adds design interest as well as finishing the edge of the garment. Many casual sports clothes call for topstitched hems, it is a good choice for knits, since you don't have to worry about finishing the hem edge first. A hem finish that is used by the designer Jean Muir, is done as follows.

Mark and press up a 1" (25mm) to 1½" (38mm) hem; finish the hem edge as indicated by the fabric. Topstitch as desired on the right side of the garment. Do one or more rows of stitching, using a matching or contrasting thread. Multiple rows of stitching add firmness to the garment edge, which is desirable on most fabrics.

Topstitched hems can be padded for a different look. Place a strip of polyester fleece between the hem and garment before stitching the hem in place. Cut the fleece so it is ¼" (6mm) narrower than the hem width. The padded hem works best if it is basted together before the final stitching.

Fused Hems

Narrow strips of fusible web can be used to hold hems in place. Cut the strip ¼" (6mm) narrower than the hem, or use pre-cut web strips. Insert the web between the hem and garment, making sure it is just below the hem edge. Follow the manufacturer's instructions for fusing. Fusible web adds body to the hem, which is an advantage on many garments. Always test fuse a hem on a scrap of fabric to see if the fused web will be invisible on the right side. You don't want a glued look or a line or demarcation.

SPECIAL HEMS

The following hems can be used in place of conventional hem finishes. They add design interest to the garment also.

Fake Cuff Hem

This hem finish can be used on both woven and knit fabrics. It gives the appearance of a separate cuff, although it is just a special way of turning and stitching the hem. Use it on short sleeve shirts (it's a perfect finish for long-sleeve shirts with worn-out elbows), the bottom edge of a casual shirt or top, and at the lower edge of pants legs for a "no-trip" cuff, wherever you want a cuff-like finish. The fake cuff hem is also attractive when used across the top of a patch pocket (see page 115).

This hem finish works best on garments with little or no flare at the hem edge. The hem width should be 1¼" (31mm). Allow more if you want a wider cuff finish.

Fold the hem up in position, wrong sides together, and pin. Fold the hem again in the same direction, making a double hem. Stitch ¼" (6mm) from the fold. Unfold the hem, and press from the wrong side. Stitch along the lower edge if desired.

Fake Band Hem

The fake band hem can be used on the sleeves and lower edges of sport shirts and casual knit tops. It gives the appearance of a separate band finish. The hem width should be 1¼" (31mm), or more, if you want the look of a wider band.

Fold up the hem in the finished position, and pin. Turn the folded hem back against the right side of the garment, so that the hem edge is even with the garment fold. Stitch the folded edge on the garment side, with a ⅛" (5mm) seam. If you stitch on the hem side, you will have problems with the cut edge of the narrow seam; it tends to curl up into the presser foot. Unfold the hem and press from the wrong side so that the seam allowance goes up into the garment.

This is a good sleeve finish for a top with a mitered or crossed-over V-neck. Make the band finish the same width as the V-neck band.

Rolled Hem

This hem is ideal for lightweight knits such as polyester interlocks, Qiana® and Nyesta®. It gives a narrow roll finish to the hem edge, which eliminates the "shadowing through" of a regular hem. It also prevents the pulled, drawn look that a regular hem can give to these luxury fabrics. It is a hem finish you will see on many designer clothes, and is very easy to do. Allow a hem width of 1¼" (31mm).

Fold up a 1¼" (31mm) hem, right sides together, and machine stitch ¼" (6mm) from the fold. Unfold the hem and wrap it over the seam allowance to the inside of the garment. Do not press — you want a soft rolled edge.

Finish the back of the hem by folding under the edge ¼" (6mm). Pin the folded edge so that it just meets the stitching line. Make sure the roll is an even width all around the hem. Catch the folded edge just to the stitching threads with a loose backstitch.

The edge can also be finished by *stitching-in-the-ditch*, from the right side. You can either turn under the raw edge ¼" (6mm) or leave it sticking up behind the rolled edge. Shorten your stitch length, and pull the roll down out of the way of the needle so the fold doesn't get caught in the stitching. If you turn under the raw edge, make sure you have it

pulled up high enough so that it becomes caught in the stitching line.

Note: Don't use the rolled hem finish around the lower edge of tuck-in tops. It will show a ridge through your pants or skirts.

EDGE FINISHES

Try some of the following edge finishes on your knit and woven garments. These are a change from the conventional hem and facing, and add interest to the garment. Many of these finishes are the same as are found on expensive ready-to-wear.

The rolled look can be duplicated around a scoop neckline or sleeveless armhole by using a separate strip of self-fabric. It is also the method to use if you want a constrasting color at the bound edge. Use the Chanel trim technique found on page 197, if you want the light look of the rolled edge. Use the bound edge technique if you want a heavier look or are working with lingerie fabric. The bound edge is also a good finish for sheer, swimsuit cover-ups or chiffon dresses.

Bound Edge

Trim away the hem or seam allowance from the edge to be bound. If you are binding a scoop neck, leave one shoulder seam unsewn. Leave the underarm seam unsewn for a sleeveless armhole, and one side seam unsewn if you are doing a hem finish.

Cut a 2" (50mm) wide strip of self or constrasting fabric for the binding piece. Cut it across the stretch for a knit, or on the bias for a woven, or knit with very little stretch.

Fold the strip in half, lengthwise, wrong sides together, and pin the cut edges to the right side of the garment edge. Stitch with a ¼″ (6mm) seam, stretching the trim strip slightly around curves.

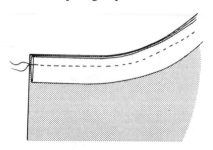

Close the unsewn seam, stitching through the trim, making sure the seam allowances are pressed up into the trim as you stitch across them.

Fold the trim up over the seam to the inside, and pin, making sure the roll is an even width around the entire bound edge. Stitch the folded edge of the trim to the first stitching line with a hand backstitch, or *stitch-in-the-ditch* on the right side. If you stitch-in-the-ditch, pull the folded edge beyond the seam so the machine's stitches will catch it.

HAND STITCH
WRONG SIDE

STITCH-IN-THE-DITCH
RIGHT SIDE

This technique can be done in reverse. Stitch the trim to the wrong side of the garment first, and then turn over to the right side. Topstitch the fold using either a straight stitch or zigzag. This will give you the look that is so popular on T-shirts.

Note: Don't use this finish on the lower edge of tuck-in tops. It will show a ridge through your pants or skirts.

Piping Finish

This edgefinish can be used around sleeveless armholes, scoop or jewel necklines, or even at sleeve and hem edges. Use a matching or contrasting fabric for the trim strip.

Cut the trim strip across the stretch for knits, or on the bias for wovens or non-stretchy knits. The trim strip should be 1″ (25mm) wide.

Trim away the seam or hem allowance of the edge to be piped. Leave one garment seam allowance open.

Fold the trim strip in half, wrong sides together, and pin to the right side of the garment, cut edges even. Stitch with a ¼″ (6mm) seam. This is easy to do if you let the edge of the wide, zigzag foot run along the fabric fold, Fig. 1. Turn the raw edges of the strip to the inside, leaving a narrow fold of fabric extending beyond the garment edge. Press lightly from the wrong side, and close the open garment seam. Press open the seam and hold the piping strip in place by machine stitching ⅛″ (3mm) from the garment fold. Doing the final stitching with a contrasting thread gives a decorative effect, Fig. 2.

FIG. 1

FIG. 2

Lettuce-Edge Finish

This edge finish gives a very delicate, ruffled look. It is suitable only for stretchy knits, such as interlocks, tricots, ribbings and jerseys.

Trim away the entire hem or seam allowance from the edge to be finished, or if you want a firmer edge, leave a ⅜″ (9mm) hem allowance. Try both ways on a scrap of your fashion fabric to see which method gives you the desired look.

Set your machine for a narrow to medium wide zigzag, with a short stitch length. The exact stitch combination can be adjusted to your liking on the test scrap.

Stitch along the cut or folded garment edge while stretching the fabric. Hold the fabric in front of and behind the presser foot. Don't stretch so hard that you cause your fabric to run. Different fabrics stretch different amounts, and this will influence the look of the finished edge. Fabrics that have lots of stretch will ruffle more than less stretchy fabrics.

The lettuce-edge is an excellent finish for tricot. It makes a lovely ruffled edge that is most attractive around the bottom edge of nightgowns and peignoirs. Use it around necklines and sleeve and hem edges of dresses and tops, and the bottom edge of pajama-type pants. It can also be used on the edge of ribbing that is being applied to the neckline and sleeve of a T-shirt. Just cut the ribbing half the regular width, lettuce-edge one side and apply to the garment.

Satin-Stitched Edge Finish

The satin-stitched edge finish is now showing up on designer's fashions. It is quick and easy to do, and gives the garment an unusual touch. It is most suitable for wool flannels, gabardines, and double knits. You do not want this edge to ripple, like the lettuce-edge, so test stitch a scrap of your fashion fabric before you decide on this finish to see if it will be satisfactory.

The satin-stitched edge finish can be used at hem edges, sleeveless armholes, necklines, and collar and pocket edges. Experiment with it for other applications.

Turn under the hem or seam allowance and zigzag along the folded edge. Adjust the stitch so it is about 1/8" (3mm) wide, and quite close together. Miter corners and points for a neat finish. *Easestitch* curves to help them turn under neatly. Re-stitch along the edge so you build up a nice satin-stitch look. Trim the seam or hem allowance close to the stitching, being careful not to cut the stitches. Steam press to remove any ripples.

Chanel Trim

Chanel trim is a matching or contrasting strip of fabric used to bind the edges of a garment. It gets its name from the famous French designer, Coco Chanel, who used it extensively on her suits. This technique can be used on both knits and woven fabrics. The initial trim application is the same for both types of fabrics, but the finishing is slightly different.

Trim away all seam or hem allowances from the garment edge that is to be bound. If the edge is faced, i.e. jacket fronts, pin the facing to the garment, wrong sides together, and trim its seam or hem allowance also. Leave one seam unsewn when applying this trim to the garment. The seam will be closed after the trim has been stitched in place, but before it is turned and finished.

Cut the trim from the desired fabric, across the stretch for knits and on the bias for wovens and firm knits. The width of the trim strip should be four times the width of the finished trim.

Apply the trim to the cut edge of the garment, right sides together, cut edges even. Stitch with the desired seam width. The width of the finished trim will be the same as the initial seam width. It can be 1/4" (6mm) to 1" (25mm) wide. Stitch accurately so that the finished trim will be even.

Press the trim out over the seam allowance and close the unsewn seam. Trim the seam allowance and turn the trim to the inside of the garment. Catch in place using one of the methods given below.

TRIM

Knit Fabrics: Secure the trim by *stitching-in-the-ditch,* on the right side. Use a short stitch length, so the machine feeds slowly; this also helps the stitches bury down in the fabric. Trim away the excess seam allowance close to the stitching.

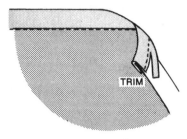

Woven Fabrics: Turn under the trim strip, on the wrong side, so the fold just covers the stitching; *slip-stitch* in place.

When applying Chanel trim around curves, stretch the trim slightly around inside (neckline, armhole) curves and ease it around outside (rounded corners of jacket fronts — patch pockets) curves. This makes the trim lie flat and neat in those areas.

BELT LOOPS

Many garments require belt loops. They can be basic, straight loops, or shaped loops. Basic loops are applied to the garment before the waistband is stitched in place. Shaped loops are applied after the waistband has been completed.

Basic Belt Loops

Cut a lengthwise strip of fabric, three times as wide as the finished loop. Use the selvage edge for one side of the belt loop strip.

Fold the loop strip, as shown, and stitch along each edge.

Cut the strip to even lengths, twice the length of the finished loop. Pin the strips to the waist of the garment, before the waistband is stitched in place.

Apply the waistband and stitch the belt loops to the garment below the waistband. Place the stitching so the finished loop will be wide enough to allow the belt to slip through easily.

Fold under the end of the belt loop and stitch to the top edge of the waistband. Backstitch for strength. Trim away any excess loop fabric.

Shaped Belt Loops

Shaped belt loops are applied after the waistband has been completed. The top edge is folded under and stitched to the top of the waistband. The bottom edge is topstitched in place below the waistband, leaving enough room for the belt.

Shaped, western belt loops are very popular on men's and women's clothing. A pattern is given in the back of the book for an easy version of the Western belt loop. Use the following instructions for construction.

Fold the belt loop piece right sides together, and stitch a narrow seam across the bottom. Stitch the side to the dot, Fig. 1. Turn to the right side, push out the point, and fold the lower end as illustrated, Fig. 2.

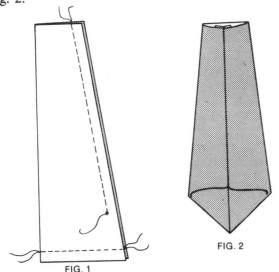

FIG. 1

FIG. 2

Stitch in place as directed above.

Support the ends of belt loops that are stitched to just a single layer of fabric by placing an extra piece of fabric behind them, on the wrong side of the garment. Stitch through all the layers.

SEWING TIPS

Hems that have to be let down usually leave a crease. A half and half solution of white vinegar and water helps remove the crease. Apply the solution to a pressing cloth and steam press.

Pleated garments will keep a sharper look at the hem edge if you edgestitch the back of each pleat on the wrong side, the length of the hem.

Never use the turned and stitched method of hem finish for knits. It is too bulky and not at all necessary, since knits don't fray. Never use seam binding on knits either. This will make a hem ridge show on the right side. The *tailor's hem* or some form of a topstitched hem is the best method to use.

Stretchy knits, such as stretch terry and velour, should have the edge finished with a big zigzag before they are hemmed. In order to keep the edge from stretching out of shape when zigzagging, use the following technique:

Attach a thread to a garment seam right at the hem edge by wrapping it around the pin, as shown. Leaving the thread attached to the spool, hold the thread taut along the edge of the fabric and zigzag over it. This keeps the hem edge from stretching out of shape. Remove the pin and pull the thread away after stitching.

Place a fine cotton cord along the inside fold of the hem on fine wool garments. This softens the hem edge for a nicer look. Hold the cord in place with large running stitches.

Do not use a machine blind-hem on pile fabrics such as corduroy, velour, or velvet. The needle tends to pick threads out of the fabric, leaving visible marks or holes on the right side.

Never use a double thread when hemming. You may think you are making it stronger; however, if you ever catch your heel in the hem, the thread will hold, but the stitch may pull out of the garment, leaving a hole.

When hand finishing Chanel trim or other bound edges, insert the needle under the threads of the first stitching line instead of in the garment fabric. The stitching will not show on the right side, and the machine stitching line will be covered on the wrong side.

NOTES

ULTRA SUEDE® FABRIC

ULTRA SUEDE® FABRIC

Although the following instructions are for Ultra Suede® fabric they can also be used for real leather and other synthetic suede fabrics, such as Amara, and Suede 21, that can utilize the flat method of construction.

Ultra Suede fabric is easy to sew! Yes, that's really true! It's easier to use than most woven fabrics and lots of knits. One of the most luxurious fabrics available today, it is used extensively in high-fashion clothes by top name designers.

Why don't more people sew it at home? For one thing, it is quite expensive — $50 per yard — and most home sewers are afraid of making a mistake on such an expensive fabric. However, as soon as you read through these instructions, you will see that Ultra Suede fabric really is easy to sew, and those designer clothes that you have dreamed about can easily be yours at a fraction of their cost.

WHAT IS ULTRA SUEDE FABRIC?

Ultra Suede fabric is a non-woven fabric made from 60% polyester and 40% non-fibrous polyurethane. It does not have a lengthwise or crosswise grain, but it does have an up and down nap. It has all the advantages of real suede leather and none of the disadvantages.

It is completely machine washable and dryable and does not shrink. Washing makes the fabric softer and helps eliminate the "rustling sound" that it has when new. Wash in warm water and dry at medium heat, being careful not to overdry. Remove the fabric from the dryer immediately for best results. It is not necessary to pre-shrink this fabric.

Ultra Suede fabric can be dry cleaned if you prefer but it isn't at all necessary. Why make your fashion garment that much more expensive with added cleaning bills if you don't have to? This is one of the fabric's big advantages over real suede. Note: While washing softens the fabric, dry cleaning preserves the original firm hand. If you want to retain a more crisp look, dry cleaning is the answer. Most ready-to-wear Ultra Suede fabric garments are marked dry clean only. This is usually because non-washable linings and bindings have been used in the construction, not because the fabric is not washable.

Garments made from Ultra Suede fabric will not shrink, ravel, pill, peel, lose their nap, or crock (meaning the color doesn't rub off as with real suede). It is wrinkle proof and lightweight, making it ideal for travel. You won't feel "worn out" wearing an Ultra Suede fabric coat or jacket as you will with heavier, real suede garments.

Ultra Suede fabric is warm like a sweater, and it does breathe. You won't perspire in it as you will when wearing other fake leathers. It acts like a wind breaker — the same as real leather — so even though it is lightweight, it can be quite warm on a cool breeze day.

Jackets and coats made from the fabric are great for outerwear. A light-colored Ultra Suede fabric trench coat is a very practical item because it is so versatile and can be machine-washed and dried whenever needed. Outerwear garments can be made water repellant by spraying with Scotch-gard®. This treatment also makes the lighter colors of suede somewhat dirt repellant.

Ultra Suede fabric doesn't water spot or stiffen when wet so you can spot-clean stains on any garment and not have to worry about left-over cleaning marks.

One word of caution — all synthetic suede fabric burns easily. A dropped cigarette ash can immediately leave a permanent mark or hole. Rubbing dry, white scouring powder on the spot can sometimes remove the burn mark if it isn't too deep. Smokers, please be careful, and non-smokers, watch out for careless smokers at crowded parties.

BEFORE YOU BEGIN

Now that you know some of the facts about Ultra Suede® fabric and are excited about this luxurious fabric, you should be ready to begin your own "Designer Fashion." But, before you rush out and buy your favorite shade, please **read through the rest of these instructions.** Some planning has to be done before you select the pattern and buy the fabric. Since Ultra Suede fabric does involve a sizeable investment, you should prepare yourself well in its cutting and stitching techniques. As was previously mentioned, Ultra Suede fabric is easy to sew, but it is different from woven fabrics, and you should be well aware of the new methods before you begin.

SELECTING PATTERNS

Ultra Suede fabric looks best in jackets, vests and coats, and, of course, the traditional shirtwaist dress made so famous by Halston. It does not drape or ease well, so avoid patterns with close-fitting curves, lots of gathers or pleats and eased seams. Remember, Ultra Suede fabric is similar to leather, and garments that are casual and loose fitting, with tailored lines, look best. Styles calling for topstitching show the fabric to best advantage. Choose patterns with yokes, patch pockets and flaps, and extensive topstitching detail.

There are some patterns available today that are designed for leather or leather-like fabrics. These have the lines that look best with suede-like fabric. You

will find that the ease in the sleeve cap is less than normal, so the sleeve can be stitched into the armhole without any puckers.

Whether you use one of the leather-adapted patterns or a regular pattern, it is suggested that you make up a trial garment first so that any pattern alterations can be done before the fabric is cut. It is not practical to alter your garment after it has been cut and sewn due to some of the types of seam construction.

A heavy muslin can be used for the trial garment, but it's more fun to pick up a denim remnant to use. Denim is good for this purpose because it has the same drape and ease characteristics of the Ultra Suede fabric, and you will get a true picture of the fit and any construction problems you will have with the suede. Of course, a denim trial garment will cost a bit more, but with a little more work you will have a wearable garment instead of just a muslin shell that you will throw away.

Things to look for when making the trial garment are length in sleeve and body, general overall fit, and suitability of the style. It's a lot easier to decide that you don't like a $6 or $8 denim jacket than it is to reject a $80 to $100 Ultra Suede fabric jacket.

SEAM VARIATIONS

Look at ready-to-wear Ultra Suede fabric garments and you will notice different seam types used. Manufacturers use the conventional, topstitched, flat, and slot seams and you have the same options. Your choice will be governed by the desired finished look. Some garments are made using one seam method exclusively, while others are made with a combination of two seam types. For example, we saw a beautiful man's sport coat, by Halston, that was made with the conventional seam method except for the lapel, collar edges and pocket flaps. These were finished with just the cut edges top-stitched together. This coat was also fully lined and was truly an elegant garment.

While all seam types work, we have found through experience that the flat method gives a smoother more leather-like look to the garment and saves you fabric in the pattern layout. The conventional seam is the one we recommend for armholes and can also be used for other seams except some method must be used to keep the seam pressed open flat if you are going to wash and dry the finished garment. We do not recommend conventional seam techniques for faced edges such as lapels, pocket flaps, etc. The edge will be quite bulky and tend to ripple after machine washable and drying. Read through the section on Seams to get more information on the various techniques.

YARDAGE REQUIREMENTS

Always check the amount of fabric needed before purchasing your Ultra Suede fabric. Yardage requirements given on pattern envelopes are usually more than actually required, and with the fabric being so expensive it doesn't make sense to buy more than you need. For example, a trench coat made from a Vogue pattern called for 4⅜ yards (3.9m) of 45″ (115cm) fabric with a nap layout. The actual garment needed only 3¼ yards (2.9m) when the flat method of seam construction was used. The pattern wasn't shortened, so you can see how much fabric was saved. At $50 per yard that is quite a savings.

After you have completed your trial garment, made any pattern alterations, and decided on the seam method, you should then layout the pattern pieces on a marked cutting board or another piece of 45″ (115cm) wide fabric. Follow the layout tips given on page 213 to help position the pattern pieces and save fabric. Measure exactly how much fabric is needed and then go to the store to purchase your Ultra Suede fabric.

SEWING NOTIONS

You don't have to use lots of special sewing notions when working with Ultra Suede fabric. However, we would like to review your usual sewing equipment, with some comments on a few items that can make construction easier.

SCISSORS
A good pair of sharp scissors is a must for cutting so that you get smooth rather than jagged edges. This is especially important when using the flat seam method since the cut edge is visible on top of the garment. Long, sharp, bent-handled shears will enable you to make smooth, long strokes for straight cuts. A pair of 6″ (15cm) trimming shears is useful for the many trimming jobs involved with Ultra Suede® fabric. Applique scissors make it easy to trim the underside of lapped seams without having to worry about cutting the garment.

PINS
Pins can be used without leaving holes as they do in real leather. Use sharp, dressmaker pins. The extra long pins (1½″-38mm) with the large heads are excellent, as they can be pushed into the fabric much more easily than the small, metal headed pins. Regular pins will soon make your fingers feel as though they have holes in them.

A word of caution about pins. While you can use dressmaker pins in your Ultra Suede fabric with no left-over pin holes, this doesn't hold true for decorative pins or the pins used on the back of convention badges. Their large size will put holes in your garment.

THIMBLE
A good fitting thimble should be used to protect your finger. If you are one of the many who say they have never been able to use a thimble, you will become an immediate convert. Ultra Suede fabric is resistant to hand needles, and you need the help of a thimble to push the needle through.

MACHINE NEEDLES
Use a size 11/75 or 12/80 machine needle when sewing. If you use topstitching thread, you will have to go to a larger needle, probably a size 16/100.

Occasionally you may have some trouble with skipped stitches. Try using a needle one size larger or one of the *Universal needles* now on the market. Sometimes changing from one brand of thread to another will solve the problem. Increasing the pressure on the presser foot and/or using the straight-stitch throat plate with the small hole can also help.

Do not use leather machine needles.

HAND NEEDLES
Use fine hand needles when basting. As we mentioned above, a thimble is a must.

There are fine leather needles available at most notions counters which penetrate Ultra Suede fabric much more easily than regular needles because they have a fine, sharp wedge at the point. These needles will really save your fingers. If you buy leather needles in a package of assorted sizes, use just the fine ones on your garment. The larger ones may leave marks in the fabric.

THREAD

Use polyester thread when sewing. It has good tensile strength. Regular size thread can be used for the flat seam method as well as the conventional seam method. Some of you may prefer to use topstitching thread for flat seams because of the heavier look it gives. That is fine if your machine can handle it, but there are some machines that just can't make good seams with this heavier thread. Make some seam samples using 4 to 6 layers of Ultra Suede fabric before beginning your garment to see how it it going to stitch. Sometimes topstitching thread will work on 2 layers of fabric but will balk at the thicker seams found at the neck, collar, pockets and flaps. You may have to decrease the bobbin tension when using this thread for both the top and bobbin thread. Ultra Suede fabric tends to grab the needle as it goes through the fabric, thereby throwing off the timing and causing skipped stitches and looping underneath. Don't be too concerned if you can't get good results with topstitching thread. Regular thread looks just fine on Ultra Suede fabric and works a lot easier.

IRON

Do not allow a bare iron to touch the Ultra Suede fabric. You will end up with an "iron mark." Always use a pressing cloth. Always test iron and press cloth on a scrap of fabric to be sure iron is not too hot and press cloth too thin. Product Note: June Tailor's Moisture Control Press Cloth is excellent.

A *Seamstress®* is excellent for applying fusible interfacing and pressing seams as well as for applying fusible web for hems. Only a seamstress can be used on the right side of the fabric and no press cloth is needed.

RULERS

A plastic "see through" ruler is a great help for the exact marking of seam allowances. The best kind to use is 2″ (5cm) wide and 18″ (45cm) long. It has red grid lines at ⅛″ (3mm) intervals over the entire surface of the ruler.

SEWING TAPES

Double faced basting tape can be used during garment construction when making conventional seams instead of hand basting. Care must be taken in positioning the tape so it isn't in the stitching line.

Disappearing Basting Tape is a new product that can be stitched through and disappears in the first washing. It's also excellent to eliminate "drag" when top stitching. We prefer the 1/8″ width.

GLUE STICK

A glue stick, available at art supply stores and many fabric stores, is a must when using the flat method of seam construction. This water soluble glue makes basting the seams quick and easy and even allows you to do some simple fitting with glued rather than stitched seams — great for fitting skirts. Product Note: We have found that Dennison's Glue Stick, Fantastic, Collins, or Talon Glue Stick to be the best glue sticks when working with Ultra Suede fabric. Other brands are available but they don't seem to be sticky enough for this napped fabric.

LIQUID GLUE

Do not use liquid fabric glue on Ultra Suede fabric. It is not water soluble and will leave a permanent mark if you happen to get it on the right side of the garment.

MARKING THE FABRIC

Construction marks should be transferred to the fabric wherever possible. Notches can be marked with small clips (never snip deeper than the notch) when seam allowances are left intact. Notches should be marked with a soft pencil or chalk on the wrong side when the flat seam method is used. A sliver of hand soap can be used to mark construction marks on the right side of the fabric.

Other construction marks should be marked on the wrong side of the fabric and transferred to the right side of the garment by running a threaded needle through the mark and leaving a long thread in the fabric.

When using the flat method of seam construction seamlines can be marked on the right side of the underneath layer with pins, Disappearing Basting Tape, or a sliver of soap.

WATER ERASABLE MARKING PEN

Another marking method suitable for this fabric is the water erasable marking pen. Marks put on either the right or wrong side of the fabric can be easily removed with a drop of clear water. The purple ink, air erasable pen fades automatically within 48 hours. So be sure to sew the seam before it disappears!

SEAMS

All Ultra Suede fabric seams must be basted together in some manner before they are machine stitched in order to prevent "creeping" of the top layer of fabric. This can be done by hand basting or use a glue stick or Disappearing Basting Tape.

Conventional Seams

If you choose to use conventional seams, you must be careful that the seams don't look bulky and unpressed when you finish. Special care must be taken to make all seams flat. Follow the instructions below to help you achieve this look.

Stitching Seams: Use one of the following methods when making conventional seams.

#1 Hand baste the seam together just inside the seamline. Machine stitch, holding the fabric taut. Remove the basting after the stitching has been completed.

#2 Tape-base the two layers of fabric together using Disappearing Basting Tape. Place the tape between the two layers of fabric about 1/8" (3 mm) short of the seamline so that it will not be caught in the stitching. Machine stitch the seam, holding the fabric taut. If you do stitch into the tape, never fear — it doesn't gum up the needle and disappears after the first washing.

Finishing Seams: Ultra Suede® fabric will not hold a press through washing; therefore, it is impossible to press open a conventional seam and have it stay flat without some sort of help. This help is provided by fusible web or topstitching. We have seen some ready-made garments with just plain, pressed-open seams that looked very flat, and it made us wonder about the pressing problem. Perhaps the garment industry used some technique that we didn't know about. We decided to experiment a bit with some seam samples and found the following:

#1 It is possible to get very flat seams if you steam them open and then pound them with a *clapper*. Use a firm surface under the seam, rather than the padded ironing board, when pounding. A child's wooden block is ideal for this.

#2 These seams will not stay pressed flat through the washing and drying process. They will have to be steamed and pounded open after each washing. Sounds like a lot of work, doesn't it? Maybe it would be better to send the garment to the dry cleaners, and let him worry about it.

We have been unable to find a way of keeping these conventional seams pressed open without help, so we suggest that you use one of the following techniques.

#1 Place ¼" (6mm) strips of fusible web under each seam allowance and fuse so that they stay flat.

#2 Press both seam allowances to one side and topstitch through all layers. Stitch ¼" (6mm) from the seamline, ⅛" (3mm) from the seamline or do two rows of topstitching, as shown.

#3 Press open the seam allowance and then topstitch ⅛" (3mm) from the seam on both sides.

Flat Seams

The flat method of seam construction gives a flat, "leather-like" look to your garment. It is very attractive and is the method used frequently on Designer clothes. This method makes it easy to get that professional look with your first Ultra Suede® fabric garment, and it is also the fastest method of construction.

The flat seam is made by trimming away the entire seam allowance from one side of the garment piece and then overlapping the trimmed garment edge over the untrimmed seam allowance until the trimmed edge lines up exactly with the seamline. It is then hand, tape, or glue basted and stitched with two rows of topstitching. The seam line on the under layer of fabric can be marked using one of the methods given on page 207.

Stitching Seams: Use one of the following methods when making flat seams.

#1 Hand Basted Seams: Baste the seams together approximately ⅛" (3mm) from the cut edge. Position the basting stitches so that they won't be caught in the machine stitching. Do the first row of machine topstitching just slightly in from the cut edge, holding the fabric taut. Make the second row of stitching ¼" (6mm) away from the first, remembering to stitch in the same direction. Remove basting, and trim away the excess seam allowance from the wrong side. Holding the scissors at an angle to the fabric will make the trimming job easier.

#2 Tape Basted Seams: Place a strip of double-faced basting tape between the layers of the flat seam so that it is ⅛" (3mm) back from the top cut edge. Do the first row of topstitching just slightly in from the cut edge. Remember to hold the fabric taut. Carefully remove the tape. Make the second row of topstitching ¼" (6mm) away from the first. Trim away excess seam allowance from the wrong side of the garment.

#3 Use Disappearing Basting Tape that can be stitched through and disappears in the first washing.

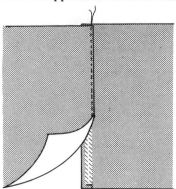

#4 Glue Basted Seams: Apply a glue stick to the wrong side of the fabric edge that has been trimmed. Keep the application about ¼" (6mm) wide. Overlap the trimmed and glued edge to meet the seamline of the other garment piece and finger press in place. Secure the seam with two rows of topstitching sewn in the same direction. Turn the garment to the wrong side and trim away the excess seam allowance. The narrow glue application will make this procedure easy because the under-edge will not be glued down. Wide glue application gives problems because you have to pull the fabric layers apart before you can trim.

When sewing multiple rows of topstitching on your garment, it is absolutely necessary to stitch each row from the same direction. Otherwise, the layers of fabric will "drag" against each other, causing ripples between the rows of stitching.

Flat Seam II

This is an alternate flat seam technique that is used when putting in a center-slot zipper (see zipper instructions page 236), or when stitching darts. Use the following procedure for making this type of flat seam.

Cut a 1" (25mm) wide strip of suede fabric as long as the seam or dart to be stitched.

Position the suede strip under the garment pieces so that the trimmed edges of the seam or dart butt together in the center of the strip.

Baste the seams together using one of the methods given in the previous flat seam section.

Make two rows of topstitching on both sides of the seam, making sure that all rows are stitched from the same direction.

Since Ultra Suede® fabric will not hold a press, the above lapped seam is good to use on the front and back pants crease. Just cut your pattern apart on the front and back crease line and use the resulting four pattern pieces to cut the fabric.

Cut a 1" (25mm) wide strip of fabric that is long enough to go along each seam, and stitch the pant legs back together using the above technique. You will always have a sharp crease down your pant legs.

STITCHING TIPS

Sew with a slightly longer stitch length than usual — 9 stitches to the inch or a stitch length of 3.5mm. Short stitches will weaken the fabric, and the stitch length tends to shorten when sewing Ultra Suede® fabric. This problem can be solved by learning to stitch under tension (no, not you — the fabric). Hold the fabric in front of and behind the presser foot and keep it taut while stitching. Don't pull the fabric through the machine — just hold it with a slight tension so that it will feed evenly.

Multiple rows of stitching and all stitching on bands, cuffs, and belts must be sewn in the same direction because of the creeping problem.

Accurate topstitching is important for that professional touch. Done badly, it can ruin the look of the whole garment, and you can't afford that. Use your machine presser foot as a guide for even top-stitching. The outside edge of most wide, zigzag feet is ¼" (6mm) from the needle. The inside edge of the right toe can also be used as an edge-stitching guide. Make some sample seams with your presser foot and see if it gives the measurements you need.

The *seam guide* on the throat plate of your machine can be used for wider lines of topstitching. If your machine does not have a seam guide, then make your own with a strip of wide adhesive tape placed to the right of the needle. Measure from the needle and mark the desired measurements on the tape. See page 26.

The top layer of waistbands, front bands, and cuffs will tend to push ahead of the bottom layers even though you have basted everything together. This can be controlled by slipping a piece of fusible web between the layers just before you do the top-stitching. Fuse the layers together remembering to use a press cloth if you are using a conventional iron. This eliminates the creeping problem and also adds a bit of stiffness to these detail areas, usually eliminating the need for interfacing.

You may backstitch topstitched seams when using regular thread, or you may prefer to *lockstitch* the ends of seams. Some people prefer to tie thread ends. Never backstitch when using topstitching thread. Pull both threads to the wrong side and tie off in a square knot; leave 3" (7.6cm) thread ends, thread through a hand needle and weave the threads ends in between the garment and the facing fabric.

Topstitching Tip: When topstitching across thick seams (such as where the collar joins the neck) the machine tends to shorten the stitch length as it approaches the seam. Prevent this problem by following these steps: stop the machine when the front of the presser foot reaches the seam; lift the presser foot and place a folded strip of fabric or cardboard the same thickness as the garment under the presser foot, so that it becomes level with the thick part of the garment. Continue stitching until

you have gone over the hump and then remove your "helper."

INTERFACING

Interfacing is optional. If you want a soft look, don't use any. If you want a more structured look, use a fusible interfacing. Non-woven fusible inter-facing works beautifully with Ultra Suede® fabric. It does not have to be pre-shrunk. Just remember not to use too heavy of an interfacing otherwise your garment will look too stiff. Woven fusible interfacing can also be used, but it must be pre-shrunk before being applied to the fabric. Sub-merge woven fusibles in a basin of hot water, let stand 10 minutes, and then spread flat or hang over the line to drip-dry. Do not pre-shrink in the machine or dry in the dryer. This will cause the fusible material to fall off.

Always test-fuse a piece of the interfacing to a piece of your fabric before applying it to the garment pieces themselves. Wash and dry the sample to make sure that the bond is strong and the inter-facing doesn't pucker. Carefully follow the fusing instructions that come with your interfacing. A *Steamstress®* iron is useful here and will help you get a good bond.

Fuse the interfacing to the wrong side of the part of the garment that shows, i.e., the under collar and the lapel facing, the upper cuff and the upper pocket flap. Use caution when applying interfacing to just part of a garment piece. A visible line of demarcation may show on the right side where the interfacing ends and the garment fabric continues. This is more apt to happen with light rather than dark colors.

Do not include interfacing in the seam allowances. Trim off an extra ⅛″ (3mm) when using interfacing on garment pieces that have had the seam allowances removed so that a line of interfacing doesn't peak out between the two layers of fabric.

Trim the interfacing for the under collar only so that it is ¼″ (6mm) smaller than the finished size of the collar around all edges so you won't have problems with peek-a-boo interfacing after the collar has been applied to the neck edge, rolled into position and stitched.

One-piece collars can have an extra piece of interfacing added just below the roll line of the under collar, if desired. This gives more support to the collar stand. If you want a really firm collar finish apply interfacing to the upper collar as well.

EXTRA INTERFACING

Collar patterns that have a separate band should have both layers of the band interfaced. This gives the extra support needed in this area.

Lapels tend not to lie flat when the facing piece is completely interfaced with a fusible. This problem can be solved by slashing the interfacing along the roll line, after you have fuse-basted it in several places; then complete the fusing process. Taping the roll line, as is done in other tailored garments, is not necessary with Ultra Suede® fabric.

SLASH

Another technique which can be used for turn-back lapels is to divide the interfacing at the roll line and apply it to the garment front and facing as shown. The interfacing should stop ⅛″ (3mm) short of the roll line on each garment piece.

To give additional stability to the chest area of a man's jacket you can fuse interfacing to the garment front as well as the front facing. Cut the interfacing so it goes just to the first dart and then curves into the armscye as shown. Any line of demarcation left by the edge of the interfacing will be masked by the front dart and the patch pocket. If you prefer, you can fuse interfacing to the entire front of the garment, just remember to trim the interfacing from the dart areas and slash it along the roll line. Woman's jacket doesn't need interfacing on the jacket front — only on the facing.

Whether interfacing the garment or not, always back buttonholes with a square of woven interfacing or lining fabric in the same color as the garment. It is best to use a piece of matching lining fabric so that a white line of interfacing will not be visible in the buttonhole opening. Woven fabric will keep horizontal buttonholes from rippling or stretching. Non-woven interfacing is ineffective.

If you are unable to find a color-matched lining or interfacing fabric, camouflage the white in the buttonhole cut with a colored pen or pencil.

LINING

To line, or not to line, that is the question. Ready-made Ultra Suede® fabric garments show a lack of uniformity in lining practices. Some Designer Fashions are fully lined, some are just partially lined, and some have no lining at all. In light of this confused state of affairs, we would like to give you some lining guidelines based on our experience of working with and wearing this luxury fabric.

Ultra Suede fabric is napped on both sides. While this doesn't present a problem in dresses and skirts, it does make putting on jackets, coats and vests somewhat difficult. You will really get "hung up" if you try to pull on an unlined Ultra Suede fabric jacket over a sweater. Linings will solve this problem for you and make your garment so much more comfortable to wear.

Ultra Suede fabric will show wear at points of strain (around collars, at elbows, and across shoulders) and where it is subjected to repeated chaffing (in underarm and crotch areas). Lining will strengthen these parts and prolong the life of the garment. Linings also cover up inside construction details such as welt pockets and darts on blazer-type jackets and men's sport coats.

After considering all the above observations, we definitely feel that linings (full or partial) should be used in Ultra Suede fabric coats, jackets and vests. Why some Designers line and others don't we can't explain, but your garment will be more comfortable to wear and more attractive if you take the time to add some lining. Also, when you consider the cost of your garment, it just makes sense to add lining if that means extending the life of your expensive investment. Follow the suggestions below for linings:

Full linings are recommended for coats and jackets having inside construction details that are best covered up, i.e., darts and set-in pockets.

Full linings can be used wherever desired for appearance's sake.

Vests should be fully lined for comfort. Ultra Suede fabric vests in better stores have just the fronts cut from suede. This type of vest is designed to be worn under jackets. The lining back allows the jacket to slip easily over the vest.

Ultra Suede fabric can be used for the back of vests that are to be worn without a jacket.

Partial linings, consisting of the upper back and sleeve lining, can be used on jackets for both men and women. Jackets with front and/or back yokes are especially adaptable to partial linings because only the yokes are lined, and the yoke seams are neatly covered by the lining.

Ultra Suede fabric pants are more comfortable if they are lined, and the lining will prolong the life of the garment. Unlined, snug pants will split out at the seat. Make a full length "drop lining" (attached only at the waist and zipper), using the pants pattern to cut the lining pieces. Or you can just make a short lining that extends only a couple of inches below the crotch.

All jacket and coat sleeves should be lined for comfort and strength. Elbows will soon wear through unlined sleeves if the garment is worn often. If this happens, you can save the garment by adding hunting patches to the elbow area in a matching or contrasting color of Ultra Suede fabric.

The area at the top of the shoulder where a woman places the strap of her shoulder bag will show wear after a period of time. Carry a different bag or hold the strap in your hand when wearing your Ultra Suede fabric garment in order to prevent this.

Lining Fabrics

Fabrics suitable for lining Ultra Suede fabric garments are lightweight polyester lining fabrics that are machine washable and dryable. Look for something that has a fairly slick surface so that it will slide over your other clothes easily. Lining fabrics should be pre-shrunk before cutting.

Some suggested fabrics are: a la creme, Caio, some of the pretty printed Ultressas and even woven, lightweight Qianas.

CUTTING THE FABRIC

The method of seam construction that you use on your Ultra Suede® fabric garment will influence the amount of fabric needed and the pattern layout. The lapped seam method uses less fabric than the conventional seam method because seam allowances are removed from some sections of the pattern. This enables you to place the pattern pieces closer together on the fabric.

You should buy your pattern and make up the trial garment even before you buy your fabric so that you will have all the length alterations done and will have decided on the method of seam construction. If you are going to use the flat seam method, you should fold the affected seam allowance out of the way and make a trial layout on your cutting board or another piece of 45″ (115cm) wide fabric. This will give you an accurate measurement for your yardage and will probably save you quite a bit of money.

General Cutting Tips

Whether you choose the flat or conventional seam method, all pattern pieces should be placed on the fabric so that the tops face the same direction. (nap layout). If you cut with the nap running up the pattern pieces, you will get a richer color. If the nap runs down, it will give a lighter, glossy look. The choice is yours—just make sure your placement of the pattern pieces is consistent. After repeated washings the nap direction seems to disappear, but initially there is quite a difference. You can "cheat" a bit on the nap with small pattern pieces. These can be tilted off grain if necessary in order to get a better fit on the fabric.

Ultra Suede fabric can be cut double. Fold the fabric wrong side out and pin the pattern pieces in position. Mark the wrong side of each cut piece with a strip of drafting tape, soap, chalk, or soft pencil immediately after it has been cut to help you in the construction process. Position the tape strips so that they will not be caught in any machine stitching.

Mark garment pieces that have not had the seam allowance trimmed with small clips at the seamline on each end of the seamline. These clips will re-

mind you of what has or hasn't been trimmed when you put the garment together.

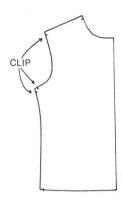

Bias markings on pattern pieces can be ignored. This is a big fabric saver. Place bias pattern pieces on the cross-grain to give them a bit of stretch.

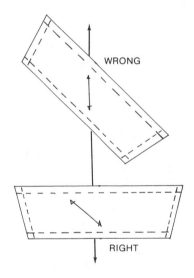

Cut all collar and cuffs on the cross-grain so they will match the nap of the rest of the garment. Positioning all pattern pieces on the fabric with the printing running in the same direction will give you the correct layout.

Waistbands should be cut on the cross-grain whenever possible. Some men's jacket patterns, calling for a waistband finish, will be too large to cut the band crosswise. You will have to piece the band at the side seams or cut the band lengthwise on the fabric. Belts should be cut lengthwise if they are longer than 45″ (115cm). Always cut long lengthwise pattern pieces first so that you will know how much fabric you have left for the other pieces.

Sleeve and garment lengths should be adjusted before pinning the pattern to the fabric. (That's what the trial garment is for.) Trim hem allowances to ¾" (19mm). If you are going to make a conventional hem, the allowance will just be turned up and stitched or fused in place. If you are going to make a faced hem you should fold up the entire hem allowance before pinning the pattern to the fabric. Then cut ¾" (19mm) wide strips of suede fabric to face the hem edges. If the hem edge is curved, the facing strips must be cut following the same curve. Make sure you allow for enough fabric to cut the facing strips. Hem widths for garments that are going to be fully lined should be 1¼" (31mm) wide. Dress and shirt hems can be left at 2" (50mm) and hand stitched using a blind tailor's hem.

Flat Seam Cutting Tips

When using the flat seam method, fold back the affected seam allowances on the pattern pieces before you pin them to the fabric. Figuring out what is going to lap over what is somewhat like working a puzzle, but it is fun to do and isn't difficult if you follow the guides given below. A good rule to follow when figuring this out is to trim away the seam allowance of the pattern piece on which you will do the topstitching. Note: When pattern pieces show a topstitching line, that seam allowance is the one to be eliminated. Generally, it doesn't matter how you lap the seams, just be consistent within the garment.

Back shoulder seams are usually lapped over front shoulder seams. Trim away the back shoulder seam

allowances. If the back shoulder seam includes a dart you may prefer to lap front over back.

Yoke seams are always lapped over the body of the garment. Trim away the yoke seam allowances.

FRONT YOKE

BACK YOKE

Side seams are usually lapped front over back. Trim away the side seam allowances on the front pattern pieces.

Garments with underarm bust darts should usually have the back side seam trimmed so that you can lap back over front. This will hide the multiple layers of fabric at the end of the dart. However, if there is a side pocket in a seam you must lap front over back.

Garments with front and/or back panels should have the seams lap front over back at each seam line. Trim away the seam allowances from the seam line closest to the front of the garment.

Waistbands, front bands and cuffs overlap the body of the garment. Their cut edges are top-stitched together rather than conventionally stitched and turned. Trim away all the seam allowances from these pieces.

Facings for waistbands, front bands and cuffs should also be trimmed, but leave ⅛″ (3mm) of the seam allowance around the outside edges. Leave the complete seam allowance at the edge that joins the body of the garment. This edge will be trimmed after being machine stitched in place. The ⅛″ (3mm) allowance around the outside edges will give you some extra fabric to work with when you do the final rows of topstitching. This "extra" helps you make sure that you always catch the underside when stitching and saves your sanity. Other instructions will have you trim both seam allowances equally, but then it is easy to lose the under-edge when topstitching.

FACING

Patch pockets and patch pocket flaps should have all the seam allowances trimmed away. Leave a ⅛″ (3mm) allowance on the flap facing for the above reason.

FLAP FACING

Facings for pocket flaps are usually cut from the same pattern piece as the flap itself. However, if you are short of fabric you can just cut a narrow facing for the pocket, as illustrated. Remember to leave a ⅛″ (3mm) allowance on the outside edges of the facing for ease of construction.

Square flaps can be cut with the lower seamline on a fold, if you have large enough pieces of fabric to accommodate this size pattern piece. Trim the seam allowances from the outside edges of the pocket. Make sure the pocket nap goes in the proper direction when stitching the flap in place.

Pocket flaps that will be sewn into yoke seams should have all their seam allowances trimmed except for the seam allowance that will go into the seam. The flap facing should be trimmed the same way, only leave a ⅛″ (3mm) allowance around the outside edges.

UPPER FLAP

FLAP FACING

Cut the pocket lining pieces from suede fabric if you have enough fabric. This looks nicer than using lining fabric, especially if the jacket is to be only partially lined. It also feels good when you put your hands in your pockets.

One-piece collars or collars with a cut on band should have the seam allowances trimmed from all four edges of the upper collar. Leave all the seam allowances intact on the under collar.

UPPER COLLAR

COLLAR FACING

Upper collars that have separate bands should have all the seam allowances except the lower edge trimmed. Trim the collar facing the same except leave a ⅛″ (3mm) allowance around the outside edges. The band that goes inside the neck of the garment should have all the seam allowances trimmed away. Leave the seam allowances intact on the outside band, for ease in stitching and placement.

UPPER COLLAR

INSIDE STAND

COLLAR FACING

OUTSIDE STAND

Front opening garments that do not have a separate front band should be cut without the front seam allowance. The facing for this garment piece should have the seam allowances trimmed to just ⅛″ (3mm).

If you are not going to line or partially line the front of a garment with a front band finish, then you should modify the shape of the band facing as illustrated. This will help prevent wear at the front neck edge, as this area is a point of strain and will need some extra protection.

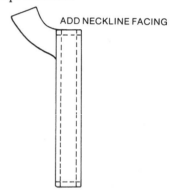

ADD NECKLINE FACING

Patterns having a straight edge at the center front, with either a band finish or a regular finish, can have the facing or band cut all-in-one so that you have a fold along the front edge rather than a cut edge. Overlap the front seamlines of the two pattern pieces and tape in place, as shown, before placing the pattern on the fabric. This method may create some layout problem because of the size of the pattern piece, so work it out before you buy your fabric.

Garments without collars should have the neckline seams trimmed away. The neckline facing should have the neckline seam trimmed to ⅛″ (3mm).

Front opening garments with a turn-back lapel and collar should have the edge at the top of the lapel trimmed to the point where the collar joins the neck edge. Trim the entire seam allowance from the garment front but leave a ⅛″ (3mm) seam allowance around the edge of the facing.

Corners that are to be sandwiched between cuffs, collars, and bands should be trimmed as shown.

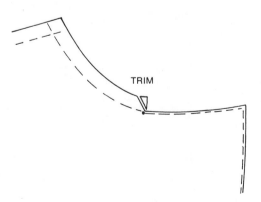

TRIM

If you are making a two piece sleeve and are using the flat seam method then eliminate the seam allowance on both sides of the upper sleeve and leave it intact on both sides of the under sleeve.

Cutting Sleeves

Whether you choose to use the conventional or flat seam method on your Ultra Suede fabric garment, the sleeve will be sewn into the armhole with a conventional seam. This technique is easier than trying to lap the armhole seam, and it gives a nicer look. Do not trim seam allowances from the armhole.

Check the amount of ease allowed in the sleeve cap of your pattern before cutting out the sleeve. Allow only 1″ (25mm), adjusting the pattern as given on page 91.

Cutting Pants

The crotch seam of pants should be sewn with a conventional seam rather than a lapped seam. This is easier to do and more comfortable to wear. The lapped seam method can be used for all other pant seams.

Cutting Linings

Cut your lining from the lining pattern pieces or from the appropriate garment pattern pieces if separate lining patterns are not given.

Cut the underarm seamline of the sleeve lining ½" (13mm) higher than the garment seamline. This allows for the ease needed to cover the underarm seam allowance.

Before you cut your fabric, carefully review your pattern pieces to make sure you are lapping things properly. A little extra time spent at this point can save you from making a costly mistake.

CONSTRUCTION TECHNIQUES

Now that your garment is cut out, you are ready to start the fun part. Watching this fabulous fabric turn into a High-Fashion garment through your sewing skills is very exciting. You will be surprised at the ease and speed of the construction, so let's get started.

DARTS

Darts in Ultra Suede fabric garments should be long, gradually tapering to a point. Short, wide darts are difficult to stitch without getting a pucker at the point. Patterns for skirts and pants that use yokes instead of darts are better choices for this fabric than patterns with conventional darts.

There are many ways of handling darts. Try all methods on scraps of fabric to see how they work and how they look. Select the method you find most suitable for your particular fashion.

Conventional Darts

Stitch the dart, gradually tapering to the point, and then use one of the following methods to finish the dart.

Finish the dart using one of the following methods:

#1 Slash open the dart along the fold and trim to ½" (13mm). Press open and pound the seam flat. Hold the seam allowance in place with thin strips of fusible web.

#2 Slash the dart open and topstitch along each side catching a 1" (25mm) square of fabric at the point of the dart as shown. This helps fill in the point of the dart and makes both sides equal.

#3 Press the dart to one side and pound. Topstitch approximately ⅛″ (3mm) from the seamline. You can stitch just one side or along both sides. This method looks nice on long, double ended darts on jacket fronts.

Lapped Darts

Skirt and pant darts and the darts at the back of the neck or shoulder can be cut open along one side, lapped, and double stitched in place. This method should be used only on fairly narrow darts because it is difficult to get a smooth point if the dart is very wide.

A small scrap of suede fabric added to the underside of the dart point, as previously described, will make the dart end smoother.

Slot Dart

The slot dart method is the best choice when stitching a wide dart such as the ones found in some vest patterns. It can also be used for regular size darts too if you desire the slot look.

Cut out the dart along the stitching lines. Bring the cut edges together and baste them to an inch wide strip of suede cut 1″ (25mm) longer than the dart opening. (Glue stick works wonders here). Topstitch along the dart edges with one or two

rows of stitching, making sure the dart edges stay butted together.

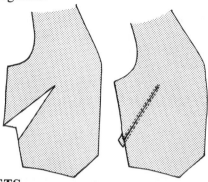

POCKETS

You will find many different types of pockets on the patterns that you might select for your Ultra Suede® fabric garment. Some will be more suitable to this fabric than others. Patch pockets with or without flaps are ideal, and the welt pockets described below will give a flatter appearance than welt pockets made with traditional stitching techniques. All the pockets are made without any turned under or faced edge for the leather-like look.

You can easily modify the pockets given in your pattern so that they utilize the following techniques.

Patch Pockets

If a buttonhole is to be placed at the top of the pocket, make sure the pocket hem is wide enough to extend below the lower end of the buttonhole. The buttonhole needs two layers of fabric plus a patch of woven lining for support.

Cut the pocket without any seam allowances. Trim the upper edges of the patch pocket hem as illustrated. This prevents the edge of the hem from peeking out along the side of the pocket after it has been stitched in place. This is important for a pocket without a flap to cover the top edge.

Fold over the hem allowance at the top edge of the pocket. Baste or glue in place and do two rows of topstitching across the top of the pocket. Another two rows of stitching can be done across the bottom edge of the hem if desired. Remember to make all rows of stitching from the same direction.

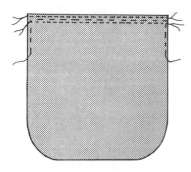

Baste or glue the pocket in position on the garment and stitch in place with two rows of topstitching. Reinforce the top corners of the pocket with back stitching or decorative stitching.

Patch Pocket With Flaps

Construct and apply the pocket as directed above.

Cut the pocket flap and facing as given on page 215. Baste the facing to the pocket flap, wrong sides together, so that ⅛″ (3mm) of the facing extends all around the edge of the flap.

Do two rows of topstitching around the three outside edges of the flap. Trim the facing even with the flap edges.

Baste or glue the flap in position on the garment and topstitch in place.

Slash Pocket With Flap

This pocket flap will have the full seam allowance left on the bottom edge of the flap and facing so that it can be sewn into the pocket slash. The pocket flap should be made before the pocket opening is cut so that the slash can be cut to fit the flap exactly. This procedure makes sure that no gaps are left at the sides of the pocket opening.

Flap Construction: Baste or glue the facing to the flap, wrong sides together, and topstitch 5/16″ (8mm) from the edge, around the three sides, as illustrated.

Edgestitch only the front edge of the flap. The sides will be edgestitched later. Trim the facing even with the edges of the flap.

Mark the seam allowance on the right side of the flap with a strip of drafting tape. Be sure that the edge of the tape is right along the seam line, and both sides of the flap below the tape are exactly the same length.

SAME LENGTH   SAME LENGTH

Pocket Construction: Cut along the pocket opening with an Exacto knife or a single-edge razor, placing a pin at the end of each side of the opening to prevent overcutting. Make sure that the opening is exactly the same length as the finished flap.

Slip the flap into the pocket slash so that the tape lines up with the cut edge of the slash. Baste or glue the flap in position and remove the drafting tape.

Topstitch the ends and across the width of the pocket through all the layers of the pocket flap and garment.

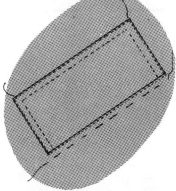

Pocket Lining: The pocket lining looks nice if Ultra Suede® fabric is used rather than lining fabric, especially if you are not going to fully line the garment. If the lining pattern is one long piece, it can be cut

along the foldline to facilitate the use of small scraps of fabric. You can even alter the shape of the lining pieces to take advantage of the suede scraps. Cut the pocket lining pieces without seam allowances if you use Ultra Suede fabric.

Baste or glue and stitch one pocket lining piece to the seam allowance of the flap.

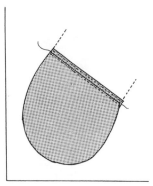

Working on the wrong side of the garment, cut two diagonal lines as shown, underneath the flap. Cut right to the stitching line, cutting the garment fabric only.

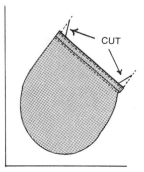

CUT

Lap the other pocket lining piec ¼" (6mm) over the free edge of fabric and baste or glue in position.

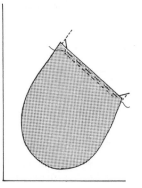

Turn the garment right side up and fold back the lower part of the garment until you see this basted seam. Machine stitch across the top of the lining piece.

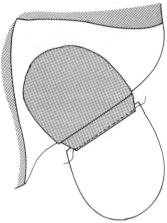

Baste or glue the pocket lining pieces together and edge-stitch.

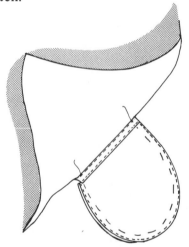

If the slash pocket is made on a garment with a front opening and facing, the pocket lining should be tucked between the facing and garment and tacked to the facing to keep it in place. Now, wasn't that easy? This is beautiful when used on a coat — make the finished flap 2″ (50mm) wide by 7″ (17.5cm) long.

Welt Pocket

This pocket is usually used for vests, but it can also be used as a chest pocket or hip pocket on a skirt, dress or pants.

Welt Construction: Delete the welt pattern piece and add 1″ (25mm) to the top of the pocket lining pattern. Cut this altered lining pattern from Ultra

Suede® fabric, making sure the turned down portion of the welt has the correct nap direction. Cut one pocket piece minus the added 1″ (25mm).

ADD 1″ (25mm)

Turn down the 1″ (25mm) welt extension, wrong sides together, baste or glue and do two rows of topstitching along the fold.

Pocket Construction: Cut along the bottom and side lines of the pocket markings with an Exacto knife or a single-edged razor. If you are making matching pockets, you must make sure that these pocket cuts are positioned and sized identically.

Slip the edgestitched welt into the slash, centering it in the opening. The right side of the welt should be against the wrong side of the garment. Baste or glue the welt in position. Edgestitch the sides and across the bottom of the welt.

RIGHT SIDE

WRONG SIDE

Baste or glue, and stitch the other pocket lining piece to the wrong side of the flap of the garment that extends down behind the stitched welt.

Baste or glue and edgestitch together the outside edges of the pocket lining pieces.

Buttonhole Pocket

See page 247.

Single Welt Pocket With Flap

Construct the welt pocket using the above instructions, but make sure the welt and pocket opening are just ½″ (13mm) wide.

Make the pocket flap following the instructions for the patch pocket flap. The finished flap should be ½″ (13mm) longer than the pocket opening. This extra ½″ (13mm) makes sure that the pocket opening will be completely covered by the flap.

Baste or glue the flap in position above the pocket opening and topstitch in place.

Flap Pocket In Yoke Seam

This flap pocket is a snap to make and can be used in the yoke seams of jackets, coats, dresses, and even pants.

Flap Construction: The flap and flap facing should have the top seam allowance left intact. The other seam allowances are completely trimmed from the flap and trimmed to just ⅛″ (3mm) on the flap facing.

Baste or glue the flap and facing wrong sides together and do two rows of topstitching around the outside edge. Trim the facing edges even with the flap.

Pocket Construction: Cut two pocket lining pieces from Ultra Suede® fabric for each pocket, measuring at least 1″ (25mm) wider than the pocket opening. Position one pocket piece on the garment, wrong sides together, centering it over the pocket marks. Baste or glue in place. Stitch an opening ½″ (13mm) shorter than the finished measurement of the pocket flap, and ⅞″ (22mm) deep. Make two rows of stitching and then trim the opening close to the stitching line.

Position the other pocket piece so that the wrong side is against the right side of the first lining piece. (It looks nicer to have the right side of the fabric visible on the inside of the garment if it isn't going to be fully lined.) Baste or glue and edgestitch the pocket pieces together.

Baste or glue the flap in position, centering it over the opening. Mark the seamline, and baste the yoke over the flap. Stitch the yoke seam with two rows of topstitching.

LININGS

Lining Ultra Suede fabric garments makes them easier to slip in and out of, as well as prolongs the life of the garment. Coats, jackets, and pants should definitely be fully or partially lined and dresses and skirts can be lined or not, as you desire.

If you choose to fully line dresses, skirts or pants, attach the lining at the neckline and zipper for dresses, and at the waistline and zipper for skirts and pants, using traditional lining techniques.

Coats look best when fully lined. Jackets can be either fully or partially lined. The type of jacket lining you choose is a matter of preference, though patterns calling for front and back yokes are more suitable to the partial lining technique than patterns without yokes.

If you are going to fully or partially line your garment and the pattern gives a back neck facing, eliminate that facing and extend the lining all the way up into the neckline. (See page 176). This gives a much nicer finish to the inside of the garment and saves some fabric.

Stitching Tip: When stitching lining fabric to suede fabric do so with the lining up and the suede next to the feed dog. Hold both layers taut as you stitch and you won't get any puckers.

Partial Linings

Partial linings consist of a full sleeve lining and a lining at the upper portion of the back and/or front of the jacket. If your pattern has front and back yokes, it is an easy matter to line just the yokes, cutting the lining pieces from the yoke patterns. Yoke linings are a good way to make a partial lining because the lower edges of the lining pieces are neatly enclosed in the yoke seams rather than hanging free. Follow the instructions below for yoke linings.

Patterns With Straight Yokes: Prepare the jacket for the lining by lapping the yoke over the body of the garment and basting the seam in place.

With the jacket wrong side up, place the yoke lining in position as shown so that the lining seamline is directly on top of the garment seam line. The right side of the lining is against the wrong side of the garment. Baste in place.

Turn the garment to the right side and edgestitch the yoke to the garment.

Working on the wrong side, trim the seam allowance to ⅜" (9mm). Fold the lining up into the finished position, wrong sides together, and pin.

Do the second row of topstitching on the right side of the jacket. Only one row of stitching will show on the lining and the seam will be neatly enclosed.

Baste the front yoke lining to the garment at the shoulder. Overlap the back shoulder over the front, leaving the back lining free. Baste the shoulder seam and machine stitch with two rows of topstitching.

Fold under the back lining seam allowance at the shoulder, and slipstitch it in place at the shoulder seam. Baste the lining at the neck edge and around the armscye.

Patterns With Shaped Yokes: Baste and machine stitch the yokes in place on the front and back of the jacket. Baste and machine stitch the shoulder seams of the jacket.

Turn under the seam allowance at the bottom edges of the yoke linings and baste. Stitch the yoke shoulder seams and press them open.

Position the lining inside the jacket (wrong sides together) and baste around the neck, front edge and armscye. *Slipstitch* the hem of the yoke linings to the yoke seam.

Patterns Without Yokes: Cut the pattern for the back lining so that it is 1" (25mm) wider than the jacket at the center back. This allows for a pleat at the center back of the lining. The lining should extend 3" (75mm) below the armhole at the sides.

Hem the lower edge of the back lining and make a 1" (25mm) wide pleat at the center back, basting across the top and bottom. Fold under the shoulder seam allowance and baste.

Position the lining in the jacket after the shoulder and side seams have been basted and machine stitched. Baste around the armscye. Slipstitch the lining to the seam line of the garment at the shoulder and side. The lower back edge of the lining will hang free.

Full Linings

Fully lined jackets and coats that are hemmed at the lower edge and sleeves should have only a 1¼" (37mm) hem allowance. Adjust the pattern of both the garment and lining pieces if necessary.

The lower edge of the lining can be machine stitched to the edge of the garment hem before the front facings are stitched in place. This technique is a good one when working with Ultra Suede fabric because hand catching the lining to the garment is somewhat difficult because of the characteristics of the suede.

Mark the hemline on the right side of the garment after all the vertical seams have been sewn but before the facing is applied. Use a chalk pencil or sliver of soap for this purpose.

Sew the vertical seams of the lining and stitch the lining to the front facings leaving the lower 2" (5cn) unstitched.

Position the lining against the garment, right sides together, so the cut edges and seams are matched; pin in place. Stitch along the edges with a ¼" (6mm) seam leaving the first and last inch (25mm) unstitched. If the garment has a vent you must also leave an unstitched section beside each side of the vent.

Turn the lining to the inside and position the facing against the front edge of the garment as it will be for the final stitching. Fold up the garment edge along the marked hemline and pin in place. Pin the top edge of the lining to the neckline edge of the garment. Smooth everything in place and you will see a neat fold of fabric fall into place at the lower edge of the lining. The garment hem will be finished with one or two rows of topstitching when the facing is finally stitched in place. Hand catch the unstitched ends of the facing in place.

If you prefer the traditional method of hand catching the lining in place at the lower edge of the garment, machine stitch ¼" (6mm) from the hem edge before you turn the hem up and it will be much easier to catch the lining to this line of stitching than to the suede fabric itself.

Sleeve Linings

The sleeve lining will be attached to the garment at one of two points during the construction process. This is determined by the type of finish at the bottom of the sleeve. Sleeves with cuffs will have the lining attached to the lower edge of the sleeve before the cuff is applied or the sleeve is sewn into the body of the garment. Sleeves without cuffs will have the lining attached to the garment after the garment sleeve has been stitched in place.

Prepare the lining for either type of sleeve according to the following instructions. If the sleeve cap ease had to be reduced for the Ultra Suede® fabric, remember to make the same alteration for the lining.

Stitch and press open the underarm seam of the sleeve lining. *Easestitch* the cap of the sleeve ⅛" (3mm) inside the seam line, between the notches. Regular stitch the remaining armscye right on the seam line. This stitching gives a guide line on which to turn and clip the sleeve seam allowance.

With wrong sides together, slip the lining down inside the garment sleeve. If the sleeve has a cuff-finish, baste the lower edge of the sleeve and lining together. This edge will later be enclosed between the two layers of cuff fabric.

If the sleeve has a hemmed finish, the lower edge of the lining will be left free at this point but then slip-stitched to the sleeve hem during the finishing of the garment.

Finish the top of the sleeve lining by turning under the seam allowance all around the sleeve edge, clipping to the seamline where necessary. Mark the notches around the edge of the sleeve with a soft pencil so that you can distinguish them from your clips. Pin the folded edge of the sleeve to the arm-scye seamline of the garment and *slipstitch* in place.

When attaching the sleeve lining to the lower edge of the sleeve do yourself a favor by machine stitching around the edge of the garment hem at ¼" (6mm) before you turn the hem up in position. If you are using a faced finish at the edge of the sleeve, machine stitch ¼" (6mm) from the upper edge of the facing before applying the facing to the sleeve.

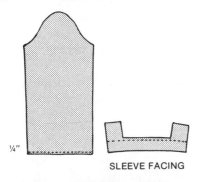

¼"

SLEEVE FACING

Finish the lining by folding under and basting ¼" (6mm) of the sleeve lining. Position the folded edge along the line of machine stitching and hand catch the fold just to the threads of the stitching line rather than trying to catch it to the Ultra Suede fabric.

FRONT FACINGS

Baste a strip of woven interfacing or color-matched lining fabric to the wrong side of the garment, underneath the buttonhole area, before you apply the front facings to coats and jackets. This will stabilize the buttonholes.

After the garment hem has been turned up, but before the shoulder seams are sewn, position the front facing against the garment front, wrong sides together. Remember the garment front has no seam allowance but the facing has a ⅛" (3mm) seam allowance remaining, so let the facing extend out beyond the garment edge ⅛" (3mm). Baste in place, (the glue stick is a must here), and topstitch the garment fronts and hem edge with two rows of stitching. Finish the two lines of stitching at the top of the lapel as shown. Trim the facing close to the finished edge of the garment front.

TRIM

FRONT BANDS

Baste or glue a strip of woven interfacing or color-matched lining fabric to the wrong side of the front band in the buttonhole area. Or you may want to use a strip of fusible web instead. Fusible web cut ¼" (6mm) narrower than band gives crispness to bands (and cuffs) and stabilizes buttonholes. It also eliminates any possibility of "drag" developing between rows of stitching.

Faced Bands

Mark the seamline on the front edge of the garment with pins or a sliver of soap. Lap the band piece over the front edge of the garment to the seam line. Baste or glue in place.

Pin and baste the band-facing in position so that ⅛″ (3mm) of facing extends beyond the edge of the top piece. Working on the right side of the garment, stitch both layers of the band to the garment with two rows of topstitching.

Pull apart the two layers of band and trim the garment seam allowance. This trimming must be done at this point — you can't get to it later.

TRIM

Baste the outside edges of the band together. The topstitching along the outside edge is done after the collar has been applied.

Bands With A Cut-On Facing

Mark the seamline on the front edge of the garment with pins or a sliver of soap. Lap the band piece over the front edge of the garment to the seamline. Baste or glue in place and stitch at 5/16″ (7mm). Trim the seam allowance of the garment front to ¼″ (6mm).

Fold the facing portion of the band back in position along the front foldline and baste again right next to the first line of basting. Edgestitch the band and facing to the garment front with one row of top-stitching.

If fusible web is being used, position it in place, fold the facing, and fuse, thus eliminating the basting along the edge.

Baste along the folded edge of the facing. This edge will be topstitched after the collar has been applied.

COLLARS

Most jackets or coats you make from Ultra Suede fabric will have a collar of some kind. The two main types of collars that you will find are collars with a separate band, and collars without bands or collars with a cut-on band. These last two collars will be applied to the garment with the same technique.

A garment having a collar with a separate band will usually have a front band finish, and the collar is applied after the shoulder seams have been sewn but before the garment side seams have been stitched. The garment calling for a collar without a band or with a cut-on band will usually have a separate front facing. The facing should be applied after the side seams are sewn but before the shoulder seams are stitched; then the shoulder seams are sewn and the collar is applied to the neck edge.

Collar With A Separate Band

Trim the seam allowances of the collar and stand pieces as given in the Cutting The Fabric section on page 211. Interface the upper collar and the inner band if you want a crisp, structured look. You can even interface both band pieces if you want a very stiff finish. Do not apply interfacing if you want a soft look. Remember to trim the interfacing 1/8" (3mm) smaller than the Ultra Suede fabric pieces so that it will not peek out from between the layers of the finished collar.

If you are lining the garment, the lining should be basted in place around the neck edge before you apply the collar. The neck edge should also be *stay-stitched* just inside the seamline and then trimmed to 3/8" (9mm). Be sure to transfer neckline notches before trimming.

Collar Construction: Baste and double topstitch the upper and under collar together around the three outside edges. The under collar should extend 1/8" (3mm) beyond the upper collar edges at this point. Trim the under collar even with the upper collar after stitching.

Topstitching Tip: When topstitching at collar and lapel points, insert a threaded needle through the point of the collar or lapel and use this "handle" to help pull the fabric under the presser foot as you stitch around the point. The machine tends to lose traction here and might begin to stitch in place, ruining your topstitching. Also, do not pivot the collar around the needle until it it emerging rather than going down into the fabric. This will avoid that pesky skipped stitch at the collar point.

Mark the seam allowance on the lower collar edge. Pin and baste the trimmed band to the collar unit — overlapping the cut edge of the inside band to the collar seam. Baste, using a large backstitch to hold everything securely.

If fusible web is desired in the collar band, cut it 1/8" (3mm) smaller around all edges than the trimmed band piece and position it on the wrong side of the band. Handle it as one with the collar band in the following steps, hand basting if necessary.

Mark the neckline seam on the wrong side of the outside band piece.

Lay the trimmed band and collar unit on top of the outside band so that the trimmed lower edge of the band is right along the marked seamline. Pin in place and baste securely across the top of the band right next to the previous basting. Hand baste in this area — the glue stick is not strong enough to hold this securely for stitching. The final topstitching that joins the collar and band will be done when the front edge of the jacket is topstitched.

The collar is now sandwiched between the two band pieces. Pull these two pieces apart and trim the collar seam allowance to ¼″ (6mm). You will not be able to get in to trim this seam once the collar has been stitched in place.

Collar Application: Clip the neckline seam to the staystitching at regular intervals as needed, and trim to ⅜″ (9mm).

Pin the inside band to the neck edge so that the trimmed lower edge of the band overlaps the staystitching ⅛″ (3mm). <u>Hand</u> baste securely in place. Now position the outside band on the neck edge so that the wrong side of the band is against the right side of the garment. Make sure both bands lie smoothly and <u>hand</u> baste in place. If fusible web has been used in the band, fuse the band layers together at this point, thus eliminating the basting step. It also eliminates any possibility of drag when the final rows of topstitching are done on the garment.

Finish the hem of the garment (see page 241) and then double topstitch the front edge and the band-collar joining seam in one operation. Trim the collar edges even, and remove any basting.

Collar Without A Band

The seam allowance of the two collar pieces should be trimmed as given on page 216. Interface the upper collar or not, as you desire. Remember to cut the interfacing ⅛″ (3mm) smaller all around. Interface the under collar as given on page 211, trimming the interfacing ¼″ (6mm) smaller around the three outside finished edges.

If you are lining the garment, the lining must be basted in place around the neck edge before you apply the collar. The neck edge should also be stay-stitched just inside the seamline and clipped at regular intervals. Do not trim the seam allowance at this time.

Draw a line marking the width of the neckline seam allowance on the wrong side of the lower edge of the upper collar.

Apply a thin strip of glue to the wrong side of the neckline edge of the collar and position the collar against the neckline seam allowance matching up construction marks and making sure the cut edge of the neckline seam meets the drawn line. Hand baste along the lower edge of the collar if you feel it is necessary.

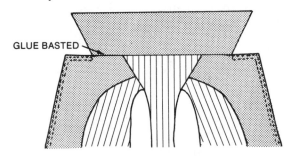

GLUE BASTED

Pin the under collar to the upper collar, wrong sides together, with ⅝" (16mm) of the under collar extending beyond the edges of the upper collar. Pin and baste or glue the neck edge of the under collar securely in position. Working on the inside of the garment, edgestitch through all layers along the lower trimmed edge of the upper collar.

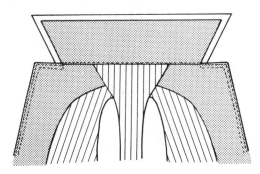

Unpin the outside edges of the collar and separate the two layers. Trim the seam allowance at the neckline.

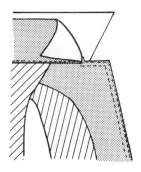

Roll the collar over your hand into the finished position and pin the two collar layers as they fall. If you have a dress form, or if you have someone to help you fit the garment on yourself you can get the proper collar roll that way. You will notice that you may have more than ⅝" (16mm) of the under collar extending beyond the edge of the upper collar at this point. This is the natural shortening of the

under collar and is what creates a nice rolled collar that stays flat and neat around your neck.

While the collar is still in the rolled position, glue the edges together and finish with two rows of topstitching.

Collar With Cut-On Band

Use the above techniques for applying the collar with a cut-on band with the option of doing two rows of topstitching where the collar joins the neckline edge instead of one row.

SLEEVE VENTS

The finish at the bottom of the sleeve will, of course, be determined by your pattern. Some sleeves will have a faced vent such as found on men's suits; some will require a vent finish combined with a cuff, and some sleeves will just have a simple hemmed edge. Read through these instructions and combine them with your pattern requirements for the desired finish.

Sleeve vents are constructed before the underarm seam of the sleeve is sewn unless the vent is part of that seam.

Slash Vent

Cut a vent facing from Ultra Suede® fabric that is 3" (76mm) wide and 1" (25mm) longer than the vent slash. Slash the sleeve along the vent marking, rounding the top of the slash.

Pin and baste the facing in the proper position wrong sides together. Make two rows of stitching around the vent slash, as illustrated.

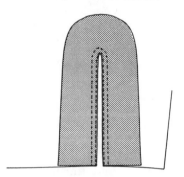

Alternate Finish: Pin and baste the facing in the proper position on the wrong side of the sleeve, but do the final topstitching around the vent when you topstitch the edges of the cuff. This is a good way to finish the cuff and vent because you make one continuous line of stitching up the ends of the cuff and vent. This method works only with cuffs that are cut flush with the sides of the vent.

Stitch the underarm seam using either the conventional or lapped seam method. If the garment is going to be lined, the sleeve lining should be stitched now and slipped down inside the garment sleeve, wrong sides together. Slash the lining along the vent line cutting it ½″ (13mm) longer than the pattern indicated. Slip the lining behind the vent facing and *slipstitch* in place. Baste the lower edge of the sleeve and lining together.

Tailored Vent

Slash the sleeve on the vent marking making the slash 4½″ (113cm) long. Face the back of the vent (the edge closest to the underarm seam) with a ¾″ (19mm) wide strip of Ultra Suede® fabric that is cut 5″ (13cm) long. Baste and double topstitch in place as illustrated.

Cut a sleeve placket piece from Ultra Suede fabric using the pattern found on the large pattern in the back of the book. Cut ⅜″ (9mm) into the sleeve at the top of the vent.

Fold the vent facing in half, wrong sides together. Baste and double topstitch the folded edge to the dot. Pull the threads through to the inside of the two layers and tie.

Working on the right side of the sleeve, sandwich the edge of the sleeve-slash in between the unstitched edges of the vent facing, overlapping the sleeve edge ⅜″ (9mm). The lower edge of the vent facing should be even with the lower edge of the sleeve. Baste in position and double topstitch as shown.

Stitch the underarm seam and apply any sleeve lining as described in the previous vent section.

Vent In A Seam

Some patterns will have a sleeve vent constructed as part of the sleeve seam. You will find this type of construction more often on men's than on women's garments. It is a very easy vent finish, and you can modify any sleeve pattern to use this type of vent if you wish by following the instruction below.

Draw a line up the back section of the sleeve starting where the vent slash is located. Cut the sleeve apart along this line and add a ⅝" (16mm) seam allowance to both sides of the cut, plus an extra ½" (13mm) in the vent area.

Now overlap the original underarm seam so that the seam lines are on top of each other. Tape in place and use this new pattern to cut your sleeves.

Baste, stitch and press open the underarm seam of the sleeve. Use thin strips of fusible web under the seam allowances to hold them flat, or edgestitch on each side of the seam.

When you line this type of sleeve, you should cut the lining from the altered sleeve pattern. Stitch the underarm seam to a point ½" (13mm) above the top of the vent opening and press the seam open. Slip the lining down inside the sleeve and baste along the lower edge. *Slipstitch* the edge of the lining to the vent edges.

Faced Vent

A tailored sleeve vent on a man's sport coat or woman's jacket is best handled with a facing. Cut the facing as follows:

Overlap the pattern pieces at the front seam until the seamlines are on top of each other; pin together. Remove the hem allowance from both sleeve pattern pieces and the vent extension of the upper sleeve. Trace around this adjusted pattern for your sleeve facing, making it ⅛" (3mm) larger around the three outside edges, 3" (7.5cm) wide on the sides of the vent, and 2" (5cm) wide at the bottom edge.

TRIM

Stitch the front seam of the sleeve using either the conventional or flat technique.

Apply interfacing to the sleeve facing is more body is desired. Cut the interfacing ¼" (6mm) smaller than the facing so it doesn't peak out from the finished sleeve. Also, machine stitch ¼" (6mm) down from the edge of the facing so you will have a line of stitching for attaching the lining.

Position the facing against the lower edge of the sleeve, wrong sides together and glue. Remember the facing is ⅛" (3mm) larger than the sleeve so it should extend out beyond the sleeve edge that much. Double topstitch around the facing as shown. End the stitching at the construction dot marking the top of the vent. Pull the threads through to the wrong side and tie. Trim the excess facing.

Baste and stitch the upper sleeve seam to the dot using the lapped seam method. This works best if the sleeve is turned inside out for the stitching. Hold the vent closed by sewing the vent buttons in place.

CUFFS

Directions are given for the two basic types of cuffs you will find on patterns, the cuff with a separate facing and the one-piece fold-over cuff. Interfacing the cuff is optional. If you decide to use it, apply the interfacing to the upper cuff piece or the half of the fold-over cuff which will form the upper cuff. Remember to trim the interfacing ⅛″ (3mm) smaller than the cuff so that it won't peek out around the edges.

Fusible web, cut to fit the finished cuff, can be used instead of interfacing, if desired. It gives a crisp look and eliminates any chance of drag when sewing the final rows of topstitching. Glue baste it in position before you begin the cuff application.

If you choose not to use interfacing or fusible web, then position a patch of color matched, woven lining fabric under the buttonhole area for support. Glue will hold the patch in place until the buttonhole is worked.

Cuff With A Separate Facing

The upper cuff piece should be trimmed of all seam allowances. The cuff facing should retain the full seam allowance at the sleeve edge and just a ⅛″ (3mm) seam allowance around the outer three edges.

Position the lining in the sleeve and baste around the lower edge. Mark the seamline at the lower edge of the sleeve. Lap the upper cuff over the seam allowance so that the trimmed edge just meets the seamline. Baste or glue in position.

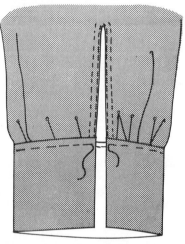

Position the cuff facing under the cuff, wrong sides together, so that ⅛″ (3mm) of the facing extends beyond the three outside edges of the upper cuff. Baste or glue securely at the sleeve edge. Double topstitch through all layers at the top edge of the cuff.

Separate the cuff pieces and trim the sleeve seam allowance. Trim away the excess seam allowance at the sleeve edge of the cuff facing also.

Baste the outer edges of the cuff and facing together. If fusible web has been used in the cuff, fuse the cuff layers together at this point, eliminating the basting step. Double topstitch around the three outer edges.

Trim the facing even with the upper cuff edge. Do both lines of stitching from the same direction.

Fold-Over Cuff

This cuff piece should have three seam allowances trimmed away, leaving just one intact at the sleeve edge.

Mark the seamline on the right side of the lower edge of the sleeve. Lap the trimmed edge of the cuff over the lower sleeve seam until the edge meets the seamline. Baste or glue in place. Trim away ¼" (6mm) of the sleeve seam allowance at the lower edge of the sleeve.

Fold the facing portion of the cuff back in the finished position, wrong sides together. The ⅝" (16mm) seam allowance will extend up into the sleeve. Baste across the top of the cuff again and then baste or glue around all three outside edges. This basting is important in order to prevent the layers of fabric from shifting during the final stitching. If fusible web has been used in the cuff this is the time to fuse the cuff layer together, thus eliminating the basting.

Double topstitch across the top of the cuff. Double topstitch around the outside edges of the cuff. It is important that these two stitching operations be done from the same direction so that a "drag" does not develop around the cuff edge. Trim away excess seam allowance at the top edge of the cuff facing.

SETTING IN SLEEVES

Always set sleeves into the armhole with a conventional seam. This method is easiest and looks best when finished.

Ultra Suede® fabric cannot handle the cap ease found in most patterns so you will have to make some alterations to your pattern before you cut the fabric. Follow the instructions given on pages 90-91 for measuring and adjusting the sleeve cap ease. Allow only 1" (25mm) of ease in the sleeve cap.

The remaining 1" (25mm) of ease must be controlled some way while you stitch the sleeve in place, and we have found this to be the easiest method.

With the suede right side up, machine stitch from notch to notch around the top of the sleeve, keeping the stitching just short of the given seamline. Use a regular stitch length, but backstitch one stitch every third forward stitch.

Now, working on the wrong side of the sleeve, pull up the bobbin thread with the point of a pin, between every backstitch. This will cause the sleeve cap to curve under, and it holds the ease in place for the final stitching.

Pin the sleeve into the armhole, matching the construction marks. Place the pins directly in the seamline for better control of the fabric ease. Baste in place and try the garment on to check the fit.

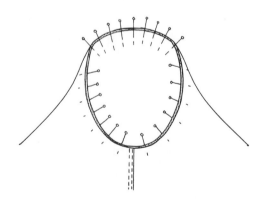

Once the fit is perfect and smooth, machine stitch the sleeve in place. Stitch a second row ¼" (6mm) in the seam allowance. Trim to this stitching. Tailored jackets and coats look nicer if you add a shoulder pad; casual jackets can also have a shoulder pad if desired. Refer to page 183 for shoulder pad information. Note: Clip the seam allowance of the Lamb's Wool or Tri-shape to the stitching line

around the seam cap. This releases the tension on the seam allowance and allows the sleeve seam to lie flat.

ZIPPERS

Some Ultra Suede fabric garments will require zippers, and these are really very easy to insert. Zippers in conventional seams will be stitched-in using the traditional techniques. However, the flat method of seam construction makes it possible to easily insert zippers that have a very flat finish. Follow the instructions below for the center-slot, lapped and fly zipper.

Center-Slot Zipper

The simplest way to insert the center-slot zipper in an Ultra Suede fabric garment is to use the Lapped Seam II method for the zipper seam.

Trim the seam allowance from both sides of the seam. Cut a 1" (25mm) wide strip of fabric the same length as the seam. Butt the trimmed edges of the seam together and center them down the length of the strip. Baste in place and edgestitch each side of the seam.

Make a slash down the center of the 1" (25mm) strip

the length of the zipper. Position the zipper under the slash and baste or glue securely.

Do the second row of topstitching ¼" (6mm) away from the first, stitching from the same direction on each side. This row of stitching holds the zipper in place, and you will have four neat rows of topstitching showing down the zipper seam.

Lapped Zipper

This method is used at the sides of skirts and pants and at the center back of pants, skirts and dresses. It is also a simple way of making a fly zipper for pants. Just add two extra rows of topstitching to outline the fly.

Trim the seam allowance from the edge of the garment that laps over the zipper. Trim the other seam

allowance a scant ⅜" (13mm) just the length of the zipper.

Zipper Tip: Use a longer zipper than necessary so it extends entirely above the waistline seam. This makes it easier to lower the back waistline seam if necessary for fitting purposes. You won't be cutting into the metal stoppers at the top of the zipper.

Position the zipper under the partially trimmed garment piece so the fabric edge is next to the zipper teeth. Glue or baste in place and edgestitch with a zipper foot the length of the zipper teeth.

Cut a facing for the other side of the garment that is 1" (25mm) wide and 1" (25mm) longer than the zipper. Lay the facing along the edge of the completely trimmed seam allowance, wrong sides together. Glue or baste and double topstitch the edge of the facing just the length of the zipper.

Mark the seamline down the length of the garment piece to which the zipper has been attached. Lap the faced side of the garment over the zipper so that the trimmed edge meets the seamline.

Baste in position. Double topstitch the remainder of the seam below the zipper.

Working on the right side of the garment, fold back the side until the zipper facing is exposed. Baste the facing to the zipper tape. Machine stitch the facing to the zipper tape with a row of machine stitching.

Slip a ¼" (6mm) strip of fusible web in between the facing and garment fabric. Fuse in place from the wrong side. This keeps the facing flat and always in the right position.

Fly Zippers

Trim away the seam allowance on the lapped over part of the garment and leave the seam allowance completely intact on the under part of the garment.

Position the zipper under the edge of the untrimmed seam allowance so the edge of the fabric is beside the zipper teeth. Glue or baste and edge-stitch with a zipper foot, close to the zipper teeth.

Cut a facing for the other side of the garment that is 2" (5cm) wide and 1" (25mm) longer than the zipper. Lay the facing along the edge of the other seam, wrong sides together. Glue or baste and double

topstitch the edge of the facing just the length of the zipper.

Mark the seamline down the length of the garment piece to which the zipper has been attached. Lay the faced side of the garment over the zipper so that the trimmed edge meets the marked seamline. Glue or baste and double topstitch the remainder of the seam below the zipper.

Glue the facing in position and finish the fly zipper with two rows of decorative topstitching 1¼" (31mm) from the edge on the right side of the garment. This stitching should also catch the zipper tape.

WAISTBANDS

You will find two types of waistbands on Ultra Suede® fabric garments, the faced waistband and the fold-over waistband. Fold-over waistbands use larger pieces of fabric than faced waistbands, so if you are short of large, un-cut pieces of fabric, you can make the waistband into a faced one and utilize smaller pieces of fabric. Just cut the waistband pattern apart along the foldline and use these two pieces to cut the waistband and facing.

Interface waistbands that are used at the top of pants and skirts or, eliminate the interfacing and just don't trim the waistline seam; it will act as interfacing. Interfacing is optional for waistbands at the bottom edge of jackets, or you can use a piece of fusible web between the waistband layer for a crisp look. In either case, a piece of woven interfacing or color-matched lining fabric should be positioned on the wrong side of the band underneath the buttonhole area.

Faced Waistbands

The upper waistband piece should have all the seam allowances trimmed away. The waistband facing should have the three outside seam allowances trimmed to ⅛" (3mm); the seam allowance that joins the body of the garment should be left intact.

Mark the seamline on the right side of the garment piece that joins the waistband. Overlap the upper waistband piece until the trimmed edge meets the seamline. Baste or glue securely in place.

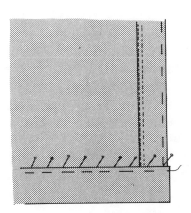

Position the waistband facing against the upper waistband, wrong sides together. The ⅛" (3mm) allowance of the facing should extend beyond the edges of the upper waistband. Baste or glue in place and then finish with a double row of topstitching.

Separate the two waistband layers and trim the seam allowance.

Pin and baste or glue the edges of the waistband together. Or a piece of fusible web cut ¼" (6mm) narrower than the waistband can be fused in place between the fabric layers and fused together at this point. Double topstitch the remaining edges of the waistband. If the garment has a collar and front facing or band that hasn't been topstitched, then continue the topstitching through these areas at this time. Make sure that all the rows of topstitching are made in the same direction.

Fold-Over Waistbands

Use the pattern piece given with the pattern, or, if you are making a waistband for pants or a skirt, cut the waistband piece 1" (25mm) longer than the top edge of the garment and 2½" (64mm) wide.

The 1″ (25mm) band extension can be placed on either side of the waist opening, as you prefer.

Mark the seamline at the waist of the garment and lap the waistband to the seamline. Baste or glue in position.

Fold the waistband down in the finished position so that ½″ (13mm) extends below the waistline seam on the wrong side. Baste or glue securely. Note: The waistline seam is left untrimmed in the waistband to give extra body. Fusible web can be added to the waistband also if desired.

Finish the waistband by making four rows of topstitching along the length of the waistband. Make sure that all the rows of stitching are done from the same direction. Trim the front edges of the

waistband even and trim away the excess seam allowance from the back of the band.

HEMS

If you look at ready-to-wear Ultra Suede® fabric garments you will see various types of hem finishes. Some garments are just cut at the desired length and left with a raw edge. We feel this gives an unfinished look and encourage you to make conventional or faced hems.

Conventional Hems

Turn up the garment along the hemline. The hem width is ¾″ (19mm) for unlined garments and 1¼″ (31mm) for lined garments. The hem allowance of the pattern should be trimmed to these widths before being pinned to the fabric.

Finish the hem by fusing with strips of fusible web or making a double row of topstitching along the lower edge. A word of caution here, fused hems sometimes get a "glued look" after repeated washings.

Hems can also be done by hand using the Tailor's hem technique given on page 193. Do a row of machine stitching ¼″ (6mm) below the hem edge first and catch the hand stitches to this stitching line instead of the suede. Much easier.

Faced Hems

Faced hems are more suitable for garments with curved edges. It is impossible to use a conventional hem finish on these garments and achieve a smooth look since Ultra Suede fabric does not ease well.

Cut facing strips ¾" (19mm) wide, using the garment piece as a pattern so that you duplicate the curve exactly. Position the facing against the garment, wrong sides together, and baste or glue. Finish with a double row of topstitching along the lower edge.

Hems At The Front Facing

Garments that are hemmed and have a fold-back or separate front facing should be finished according to the following instructions.

Conventional Hem: Fold the hem up and baste or glue. Trim the front edge of the hem so that it extends only ½" (13mm) into the facing. Fold the facing back in the finished position. Baste or glue in position and trim after it has been stitched across the lower edge.

Note: A conventional hem can be left 2" (5cm) wide — then you have the option of lowering the hemline at a later date.

Finish the lower edge by fusing the hem with strips of fusible web or double topstitching along the lower edge of the hem. If you are topstitching the hem edge, then topstitch the entire jacket at this time, going up the fronts, across the collar and across the bottom edges in one operation. Make both rows of stitching from the same direction.

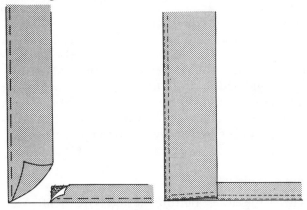

Faced Hem: The lower edge of the facing should be trimmed ⅛" (3mm) wider than the lower edge of the garment.

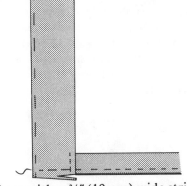

Face the hem with a ¾" (19mm) wide strip of Ultra Suede® fabric placed wrong sides together with the facing extending ⅛" (3mm) below the garment edge. The hem strip should extend just ½" (13mm) into the facing at the front edge. Baste or glue the hem facing in place and finish by double topstitching as above. Trim all edges even.

BUTTONHOLES

All buttonholes should be backed by interfacing to prevent rippling and stretching. A square or strip of woven interfacing, or better yet, a color-matched lining fabric should be used. Color-matched lining will avoid having a strip of white showing in the buttonhole opening.

There are four methods of making buttonholes in Ultra Suede fabric. All are easy, but the bound buttonhole does require precise marking and cutting. It is suggested that you try the various buttonhole methods on scraps of fabric to see which one works best for you. You will also work out any construction problems before you begin work on the garment.

Buttonhole I

This is the easiest buttonhole and is frequently seen on Designer fashions.

Using 14 stitches to the inch (or a stitch length of 2mm), stitch a rectangle the desired length and ⅛" (3mm) wide at each buttonhole location. Count the stitches along each side to make sure all the buttonholes are the same size. Cut the buttonholes open using an Exacto knife, buttonhole cutter, or a single-edged razor blade.

Buttonhole II

Do a regular machine buttonhole. These look best when corded. See your machine instruction book for cording instructions.

Buttonhole III

This is the easiest bound buttonhole, and it gives a nice flat look. Make the front part of this buttonhole before the facing is attached to the garment. If the buttonholes are being made in a front band, waistband or cuff, make the front side of the buttonholes before you attach these pieces to the garment.

Make a template the exact size of the buttonhole opening. The cardboard from bias or seam tape makes a good template. Cut the buttonhole ¼"

(6mm) wide and the exact length of the buttonhole. The distance from the front edge of the buttonhole to the edge of the cardboard should be the same distance from the front edge of the buttonhole to the edge of the garment. This will make the positioning of the template easier.

Use the template to cut the buttonhole "windows" on the garment piece. Make sure the windows are placed exactly where they are supposed to be before cutting. Use an Exacto knife, buttonhole cutter, or a single-edge razor blade to cut the openings.

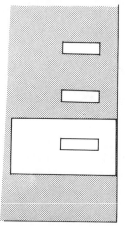

Cut two strips of fabric 1"x2" (25mmx50mm) for each buttonhole. (The strips should be 1" (25mm) longer than the buttonhole opening). Place the two strips right sides together and machine baste down the center of the strips.

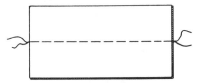

Press the strips open and position them under the buttonhole windows, centering them in the opening. Baste securely around the outside edges of the window or glue in place.

After the facing has been attached to the garment, baste or glue around the buttonhole again, through the facing layer. Finish the buttonhole by edgestitching around the buttonhole window. Use a zipper foot here for greater visibility.

Remove any basting stitches, including the ones across the buttonhole openings, and cut a window or slit on the facing side just inside the stitched box.

Note: Do not baste or glue the buttonhole to the facing until after the facing has been double top-stitchd in place. Sometimes the facing will shift a little during the topstitching and this would cause a wrinkling around the buttonhole if it had been finished.

Buttonhole IV

Because this bound buttonhole does not have any stitches visible from the right side, it is very elegant looking. Remember that the front of the buttonhole is constructed before the facing is attached to the garment.

Cut two strips of fabric 1″ x 2″ (25mm x 50mm) or 1″ (25mm) longer than each buttonhole opening.

Mark the exact position and width of each buttonhole with a fine pencil or basting thread on the right side of the garment. Double check your marks to make sure they are accurate.

Place one buttonhole strip along the buttonhole line, right sides together, so that at least ½″ (13mm) extends beyond each end of the buttonhole. Baste and stitch ⅛″ (3mm) from the edge, the exact length of the buttonhole.

Position the second strip on the right side of the garment so that its cut edge butts against the cut edge of the first strip. Baste in position and stitch as for the first strip. It helps if you count stitches so that the stitching lines are the same length.

From the wrong side, cut the buttonhole open as shown, leaving a good-sized wedge at each end. Do not cut the strips of fabric — just the garment fabric.

Turn the strips to the wrong side. Open the ⅛″ (3mm) seam and flatten it with your fingernail.

243

Wrap the buttonhole strips over the open seams and baste in position, as illustrated.

Fold back the garment at each side of the buttonhole and machine stitch across the base of each wedge.

Baste or glue and topstitch the front facing to the garment. Baste around each buttonhole going through the facing layer at this time or glue the facing in place.

Set the machine for 16 stitches to the inch (stitch length of slightly less than 2mm) and finish the buttonhole by *stitching-in-the-ditch* around each buttonhole. Stitch slowly, using a zipper foot for greater visibility; you don't want any of this stitching to show. Do this by hand if you can't bury stitches in the seam.

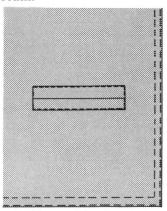

Remove all the basting and cut a window or a slit in the facing of the garment just inside the stitched box of each buttonhole.

LEFT-OVER PROJECTS

Don't throw away any of those scraps of Ultra Suede® fabric. At the price you paid, they are worth lots of money. They can be used for High-Fashion touches on other garments and clever craft projects. A few suggestions are given below. You'll probably think up more for yourself.

WRAP BELT

Cut a strip of Ultra Suede fabric across the width 3″ (7.5cm) to 3½″ (8.7cm) wide. Taper the ends and tie in a square knot for an instant high-fashion accent belt.

PATCHES

What can be more fun than Ultra Suede fabric patches on jeans? Use various colors, cut in exciting shapes, and you will really add a touch of class to those old favorites. Little kids love the patches on their clothes, too!

BUTTONS

Make covered buttons and use them on other garments as well as your Ultra Suede® fabric ones. They really add interest and are machine washable to boot.

BUTTONHOLES

Make bound buttonholes using Ultra Suede fabric for the lips. This looks especially nice on corduroy jackets. Use the buttonhole method given on page 243 (Buttonhole IV).

PIPING

Use narrow strips of Ultra Suede fabric to pipe collars, yokes, pockets, cuffs and anything else you can think of when making garments from other fabrics. Piping adds the look of real leather to the garment, giving none of the stitching and cleaning problems.

Piping Instructions

To make piping, cut ¾″ (19mm) wide strips of Ultra Suede fabric on the crossgrain. Fold the strips in half, wrong sides together, and stitch ⅛″ (3mm) from the fold.

Baste the strip to the garment section to be piped so that the stitching on the piping lies along the seamline on the right side of the garment. Clip the piping to the stitching when going around points, corners and curves.

Pin the garment pieces together, right side to right side, so that the suede strip is sandwiched in between. Stitch the seam and then trim, turn and press.

FASHION ACCENTS

Use pieces of Ultra Suede fabric to accent patch and welt pockets. It also looks nice applied to the collars of sports coats. Make a Hunting jacket by stitching Ultra Suede fabric patches to the shoulder and elbows. The shoulder patch goes on the right side unless, of course, the man is left handed.

Make a vest with an Ultra Suede® fabric front and a sweater knit back. Or stitch together patches of various colors of Ultra Suede fabric for a patchwork vest.

Design a Western scene out of Ultra Suede fabric scraps and zigzag the pieces to the back yoke of a denim jacket. (You can buy a similar jacket in the store for $250).

Make a braided belt from strips of suede trimmed from seams. Use the braid for a tie belt or a regular belt with a buckle. You can also hand stitch the braid to a denim work shirt or jacket for a new look.

Wide belts and purses made from Ultra Suede fabric are unusual. There are many patterns available for these.

Use small scraps for appliques or miniature patchworks. Ultra Suede fabric scraps are also great for cleaning glasses. They would even make a good eyeglass case or liner.

SWEATER TRIMS

Narrow strips of Ultra Suede fabric can be used to accent the neck and sleeve trim of men's and women's sweaters. Cut the strips ⅜" or ½" (9mm or 13mm) wide across the grain of the fabric.

Turtleneck Trim

Use a regular turtleneck sweater pattern, but cut out the entire neckline 2" (50mm) larger than the pattern requirement. This lowering allows the sweater to slip over the head after the Ultra Suede fabric has been applied.

FRONT   BACK

Cut the turtleneck strip 8" (20cm) wide and long enough to stretch around the head and then fit comfortably around the neck. Stitch the narrow edges of the collar, right sides together, and then finger press the seam open. Fold the collar in half, wrong sides together; divide and mark the cut edge into four equal sections.

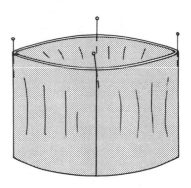

With the garment inside out, divide and mark the neckline into four equal sections. Slip the prepared collar down into the neckline and pin the edges together, matching up the quarter marks. The collar seam should be placed at the center back. Stitch the neckline with a ¼" (6mm) seam.

Pin the Ultra Suede® fabric strip to the neckline so that the lower edge runs right on the neckline seam.

Lap the edges of the strip at the center back and attach to the collar with two rows of topstitching.

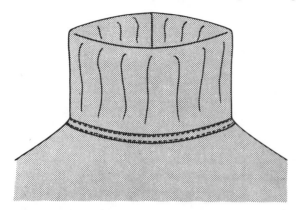

V-Neck Trim

Topstitch one or two narrow strips of Ultra Suede fabric to the band of the V-neck before it is attached to the sweater. Baste and double topstitch the strips to the neckband before you fold it into the finished position, and stitch it to the garment.

Cuff Trim

Stitch narrow strips of Ultra Suede fabric around the cuffs of sweaters to give you a complete fashion look. Apply the strips to the cuff trim before folding and applying to the sleeve opening. Be sure cuff will go over hand — Ultra Suede cuts down on stretch of cuff.

There is no end to the things you can do with all those expensive scraps. Using them up is almost as exciting as making the actual garment. Have fun!

Buttonhole Pocket

Use buttonhole method no. 3 on page 242 when doing a double welt pocket, except cut the pocket opening ½" (13mm) wide and as long as indicated on the pattern. Cut three suede strips 2" (5cm) wide and 1" (25mm) longer than the pocket opening.

Prepare two of the strips as described for the buttonhole. Slip a pocket lining piece between the layers of the lower welt strip, after the strips have been basted together and pressed open. Hand or glue baste the lining in place.

Center the prepared strips behind the pocket opening and hand or glue baste in place. Edgestitch around the pocket opening using a zipper foot, if desired, for greater visibility.

Stitch the remaining suede strips to the top of the other pocket lining piece lapping the suede ¼" (6mm) over the lining, and edgestitch.

Position the lining/suede piece behind the pocket opening so the top of the suede strip is even with the top edge of the upper welt strip. If the lower edge of the pocket lining doesn't match, don't worry; just trim it even after the pocket is completed.

With the right side of the garment up, fold down the garment to expose the seam allowance of the upper welt strip. Hand or glue baste this seam allowance to the suede strip at the top of the second lining piece. Machine stitch across the seam allowance, catching the top of the pocket piece underneath.

Fold over the side of the garment to expose the sides of the pocket lining pieces and close the pocket by stitching down the side, across the bottom, and up the other side.

KNIT KNACKS

Knits are fun to sew and easy to wear and care for. A large portion of our wardrobes is made from these comfortable and attractive fabrics. We would like to give you some new ideas for neckline finishes and waistband techniques. Patterns and neckline overlays for most of the following neckline finishes are found at the back of the book.

TAB FRONT NECKLINE

The tab front neckline can be used on dressy or casual clothes for the whole family. Use it for pullover sports shirts for men and boys; use it for tailored blouses or dresses for women and girls as well as casual knit tops. The tab can be made from matching or contrasting fabric. Use buttons or decorative gripper-snaps for the closure.

While the instructions for this neckline finish are given in the Knit Knacks section, the technique can also be used for woven fabrics. The only difference is that you must *clean finish* the facing edges so they won't fray, and *staystitch* the bottom of the tab area so it won't fray when you clip into the corners.

THE PATTERN

Use a "knits only" pattern that has been cut out on the turtleneck line, or use a regular blouse or shirt pattern that has a jewel, or high round neckline. Allow for just a ¼" seam at the neckline edge. Adjust your pattern if necessary. The pattern can have set-in or raglan sleeves, whichever you prefer. Cut out your fashion fabric so that there is no seam down the center front or center back. Press a crease down the center front that is the length of the finished tab.

You must make your own pattern for the tab facing, which is an easy thing to do. First, decide upon the finished length and width of the tab. Men's and women's tabs are usually 9" (22.5 cm) to 10" (25mm) long; use a shorter tab for small children. The tab width is 1½" (38mm) for ladies, 1½" (38mm) to 2" (50mm) for men and 1" (25mm) for small children. The following instructions are for a 1½" (38mm) wide tab. Instructions for other widths will be given at the end of this section.

Make the pattern for your tab on a 15" (38cm) square of pattern or tissue paper. Draw a line 2½" (6cm) from the edge of the square. Lay the square of paper over the front neckline of the garment pattern so the drawn line is on the center front line. Trace along the neckline edge and 2½" (6cm) along the shoulder edge.

If you are using a raglan sleeve pattern, extend the neck facing line to the center of the sleeve or the back sleeve edge. Do this by overlapping the garment front and sleeve front patterns until the seamlines meet; pin in place. Position the square of pattern paper over these two pieces, as described above, and trace off the neck edge and 2½" (6cm) of the center or back of the sleeve.

The lower edge of the tab facing should be marked 1" (25mm) below the finished length of the tab. Remember to allow for a seam width at the top of the tab facing for the neckline seam when figuring the finished length.

Draw a line 2" (50mm) to the left of the center front line and connect it to the end of the shoulder line with a nice curve. This is the cutting line for the edge of the tab facing.

Draw a line ¾" (19mm) to the right of the center front line and mark it "foldline". This will leave

1¾" (44mm) in the tab area—1½" (38mm) for the actual tab and ¼" (6mm) for a seam.

Fold the pattern square along the marked foldline, and cut out the tab facing pattern. Cut at right angles to the fold for at least ½" (13mm) when cutting along the neck edge. This gives the neck edge the proper curve. Your tab facing should now look like this.

Cut two tab facings from matching or contrasting fabric using the pattern you just created. Be aware of the part of the tab facing that will show on the finished garment. If you are working with a striped, plaid or printed fabric, position the facing pattern so that the finished tab will compliment the garment.

Cut the garment from your fashion fabric. If you are using an interlock knit, make sure the runs go up the garment—not down. You wouldn't want to have runs start in the corners of the tab. Striped fabrics should be cut so that the tab ends on, not in the middle of a stripe. Adjust the length of the tab or reposition the garment pattern on the fashion fabric so this happens.

Using a sliver of soap or *tailor's chalk* draw two lines on the right side of the garment front, ½" (13 mm) away from the center front crease. These lines should be the exact length of the finished tab plus the neckline seam width; they will be guidelines for the initial tab placement.

Apply a 1¾″ (44mm) wide strip of fusible interfacing to the wrong side of each tab piece, as shown. This interfacing stabilizes the button and buttonhole area and the vertical seams, Fig. 1. Press over the front portion of each facing piece along the foldline (interfacing edge), wrong sides together, Fig. 2. The folded-over portion will show on the finished garment.

FIG. 1   FIG. 2

If you are working with a woven fabric, stitch a half-box around the bottom of the two chalk lines. The stitching should be a scant ¼″ (6mm) to the outside of each line and straight across the bottom. This stitching reinforces the lower edge of the tab and keeps it from fraying.

Position the right side of the tab facings on the right side of the garment front so that the cut edges butt right against the chalk-marked lines. The lower edges of the tab facings should be even. Square off

the bottoms of the tab area with a chalk mark. Stitch both tab facings from the top to the bottom with a ¼″ (6mm) seam; make sure the stitching lines end exactly across from each other at the bottom of the box. Back tack both sides for strength. The two stitching lines should be exactly 1½″ (38mm) apart. Check with a ruler to make sure; if they aren't, restitch to make them exact.

Cut the garment along the edge of each tab facing to within 1″ (25mm) of the bottom chalk mark — you are cutting on the lines you first chalked onto the garment front. Turn the garment to the wrong side and cut diagonally to the ends of the tab stitching line so that a large wedge is formed. Cut the garment fabric only — not any of the facing fabric, and make sure the cuts go right to the ends of the stitching so that the bottom of the tab will be square and neat.

Press the seam allowances into the tab if you are going to topstitch the sides of the finished tab. This gives a sporty look to the finished garment. Press the seam allowances out into the shirt if you are not going to topstitch the tab. This gives a more dressy finish.

Lay the garment out flat on a table and fold back the facings along the pressed-in foldline. Position the tab facings right over left for a woman and left over right for a man. Tuck the tails of the tabs down into the opening at the bottom of the tab area making sure the top tab completely covers the lower tab especially at the bottom of the tab. Secure this area with a small piece of tape or a few hand stitches to make sure it stays in the proper position while you do the final stitching. Pin the upper edge of the facings in place along the neck line.

Lift up the bottom of the garment until the wedge and tails of the tab facings are exposed. Hand baste across the base of the wedge and then check the right side of the garment to make sure there is no pulling in the corner of the tab and everything lies smoothly. Adjust your basting if necessary and machine stitch across the base of the wedge. If you wish to topstitch the tab and collar, do not stitch across the base of the wedge at this time — wait until you have applied the collar—otherwise you cannot topstitch all the way down the sides of the tab.

Stitch and press the garment shoulder seams. Measure around the garment neck edge from the folded edge of each tab. Walk the tape measure around the seamline, not the cut edge, so that you get a true measurement of the finished neckline.

Use the collar pattern with the cut-on stand that is found in the pattern section in the back of the book. Measure the neck edge of the collar — minus the seam allowance — and adjust the collar length at the center back until it exactly matches the neckline measurement. Interface and stitch the collar

pieces together with a ¼" (6mm) seam, as described on page 81.

ADD LENGTH HERE

Pin the under collar only to the right side of the neckline, matching up the center back and making sure the front edges of the collar are even with the tab facing fold. Finger-press open the seam allowance at the front edge of the collar and secure the front edge of the collar to the tab facing fold with a few hand stitches. This will keep the collar in the proper position while machine stitching so you won't get a "bump" at the finished edge of the collar.

Stitch the under collar to the neckline, starting at the front edge on each side of the garment and stitch to the center back. This method of stitching prevents a build up of excess fabric at one side of the collar which will also cause a "bump" at the front edge of the collar. Mark the upper collar with a small clip at the shoulder seam.

Wrap the upper collar around the front edge of the collar and facing, right sides together, so that the clip mark on the upper collar edge meets the shoulder seam on the inside of the garment. Making sure the seam at the front edge of the collar stays pressed open, stitch again along the neckline seam as far as you can go. The garment and tab facing are sandwiched between the upper and under collar at this point. Wrap the upper collar around snugly so that you don't get a "stair step" finish at the front edge of the collar and facing. *Grade* and clip the seam as necessary.

The collar can also be applied using the method given on pages 84-85.

Turn the collar to the finished position. Fold under a narrow seam around the back of the collar and catch it in place with hand or machine stitching.

The collar and tab facing edges can now be topstitched, if desired. Start at the bottom on the inside of the right tab, stitch up the tab, around the collar and down the other tab to the bottom. Pin or baste the two layers of each tab together and topstitch the inside edge of each tab. Make sure you stitch each tab in the same direction as the first stitching on the outside edges of the tab. This is to prevent a "drag" from forming between the two topstitched areas. Finish the lower edge of the tab by lapping the facings and stitching them as directed previously. For a finishing touch — stitch a large X at the bottom of the tab, as shown. Make it 1½" (38mm) square.

Make vertical buttonholes in the tab as needed. Dressy blouses or shirts can be worn without any buttons, if preferred.

Designer Note: Very expensive, classic long dresses are often made out of matte jersey or Qiana®. Make a longer tab — 12" (30cm) or more — and fill in the neckline with jewelry. A classic shirt can be made using the tab neckline and the Wing Cuff, see page 103. These shirts look neater than the standard shirt that opens all the way down the front. There is less bulk and no buttons at the waistline to make unsightly bulges.

FORMULA FOR VARYING TAB FRONT WIDTHS

The distance of the section between the center front line and the edge of the pattern square will change for the different tab widths. Follow the chart below.

1" (25mm) finished tab	1¾" (44mm) from center front line
1½" (38mm) finished tab	2½" (63mm) from center front line
2" (50mm) finished tab	3¼" (81mm) from center front line

V-NECK COLLAR ON A BAND

Many knit tops currently in vogue today have a V-neck finish with a collar attached to the band. Usually this is a separate collar topstitched in place around the back of the neck. The V-neck technique contained in this section, which has the collar cut as part of the band, is easier to apply and less bulky than the band with the separate collar. The separate collar band finish tends to gap a bit around the neckline because of the added weight of the separate collar.

This neckline finish is usually seen on sports clothes, but it can also be very elegant when made up in a dressy knit for evening wear. The band and collar can be cut from the same fabric as the garment, or you can use a contrasting color. It is also possible to use ribbing for the band and collar, but select a firm rib. It is much easier to work with than the very stretchy kind.

Garment Pattern

Use any basic top or dress pattern for this garment. The neckline will pull over the head so cut the front and back pieces without center seams.

Use the turtleneck or high neckline on the pattern. When working with a fabric that has a wide horizontal stripe, cut the V so the point ends ½" (13mm) above the edge of a stripe. The finished V will then end on the stripe for an attractive finish.

Cut a V in the garment front before the shoulder seams are sewn. The length of the V is up to you, but mid-bust makes a comfortable depth. Just remember that some of the cut will be filled in with band, so you must cut lower than the desired finished depth. Refer to page 263 for V-neck cutting information.

Collar Pattern

Use the V-neck collar pattern found in the back of the book. Notice that two collar shapes are given: a straight and a pointed collar. Use the desired collar line.

The pattern has "fold" marked on two edges. Fold the collar fabric as indicated and position the pattern so that both the marked edges are on a fabric fold. The grainline should be on a lengthwise rib of the fabric.

The collar will look like this when cut.

Collar Construction

Apply a lightweight fabric interfacing to the upper half of the collar when working with lightweight knits. Fold the collar in half, right sides together, and stitch with a ¼" (6mm) seam.

Turn the collar right sides out and press. Topstitch around the outside edges if you want a sporty look. Use either matching or contrasting thread.

Collar Application

The collar can be applied with either a crossed-over or mitered trim at the point of the V. Solid color fabrics look nice with either finish. Whenever striped fabric is used for the garment, the mitered finish should be used. This design is more compatible with the stripes than the cross-over finish.

Stitch and press the shoulder seams of the garment. Insert a pin from the wrong side of the garment ½" (13mm) below the point of the V. This will be referred to as the point pin.

Pin the center back of the collar to the center back of the garment, right sides together. Pin the cut edges of the band evenly down each side of the V so that an equal amount of band extends beyond the point pin. Follow one of the methods below for stitching and finishing the band.

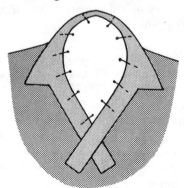

Mitered V-neck: Unpin approximately 3″ (7.5cm) of the left side of the band. Position the right side of the band over the point pin at the ¼″ (6mm) seamline of the band. Pin in place. Mark where the point pin comes through the band and then remove the point pin, Fig. 1. Start stitching the right side of the band at the point pin mark; stitch up around the back of the neck and down the other side to within 3″ (7.5cm) of the point of the V. Fig. 2.

FIG. 2

Fold back the right side of the band and pin out of the way. Insert the point pin from the wrong side of the garment again, right at the place where the stitching line started. Position the rest of the left side of the band down the V so that the point pin pierces the band at the ¼″ (6mm) seamline. The ends of the bands below the point pin should be of equal length. Check and adjust if necessary; otherwise the point of the V will pull off to one side when finished. Remove the point pin and complete the stitching on the left side of the trim from the point pin mark up to the end of the seam.

The stitching lines should meet exactly at the point of the V. If they don't meet on the first stitching, turn the garment to the wrong side and correct the stitching where you can see it a little better. Clip just the garment fabric to the stitching lines at the

point of the V and pull the band pieces through to the wrong side.

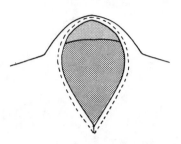

Determine the miter stitching line by folding the garment exactly down the center front and then placing a ruler along the fold so that it goes up through the bands. Draw a line along the edge of the ruler, in the band area, and stitch this line for a perfect miter.

Trim the band ends to about 2″ (50mm) and press open the miter at the point of the V. Press the entire neckline seam allowance out into the garment. Finish the seam with a row of wide zigzag along the edge, catching in the trimmed edges of the bands as you stitch around the point of the V. Trim away the ends of the bands even with the edge of the seam allowance.

Crossed-over V-neck: Position the collar and band in the neckline as described above, using the point pin as a guide. Start the stitching line at the point of the V and stitch around the neckline to within 2" (50mm) of the V on the other side.

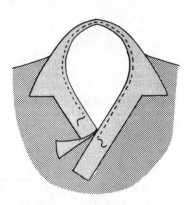

Clip the garment down to the stitching line at the point of the V. Lay it out on a flat surface, right side up, and position the bands as given below.

Tuck the free end of the band that was not sewn to the point, down inside the V. Tuck the free end of the other band through the small seam opening on the side of the V. Adjust the pieces of band until the garment front lies flat. Pin the two pieces in position at the point of the V.

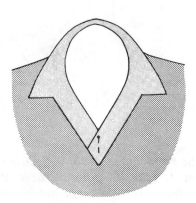

Fold over the garment front and close the open seam by sewing through the garment and two bands with a ¼" (6mm) seam. Sew from the point of the V up across the two bands. Zigzag along the edge of the neckline seam. Trim away any excess band for a neat finish.

Note: If you are using ribbing for the collar, stretch it slightly when pinning it to the neckline of the garment. Ribbing tends to loosen up in the washing process, which will give you a floppy band and collar if the ribbing isn't stretched when applied. The amount of stretch will depend on the amount of stretch the ribbing has. Soft ribs will need more stretching than firm ones. In any case, the ribbing should never be stretched so much that the neck edge ripples.

DRAPED NECKLINE

This graceful, draped neckline finish is flattering to everyone except those figures with large bustlines. Use it on dressy knit tops or add it to a long, slim dress for elegant evening or at-home wear. It should be made from soft, drapey knits such as Qiana®, Nyesta® or lightweight interlocks. Firmer fabrics will not fall into the soft folds that make this neckline so attractive. See page 248.

By using just the collar pattern, a lovely scarf can be made out of 5/8 yard of fabric.

Any basic top or dress pattern can be used for this neckline finish. Since the draped collar will slip easily over the head, a zipper opening is not necessary. Cut the back and front of the garment with the center line on a fabric fold. The collar pattern piece will require an extra ⅝ yard (57cm) of 60" (152 cm) fabric. A long sleeve top will need 1⅝ yards (148cm) of 45" (114cm) fabric or 1½ yards (137cm) of 60" (152cm) fabric. Use the draped collar and overlay pattern found in the back of the book.

Collar Pattern

Make a diagonal fold on the fabric and cut out the collar with the pattern positioned along the fold-line as indicated.

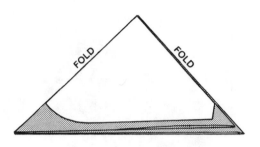

Overlay Pattern

Use the overlay pattern to alter the neckline of the garment after the shoulder seams have been completed. Fold the garment exactly along the center front and center back and place the overlay in place on the garment, matching up the center fronts and backs. Re-cut the neckline along the overlay edge.

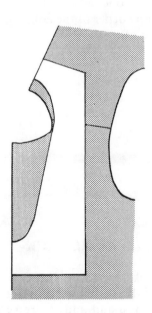

Collar Application

Fold the collar so that the back notches meet, right sides together. Stitch as indicated with a ¼″ (6mm) seam. Finger-press open the seam and turn the col-

lar right side out so that the short center back seams lie on top of each other.

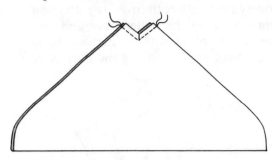

Mark the center front of the collar with a small clip. Pin the collar to the garment, right sides together, making sure the collar is distributed evenly around the neckline, lining up center front and center back. Stitch the collar in place with a ¼″ (6mm) seam.

Now finish the garment according to the chosen style. This neckline looks particularly nice with long, tight sleeves finished with a rolled hem found on page 195.

GATHERED TURTLENECK COLLAR

This unusual version of a turtleneck is fun to make and adds a beautiful high-fashion touch to your tops and dresses. The softly gathered turtleneck is easy to wear and can be as casual or dressy as the fabric indicates.

Use any basic top or dress pattern with set-in or raglan sleeves, and a high round neckline. An exposed zipper opening is used down the back of the garment, so place the center back line of the pattern on a fabric fold when cutting. Soft, drapey knits adapt well to this style, although soft, lightweight wovens can also be used.

Collar Pattern

The pattern for the collar is found in the back of the book along with the overlay pattern that is used to modify the neck opening for the new finish. When using knit fabrics, cut the collar on the cross grain. Cut the collar on the bias for woven fabrics or knits that have no stretch (some Qianas®).

Overlay Pattern

The overlay pattern is used to re-cut the neckline after the shoulder seams of the garment have been completed. Fold the garment down the center front and center back, making sure that the folds are accurately made. Place the overlay pattern on the garment, lining up the center front and center back edge of the overlay with the garment folds. Re-cut the garment neckline along the overlay curve.

Collar Construction

Make two rows of machine gathering along both short ends of the collar between the marks. The first gather line should be close to the collar edge and the second about ¼" (6mm) away.

Make a 1" (25mm) slash down the center back of the garment. Pin the collar to the neckline, right sides together, so that the gathered edges of the collar are even with the edges of the center back slash. Stitch in place with a ¼" (6mm) seam.

Pull up and adjust the gathered edges of the collar until they are ¼" (6mm) shorter than the length of the turned back facing.

Insert an exposed zipper in the center back of the garment following the instructions given on page 146. The top of the zipper should go right up to the end of the gathers at the top edge of the collar. Be careful that you catch the gathers in evenly when stitching the collar to the zipper tape.

Finish the collar by opening the zipper, folding the facing down over the zipper tape so that the end of the facing extends ¼" (6mm) below the neckline seam. Using a zipper foot, stitch through all the layers just slightly back of the zipper teeth. If you get too close here, the gathers will get caught in the zipper when it is opened and closed. Trim the zipper tape at the top corner of the collar and turn the facing right side out.

COWL NECK

The cowl neck knit top or dress is attractive and very comfortable to wear. It is one of the easiest neckline finishes, and adds a dressy touch to your wardrobe.

Use a regular T-shirt pattern that has a turtleneck or high round neckline. Trim the neckline ½" (13mm) larger at the shoulder and around the back of the neck. Drop the center 2½" (6cm) lower than the pattern neckline. Stitch and press the shoulder seams.

Measure around the neckline and cut the cowl collar the same measurement plus ½″ (13mm) for seams. This measurement should be cut on the crossgrain of the knit or the grain with the most stretch. The collar width should be approximately 16″ (41cm), or whatever width of fabric you have left over.

Stitch the ends of the collar with a ¼″ (6mm) seam and press open. Fold the collar piece lengthwise with the wrong sides together. Mark the cut edges of the collar into four equal sections, placing the first pin at the collar seamline.

Divide the garment neck edge into four equal sections. With the garment inside out, slip the collar down into the neckline, matching up the pin marks. Pin together and stitch with a ¼″ (6mm) seam. Overcast the seam edge, and you now have a graceful cowl neck top or dress.

Most knit fabrics can use a pull-on waistband finish, unless the difference between a person's hip and waist measurement is more than 10″ (25cm). When the difference is too great, a waistband that is large enough to fit around the hips will gather around the waist. Fortunately, (or unfortunately, as the case may be) the waist usually increases in size with the hips, so very few people have the above problem. If you do, use a waistband with a zipper opening on your knit garments.

Waistband Elastic

Choose a good quality elastic for your pull-on waistband. The usual width is 1″ (25mm), but it can be narrower or wider, as you prefer. The elastic must be able to withstand repeated washing or drycleanings. It is such a bother to have to replace stretched-out elastic.

Buy only elastic that is recommended for waistband application, and marked dry cleanable. Some elastic is too soft for waistband use and will not hold the garment properly. Certain types of elastics will deteriorate in the dry cleaning process, so avoid any elastic that isn't marked "dry cleanable."

Various waistband elastics have different degrees of firmness. Choose the kind that is most comfortable for you. Some elastics are constructed so they won't roll; these are a good choice for waistbands.

Waistband elastic twists for two reasons; the elastic is too tight or the casing is too wide. Adjust the casing width to accommodate the elastic width. The casing should be just ⅛″ (3mm) wider than the elastic.

Turned-Over Elastic Casing Waistband

Allow twice the width of the elastic plus ½″ (13mm) for the turned-over casing at the top edge of the garment. Measure the elastic around the waist for a snug but comfortable fit, and cut, allowing for a ½″ (13mm) overlap.

Leave a section of one garment seam unsewn, as illustrated. The top ⅜″ (9mm) should be securely stitched, and the opening should be the width of the elastic. The elastic is inserted through this opening.

Turn down the casing on the fold line and edge stitch ⅛″ (3mm) from the fold. Stitch ¼″ (6mm) above the lower edge of the casing. Use a narrow zigzag stitch, or stretch the fabric while stitching with a straight stitch. Straight stitching gives a more professional look.

Insert the elastic into the casing, using a large safety pin. Make sure the elastic doesn't twist as you pull it through. Join the ends of the elastic with a ½″ (25mm) overlap. Stitch securely.

Note: fasten the ends of the elastic with a safety pin for the first few wearings and washings to make sure the elastic length is comfortable. Elastic can shrink or relax after use.

Distribute the waist ease evenly around the elastic, and then secure the elastic at each seamline by *stitching-in-the-ditch*. This keeps the elastic in position and prevents twisting.

If the elastic ever needs replacing, it is simple to unpick the seam stitching, remove the elastic through the opening, and insert a new piece.

Separate Casing Waistband

A separate, casing waistband gives a more finished look to the waistline, and is a good technique to use if you are going to wear the pants or skirt with a tucked-in blouse or shirt.

Adjust the fit of the garment at the waistline, and leave just a ½″ (13mm) seam allowance above the waistline. Cut the waistband across the width of the fabric, or lengthwise if that direction has more stretch. The waistband width should be twice the width of the elastic plus 1″ (25mm). The length of the waistband should be 1″ (25mm) larger than the waist measurement.

Join the ends of the waistband with a ½″ (13mm) seam, right sides together. Stitch for ½″ (13mm), backstitch, leave a gap the width of the elastic, backstitch and finish the seam. The seam opening is used for inserting the elastic.

Check to see if the waistband is the right size by folding it in half; step into it and pull it up over the hips to the waist. Cut a new waistband or piece this one if the fabric doesn't have enough stretch.

Press open the seam and edgestitch the seam allowances to the waistband. This will make it easier to thread the elastic through the casing; the safety pin won't get caught behind the pressed-open seam allowances.

Apply the waistband to the garment, right sides together, with a ½″ (13mm) seam. Place the waistband seam at the center back, and evenly distribute the garment around the waistband.

Fold over the waistband to the inside so that ⅜″ (9mm) extends below the waist seam. Pin all around to make sure the waistband is turned smoothly. The final stitching can be done using one of the following methods.

Method #1: Catch the waistband in place by *stitching-in-the-ditch*. Use a regular straight stitch, and stretch the garment and waistband as you sew.

Method #2: Press open the waistline seam, and position the waistband as shown, seam edges even. Secure the back part of the waistband by zigzagging the two seam allowances together as close to the seamline as possible. This method gives a very flat finish, and doesn't require stitching on the right side. It also has lots of "give" because it is stitched with a zigzag instead of a straight stitch.

Insert and finish the elastic as described for the turned-over waistband.

SEWING TIPS

CUTTING ROUND AND V-NECKLINES

Care must be taken when cutting round and V-necklines so that the round neck will look round and the V-neck will look like a V when the garment is finished. It is very easy to give a little point to round necks and make V-necks look round if you don't follow the correct cutting procedure.

Always cut V-necks with a slight outward curve rather than just a straight line. V-necks tend to pull away from the center front when worn and the curved line will retain the proper shape of the V. Low V-necks should be cut with an exaggerated V at the point; otherwise they will spread apart when worn and become a bit too revealing.

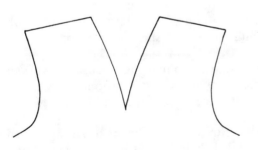

When cutting a deep V, square off the shoulder line about ¼″ (6mm) at the neck edge only. This will make the garment hug the body rather than fall away from it. Another way to make the V-neck hug the body better is to cut the shoulder ¼″ (6mm) wider at the neck edge and ¼″ (6mm) narrower at

the shoulder. The shoulder length will remain the same, but the garment will fit better.

Cut V-neck facings ⅛″ (3mm) smaller at the center fold so that the facing is ¼″ (6mm) narrower than the garment. Ease the V-neck to fit the facing and you will get a V-neck that stays snug against your body rather than one that gaps.

263

Always square off the pattern for ½″ (13mm) at the center front or center back when cutting round or scoop necklines. This eliminates the little dip you so often see on self-cut necklines.

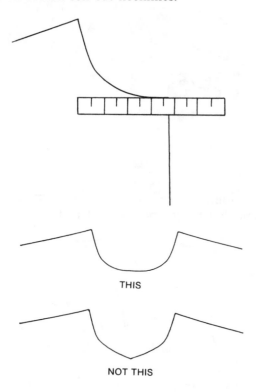

THIS

NOT THIS

Low cut round necklines should have the shoulder squared off also. This keeps the garment against the body rather than gapping away from your bustline.

A length of narrow elastic cut to fit comfortably around the rib cage can be attached to low necked gowns to keep them in place. Sew a hook and eye at the ends of the elastic and attach the center of the elastic to the center front seam of the neckline facing. Hook the elastic before you zip up the garment and dance and party in comfort.

MISCELLANEOUS SEWING TIPS

A chair on wheels is handy to have at the sewing machine, but all too often the wheels become sluggish because of a buildup of thread pieces around the casters. These threads can be removed easily by running a sharp hacksaw blade back and forth in the caster crevice a few times. Use your fingers or a tweezer to remove the cut threads.

Ordinary plastic bag material can be used as a temporary fusing material when applying appliques. Cut out a piece of plastic slightly larger than the applique and position it between the garment and applique. Cover the applique with a pressing cloth or paper towel and press — this makes sure you don't get any melted plastic on the iron.

Are you a "chicken clipper?" Bound buttonholes, set-in pockets, tab front necklines, and some zipper applications have corners that require clipping. It is important that you clip right to the stitching — not a fraction of an inch back from it — so that the corner turns smoothly. Too many people are afraid to clip all the way, and they end up with a "homemade" look. Don't be a "chicken clipper."

When stitching boxes that have to be cut open and turned — as for bound buttonholes and set-in pockets — start the stitching on a side of the box, not in a corner. This prevents a buildup of thread in the corner which will interfere with a perfect turn.

People who use a lot of "knits only" patterns soon get a collection of pattern pieces that can be hard to store. Cardboard tubes from paper towel rolls or toilet tissue can be used to store individual patterns. Roll up each pattern, slip it in the tube, label it and store on a shelf or in a box.

Small-parts cabinets that are used in workshops are also handy in the sewing room. They give lots of ideal storage space for many small sewing items.

Many times you will want to zigzag the edge of a knit fabric before you turn up the hem, but you find the cut edge stretches out of shape when stitched. This is common on stretch terries, velours and many other loosely knit fabrics. They can be zigzagged if you will first wrap a heavy thread around a pin that has been inserted at the hem edge and then stitch over this heavy thread with your zigzag - hold the thread taut while stitching. The thread stabilizes the cut edge and keeps it from stretching out of shape. Just make sure you don't catch the thread in the zigzag stitching. Once the zigzagging has been completed, pull the thread away.

Spaghetti straps or narrow tubing can be easily stitched and turned with the aid of a large bobby pin. Cut and stitch the strap as you normally would. Use a small zigzag stitch so that the seam has some give when you turn it. Cut a small notch out of the folded edge about ⅜" (9mm) down from the end of the strap. Slip the bobby pin over the end of the strap, inserting it through the notch as shown. Use the bobby pin to help turn the tubing.

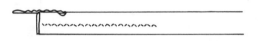

Always make an extra pair of pants when making a pants suit that uses white fabric for the pants. It seems the pants get worn more than the coordinating top and show wear much faster. (White also tends to look slightly gray after a while.) An extra pair of pants prolongs the life of the pant suit.

For perfect control and to eliminate broken threads when gathering, set the machine for zigzag with the longest stitch length and the widest stitch width. Zigzag over topstitching or heavy duty thread, making one row at 1/2" (13mm) and the other row at 3/4" (20mm). (The second row will be removed after the garment is completed.) An entire gathered skirt can be stitched in a continuous length. Draw the gathers up along the heavy thread (it'll never break); adjust the gathers; match the notches and stitch the seam allowance at 5/8" (15mm).

Eliminate the shadowing through of side seam pockets on light colored and lightweight fabrics (even when underlined) by making the pockets out of sheer nylon tricot in a natural color. It makes strong, lightweight pockets, but you will never see them.

To prevent side seam pockets from peeking out at the side of the skirt, make them into "kangaroo pockets." Make the two pockets out of two pieces of sheer tricot cut 8" (20cm) and the width and shape of the skirt front. Stitch the outline of the pocket on each side of the fabric pieces to prevent things getting lost in the front of your skirt.

For perfectly matched pocket flaps make a pattern, or template, of the finished flap from a piece of heavy, fusible interfacing. (The inferfacing is rough and "grabs" the flap fabric.) When stitching the flap and flap facing together, pin the pattern on top of the two fabric layers and use the cut edge as a guide for your stitching. Just be careful not to catch the pattern in your stitching. Now you have two identical pocket flaps.

LINED SKIRT WITH SEAM FINISH

Lined skirts are practical and comfortable to wear. The most common way of lining a skirt is to make a separate lining and attach it to the waistline before the waistband is applied. This technique is called a drum lining. The following instructions give another way of lining a skirt that includes a neat seam finish in the process. The result is really an underlined skirt, but it serves the same purpose as lining with the advantages of taking care of fraying seam edges and eliminating the problem of seam and dart "show-through" on light colored or lightweight fabrics.

Cut the skirt pieces from the fashion fabric as given in the pattern. Cut the skirt lining from the same pattern pieces but add 5/8" (16mm) to each vertical seam so each lining piece is 1¼" (32mm) wider than the matching skirt piece.

With the right sides together, pin the matching skirt and lining pieces so the vertical edges meet. Stitch with a scant ¼" (6mm) seam. Note: on very heavy or bulky fabrics a 1/8" (3mm) seam works better.

Turn the skirt/lining assembly right sides out and place it skirt fabric side up on the ironing board. Smooth out the fabric layers and notice how the lining fabric curls around the skirt fabric edges, enclosing them neatly. Press to set the edges.

Repeat this procedure on each skirt piece and then mark and stitch any darts. Before stitching the dart, machine baste down the center and a bit beyond the end of each one (see page 63) so the fabric layers stay snugly together when the dart is stitched. This is especially important for smooth dart points.

Now construct the skirt as given in the directions, applying the zipper and waistband. Be sure to use a seam roll when pressing open the vertical seams so impressions won't show on the right side.

To finish, fold up the hem and pin or baste along the fold. Trim any lining fabric that shows above the skirt fabric at the hem edge. Now carefully zigzag the lining and fashion fabric edges together making sure they stay even.

Finish the hem edge as desired and work the hem with the tailor's hem technique given on page 193. Make sure you catch only the lining fabric on the garment side of the hem; this prevents the hem from showing on the right side.

This technique can be used to line pants, dresses, and jackets — wherever you want to prevent seam and dart "show-through," and when working with a fabric that frays readily. Just add 5/8" (16mm) to all vertical seams of the lining fabric. Sorry, it only works on vertical seams, not horizontal or crotch seams.

INDEX

NOTES

NOTES

NOTES

NOTES

NOTES

NOTES

NOTES

NOTES